Exodus to Shanghai

PALGRAVE *Studies in Oral History*

Series Editors: Linda Shopes and Bruce M. Stave

Editorial Board

The Order Has Been Carried Out: History, Memory, and Meaning of a Nazi Massacre in Rome, by Alessandro Portelli (2003)

Sticking to the Union: An Oral History of the Life and Times of Julia Ruuttila, by Sandy Polishuk (2003)

To Wear the Dust of War: From Bialystok to Shanghai to the Promised Land, an Oral History, by Samuel Iwry, edited by L. J. H. Kelley (2004)

Education as My Agenda: Gertrude Williams, Race, and the Baltimore Public Schools, by Jo Ann Robinson (2005)

Remembering: Oral History Performance, edited by Della Pollock (2005)

Postmemories of Terror: A New Generation Copes with the Legacy of the "Dirty War," by Susana Kaiser (2005)

Growing Up in The People's Republic: Conversations between Two Daughters of China's Revolution, by Ye Weili and Ma Xiaodong (2005)

Life and Death in the Delta: African American Narratives of Violence, Resilience, and Social Change, by Kim Lacy Rogers (2006)

Creating Choice: A Community Responds to the Need for Abortion and Birth Control, 1961–1973, by David P. Cline (2006)

Voices from This Long Brown Land: Oral Recollections of Owens Valley Lives and Manzanar Pasts, by Jane Wehrey (2006)

Radicals, Rhetoric, and the War: The University of Nevada in the Wake of Kent State, by Brad E. Lucas (2006)

The Unquiet Nisei: An Oral History of the Life of Sue Kunitomi Embrey, by Diana Meyers Bahr (2007)

Sisters in the Brotherhoods: Working Women Organizing for Equality in New York City, by Jane LaTour (2008)

Iraq's Last Jews: Stories of Daily Life, Upheaval, and Escape from Modern Babylon, edited by Tamar Morad, Dennis Shasha, and Robert Shasha (2008)

Soldiers and Citizens: An Oral History of Operation Iraqi Freedom from the Battlefield to the Pentagon, by Carl Mirra (2008)

Overcoming Katrina: African American Voices from the Crescent City and Beyond, by D'Ann R. Penner and Keith C. Ferdinand (2009)

Bringing Desegregation Home: Memories of the Struggle toward School Integration in Rural North Carolina, by Kate Willink (2009)

I Saw It Coming: Worker Narratives of Plant Closings and Job Loss, by Tracy E. K'Meyer and Joy L. Hart (2010)

Speaking History: Oral Histories of the American Past, 1865-Present, by Sue Armitage and Laurie Mercier (2010)

Surviving Bhopal: Dancing Bodies, Written Texts, and Oral Testimonials of Women in the Wake of an Industrial Disaster, by Suroopa Mukherjee (2010)

Living with Jim Crow: African American Women and Memories of the Segregated South, by Anne Valk and Leslie Brown (2010)

Gulag Voices: Oral Histories of Soviet Incarceration and Exile, by Jehanne M. Gheith and Katherine R. Jolluck (2011)

Detained without Cause: Muslims' Stories of Detention and Deportation in America after 9/11, by Irum Shiekh (2011)

Soviet Communal Living: An Oral History of the Kommunalka, by Paola Messana (2011)

No Room of Her Own: Women's Stories of Homelessness, Life, Death, and Resistance, by Desiree Hellegers (2011)

Exodus to Shanghai

Stories of Escape from the Third Reich

Steve Hochstadt

palgrave
macmillan

First published in 2012 by
PALGRAVE MACMILLAN®
in the United States—a division of St. Martin's Press LLC,
175 Fifth Avenue, New York, NY 10010.

Where this book is distributed in the UK, Europe and the rest of the world, this is by Palgrave Macmillan, a division of Macmillan Publishers Limited, registered in England, company number 785998, of Houndmills, Basingstoke, Hampshire RG21 6XS.

Palgrave Macmillan is the global academic imprint of the above companies and has companies and representatives throughout the world.

Palgrave® and Macmillan® are registered trademarks in the United States, the United Kingdom, Europe and other countries.

ISBN HC: 978–1–137–00670–7
ISBN PBK: 978–1–137–00671–4

Library of Congress Cataloging-in-Publication Data

Hochstadt, Steve, 1948–
    Exodus to Shanghai : stories of escape from the Third Reich / Steve Hochstadt.
        p. cm.—(Palgrave studies in oral history series)
    ISBN 978–1–137–00670–7 (alk. paper)—
    ISBN 978–1–137–00671–4 (alk. paper)
    1. Jewish refugees—China—Shanghai—Biography. 2. Jews—China—Shanghai—Biography. 3. Jews, German—China—Shanghai—Biography. 4. World War, 1939–1945—Jews—China—Shanghai—Biography. 5. Shanghai (China)—Ethnic relations. 6. Holocaust, Jewish (1939–1945)—Biography. I. Title.

DS135.C5H62 2012
940.53′18092251132—dc23   2012005098

A catalogue record of the book is available from the British Library.

Design by Newgen Imaging Systems (P) Ltd., Chennai, India.

First edition: July 2012

10 9 8 7 6 5 4 3 2 1

Printed in the United States of America.

This work is dedicated to my grandparents, Amalia and Josef Hochsädt, and to all the Shanghai Jews who have offered me their memories.

Contents

List of Images

Cover photo, courtesy of U. S. Holocaust Memorial Museum

Photographs of the Narrators

Chart

Maps

Historical Photographs

Acknowledgments

My greatest debt is to the 100 former Shanghai Jews who were generous with their time, their hospitality, and their memories. The tape recordings of our interviews have been deposited in the Special Collections of Ladd Library at Bates College, where I taught for 27 years. Some of these interviews are accessible over the Internet, as sound files and transcripts, at the website www.bates.edu. Eventually all will be publically accessible in this manner.

Many people offered me invaluable help in understanding the Shanghai experience. Nicci Leamon of Maine carefully transcribed most of these interviews, and dozens of others. Karin Grimme worked on many interviews in German. Seventy students at Bates College did the rest, notably Jennifer Gibson and Scott Pugh. My associations with the Sino-Judaic Institute and with Ralph Hirsch of the Council on the Jewish Experience in Shanghai provided contacts and information. The collections of documents at the Bundesarchiv in Berlin-Lichterfelde and the United States Holocaust Memorial Museum, among many other archives in Europe and the United States, show that these Shanghai stories typified thousands of refugee experiences. They also provide sad proof of how much our American government knew about the plight of Jews in Europe and China, and of how little help was offered.

Support for a worldwide interview process was given by the Memorial Foundation for Jewish Culture, the Lucius N. Littauer Foundation, and the Dimmer-Bergstrom Fund, as well as Bates College.

My many conversations with Danny Danforth, a Bates College anthropologist who studies the identity formation of Macedonians, have contributed to my ideas about interviewing and transcribing.

Creating a book out of a manuscript is a project in itself. The structure and contents of this volume have been significantly improved by the suggestions of Eric Weitz and Elizabeth Tobin, the two editors of Palgrave's oral history series, Linda Shopes and Bruce Staples, and Chris Chappell, editor for history. Sarah Whalen and Erin Ivy were my daily contacts with Palgrave about all the details needed to produce the book.

Bates College gave me an intellectual and professional home during this entire project, providing technical assistance and financial support for my work. My colleagues in the History Department gave that home a familial character. Special Collections at the Ladd Library now houses the original interview tapes and copies of the transcripts. More recently, Illinois College has supported me during the final stages of writing.

My family assumes that writing about Shanghai Jews is what I should be doing. They have shown remarkable patience as this book slowly took shape. For that I am constantly grateful.

Series Editors' Foreword

The Holocaust has been well documented by the written records kept and preserved by the Nazis, who incriminated themselves. Seven hundred million mimeographed pages served as evidence during the Nuremberg war crimes trials after World War II. Such record keeping chronicled the atrocities in a cold and mechanical fashion from the perspective of Hitler's evil minions. However, a more human face is revealed in the stories of those who suffered—narratives related through oral histories conducted primarily since the 1970s. While emphasis has been placed on those Jews who survived the concentration camps, a more fortunate group escaped the immediate terrors of the Third Reich. They fled to other nations willing to allow them entrance. This was not an easy task because of diplomatic and administrative obstacles that called for special letters of permission, visas, and other requirements of immigration. Moreover, prejudice against the refugees raised barriers to sanctuary in many nations, including the United States.

The one place that permitted free entry, at least until 1939, was Shanghai, China, a location that few European Jews thought desirable. One of the early volumes in this series, *To Wear the Dust of War,* tells the story of a single individual, Samuel Iwry, who escaped from Lithuania to the Shanghai ghetto, where he resided for six years before becoming a successful academic in America. In *Exodus to Shanghai: Stories of Escape from the Third Reich,* Steve Hochstadt offers a fully textured account of Jewish life in Shanghai during World War II that captures the drama and pathos of that experience while revealing the community that 16,000 Jews constructed in a strange and exotic place. Nor does he neglect the lives they left behind in Europe, their often quite challenging journey, and the inventive ways they coped with life in Shanghai. The study is based on the accounts of 13 narrators chosen from more than 100 interviews he has conducted and represents their collective memory. Effectively employing oral history to humanize a relatively little known aspect of the Holocaust experience, Hochstadt allows his narrators to speak for themselves so that, in his words, "conversation about the past brings forth the passion that is often harder to perceive in written narratives." It is this passion, emotion, and intimacy that gives value to this volume and demonstrates the power of oral history. However, it requires the creative act of the historian to effectively make sense of such material—to select, analyze, order, and edit so that an overall synthesis enhances our understanding of a subject. Hochstadt accomplishes that goal while being sensitive to the fragility of memory that clouds all work in oral history.

This volume not only complements Samuel Iwry's individual story, but also adds to the *Palgrave Studies in Oral History* series' existing contribution to Jewish and Chinese history with works such as *Iraq's Last Jews* and *Growing up in the People's Republic*. It also fits well with an increasing number of volumes devoted to human rights and social justice in our effort to bring the best in oral history to scholars, students, and the reading public.

Bruce M. Stave
University of Connecticut
Linda Shopes
Carlisle, Pennsylvania

Introduction

In the final months before world war and mass murder began, about 16,000 Jews fled Nazi persecution in the new Greater Germany, crossing the globe to Shanghai. Stripped of their citizenship, homes, jobs, and possessions, Jews threw their lives into suitcases and boarded ships or trains headed east.

In a world controlled by states that carefully scrutinized every potential Jewish immigrant and then refused entry to most of them, Shanghai was an open door, at least until late 1939. The hard-to-believe claims that refugees could enter Shanghai without anyone's permission were true: when they stepped off the boat on the Bund, the banking center of Asia, nobody asked to see their papers.

They landed in one of the world's most cosmopolitan cities. During a century of Western imperial control, Shanghai developed into a global crossroads for goods and people. In the late 1930s, Western businessmen struggled to maintain colonial control, while Chinese and Japanese armies battled for military supremacy. This contest among nationalities, carried out by capitalists, gangsters, politicians, and soldiers over trade, textiles, and opium, gave Shanghai a worldwide reputation for lawlessness, but also a unique openness to strangers.

Without material resources, political rights, or physical safety, but with the crucial financial help of Jews around the world, including Baghdadi and Russian Jews in Shanghai, the refugees built a society of survival. Under the watchful and not entirely unsympathetic eyes of the Japanese military, a central European Jewish community appeared out of nowhere in 1939, creating familiar institutions in an unfamiliar environment. They survived six years of tropical heat, deadly diseases, near starvation, and even Japanese ghettoization to greet their American liberators in August 1945. This vibrant but temporary society then scattered across the globe, joining Jewish communities in North and South America, Europe, Australia, and the Middle East.

Since 1945, the dimensions of human destruction in Europe, which the refugees had barely escaped, slowly penetrated to the soul of Western consciousness. Although the lawyers and historians at Nürnberg detailed the behavior of the perpetrators in 1946, it took the more gradual collection of a library of survivors' testimonies in most of the world's languages to effectively spread this terrible knowledge. Yet for decades, Shanghai refugees told their stories away from public view. Like Martin Beutler, of eastern Berlin, who lived through extreme poverty and the divorce of his parents in Shanghai, many were reluctant to place their experiences next to those who had barely escaped death in Europe.

> *If one sits across from such people, then one feels very small. Therefore I thought, what does it matter if you, Martin Beutler, now add your two cents? It is not so important what happened to me, certainly not that one should always be telling others, "Look at everything that happened to me."* [1]

David Kranzler published the first scholarly analysis of the Shanghai Jewish experience in 1976. But until the 1990s, the survival of thousands of Jews in Shanghai was not well-known. Since then, a few historians and documentary filmmakers have sketched the broad outlines of the Shanghai story.[2] A small number of former refugees have traced their individual journeys, stretching over a decade, from persecution to freedom.[3] The list of novels inspired by the drama of refugee flight and survival keeps growing.[4]

This book takes another step toward defining the history of the unique stream of Jewish refugees to Shanghai. What did these recent escapees from the prison of Nazi Germany think as they traveled beyond the boundaries of their known world? Despite their utter lack of tangible resources, what institutions did they create to represent their view of themselves? How were they treated by the Chinese population and the Japanese military? How did children grow up during a decade in Shanghai?

The 13 narrators here give a spectrum of answers to each historical question. They embody the variety and similarities that characterized the Shanghai ordeal for thousands of Jewish refugees. *Exodus to Shanghai* is their collective memoir.

These stories of life and death tell more than the history of Jews in Shanghai. Although many more refugees managed to get into the United States, the size and shape of the Jewish refugee stream to China is uniquely instructive about the whole flight from the Third Reich. Their last-minute escape, their middling social position, and their lack of integration in their

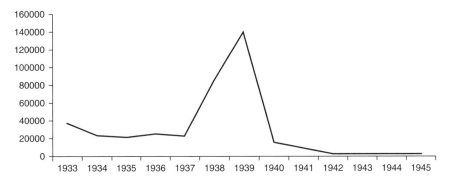

Chart 1   Jewish Refugees from the Third Reich, 1933–1945

temporary Chinese home created experiences that allow us to better understand the hundreds of thousands of German-speaking Jews displaced by the Holocaust.

The total number of refugee Jews remains frustratingly uncertain. Not only are we unsure exactly how many self-identified Jews lived in Germany at any time during the Nazi regime, but the Nürnberg Laws redefined "Jew" to include many other Germans. Counting those who managed to leave Europe before the Holocaust began is similarly frustrating. Crossing border after border, maneuvering through multinational bureaucracies that were trying to prevent their entry, hiding from all authorities, and landing in countries big and small across the world, the number of refugees from Nazi Germany can only be approximated.[5] That number acquires emotional significance, because it represents the majority of Jews who survived to carry their German Jewish culture to new homes.

Probably about half of the 525,000 German Jews and somewhat more than half of the 200,000 Austrian Jews escaped from the Third Reich.[6] The collective response to escalating Nazi persecution takes visual form in the chart above. An initial wave of refugees in 1933 was followed by a continuous stream from 1934 to 1937 as Jews were progressively excluded from the German economy and their possessions confiscated. In 1938, two sudden and violent events created an explosion of refugee flight: the incorporation of Austria into the Reich in March and the Kristallnacht pogrom in November. The 16,000 Jews who headed to Shanghai were a significant portion of this final desperate surge, as the remaining hundreds of thousands of Jews tried to get out of Nazi Germany.[7] The invasion of Poland in September 1939 did not end this flight, but did greatly increase its difficulty. Heinrich Himmler forbade all Jewish emigration on October 23, 1941, when the Nazi government turned its energies toward mass murder.

Not all of those who left Nazi Germany survived the Holocaust. Perhaps 20 percent or more settled in other European countries and were eventually captured and deported.[8] That leaves perhaps 300,000 who escaped from Europe. Of those, well over half left in the frantic but brief period between the *Anschluss* of Austria in March 1938 and the beginning of war in September 1939. The 16,000 who reached Shanghai made up about one of every 13 refugees during this "panic emigration," and probably one in 10 of those who left in 1939.[9] The more we know about their lives, the better we can understand both the intensified persecution that propelled them to flee and what it meant to become a refugee.

Who were the Shanghai Jews? The Jews from Germany, Austria, and Czechoslovakia who arrived in Shanghai represent a cross section of all refugees. Not famous like Einstein and Freud, not rich like the bankers Max Warburg or Louis Nathaniel de Rothschild, the brief flood of desperate Jews into Shanghai is the most significant self-contained example of what Wolfgang Benz called "the exile of the little people."[10]

Unlike those who were able to find refuge in desirable places, like the United States or England, the refugees to China were willing to risk anything to flee toward unknown and disreputable Shanghai. Our knowledge of Auschwitz makes the decision to flee seem obvious, but in 1938 nobody predicted a Holocaust. Gérard Kohbieter recognized the danger.

I heard the grown-ups talking, man, and what was happening and what happened, this one got busted, that one got busted, and businesses were closing. Meanwhile the jokes were going, how this can't last forever, you know. There was a significant joke about how two Jews meet on the Kurfürstendamm in 1960 and one says to the other, "Six months I give him." But I wasn't taken in by that. I felt danger. It was like a cat reacts to people who are real nervous, cats stay away from them, they don't hop in their lap. It felt dangerous, all those clowns walking around, man, with this super-masculinity, this marching, this macho thing, God in heaven, and it was directed at us. I wasn't particularly a religious Jew or anything like that. I felt unsafe.

Recognition of the necessity to flee was only the first step. Where to go? The obvious and desirable destinations were impossible. Immigration to Palestine had already been severely reduced by the British in 1936. In May 1939, the "White Paper" effectively closed Palestine to legal Jewish entry, although thousands arrived illegally. American officials did not reduce the official quota for the yearly entry of Germans to the United States, but the State Department threw up a bureaucratic wall to limit Jewish immigration. The wait for a visa to the United States was years long.

Families had to make wrenching and fateful decisions, like the one that Eric Reisman's parents faced:

My mother and father had the opportunity at the time, the mothers could go to England as housekeepers and take one child along, that was permitted, and the English would give visas to housekeepers. And my father said, "No, we're going to stay together. Together we can bear the hardships much easier than if we were separated from each other." So we stayed together, and we were able to get out as a family, and that was my father's doing. My mother, in turn, was able to care for us and nurture us, including my father, because he sometimes came home very disillusioned, and my mother was able to give him the strength in order to bear through those kind of turmoils in our life.

Getting out of the Third Reich began the journey of a lifetime. These Shanghai refugees faced a struggle for survival over the next decade, as Otto Schnepp describes:

People died in the streets. You literally step over bodies. I can't see how people would not be affected by seeing poverty and starvation and disease and death as an everyday occurrence on the streets of Shanghai. Shanghai does not get cold, it rarely gets below freezing, but I remember from somewhere a statistic that in Shanghai on a cold winter night about a hundred people would die in the streets.

War created additional challenges, including confinement to the Hongkou district by the Japanese and bombings by American planes.

Even after the war was over, and all of our narrators landed in the United States in the late 1940s, it took years to find security again. It was never easy to put aside the identity of a refugee. Near the end of her life, Lisbeth Loewenberg talked about landing in San Francisco in 1948 and the heavy psychological baggage she brought from Shanghai.

My first job that I found after one week, that was with Collier's *magazine. This place took subscriptions, they had salesmen go running around and selling subscriptions to* Collier's *and* Good Housekeeping *and* Cosmopolitan, *and so on, and I processed these orders. People took subscriptions for one year. I said, "But how do people know that after one year they will still be at that address?" I couldn't believe in permanence anymore. But you don't know where you are going to be tomorrow, was my reaction. And life has actually always seemed to me not permanent. It's all just transitory.*

Exodus to Shanghai traces the arc from continent to continent, from life to life, from desperate flight through years of uncertainty to the eventual peace of postwar America.

I am not the author of these stories. Over the past 20 years, I have walked into the homes of dozens of strangers and asked them to tell me their lives. They chose their own words and told their own tales. Blending their European heritage and hard-won lessons from Shanghai, speaking with a confidence born of the most trying circumstances, their words offer us both history and wisdom. None of them spoke English as their first language, but all of them knew how to say what they meant, how to transmute scenes in their minds into the spoken word. The singular fluency with which my interview partners described what they had seen and done, repeated over 100 interviews between 1989 and 1999, convinced me that they should relate their own stories in their own voices.

This book offers a fresh way to read Holocaust oral history by allowing survivors to speak directly to us. Just as they told me, a stranger in their living rooms, their family stories, they now tell them to readers everywhere. Out of many interviews, I chose 13 narrators whose stories add up to a history of mass flight and community survival. Among Shanghai Jews, none of the stories here is surprising.

They are an extraordinary group of ordinary people. None have familiar names, but they all look back on lifetimes of remarkable worldly experiences. They talk about fascist Germany and wartime China, about living under the hegemony of Nazis, Japanese, and Americans. Remaking their lives over and over, they show us great political forces operating at the human scale. These pieces of the broader mosaic, a world of Jewish reactions to unprecedented and unpredictable Nazi terror, also recreate the history of the twentieth century.

Because the experiences of Holocaust survivors are unimaginable for the rest of us, their choices of words are crucial to their ability to communicate across this gulf in understanding. My many conversations with survivors have taught me the humbling lesson that I can best express their history by letting them speak. I want to bring the curiosity, empathy, astonishment, and friendship of our conversations to the world. Conversation is like life, not a smooth narrative, but a spontaneous creation. Because we see our listeners, we can be more revealing.

Conversation about the past brings forth the passion that is often harder to perceive in written narratives. Although the conversational moment is past, something of the emotion and intimacy of our interviews remains in these printed words.

Paul Thompson, one of the pioneers of the practice of oral history, explains the pitfalls of trying to transform speech into print.

> The spoken word can very easily be mutilated in being taken down on paper and then transferred to the printed page. There is already an inevitable loss of gesture, tone, and timing. Much more serious is the distortion when the spoken word is drilled into the orders of written prose.... The rhythms and tones of speech are quite distinct from those of prose.[11]

Transcribing flattens out the emphases, eliminates pauses, and sometimes obscures those emotions that communicate so much to a listener. The language of interviews is immediate, emotional, unpolished, and spontaneous.[12] Of course, printed words cannot reproduce a voice.

I have nevertheless tried to preserve as much as possible of the distinctive voice of each narrator, his or her particular way of speaking. I have included here indications where the narrators laughed as important clues to their intended, sometimes ironic, meaning. I hope that these voices become familiar over the course of reading this book so that each narrator becomes an acquaintance whose unique expressiveness draws the reader into their story, just as I was drawn in during the interviews.

My work also appears on every page. Eyewitnesses tell great stories, but they do not necessarily create good history. Recounting experiences and writing history have different purposes and thus are distinct ways of telling about the past. The narrowness and personal nature of the participants' perspective both heightens the passion of their stories and limits their applicability to others. Historians seek a broad and reasoned understanding of a subject from the outside, while eyewitnesses relate their specific experiences from the inside, guided by memory and emotion. I attempt to bridge these gaps by using the historian's techniques to present the words of eyewitnesses. For the structure and emphases of this history, I take responsibility.

All the words quoted in these chapters were spoken by the narrators. But these stories do not appear here exactly as they were told. Transcripts of interviews are difficult to read. As in any conversation, we change direction in the middle of sentences, interrupt, correct, or repeat ourselves. Not everything said is equally interesting. I have selected a third to a half of the content of the interviews.

A notable difference between written history and spoken interview is chronology. In conversation, memorable moments bubble to the surface, one after another. We tell stories backward and add crucial information later. The principle of chronology is rarely one of the teller's purposes. I encourage the reader to someday pore through a transcript of a Holocaust survivor interview to experience how much insight into personality and the personal meaning of memory can be read into the twists and turns of such conversations.[13]

I open the first chapter by quoting Lotte Schwarz: "*I come from a little town in Germany, it's in the Sachsen-Thüringen area.*" She said exactly those words in that way, but halfway through our interview. The beginning of the next section, from Ernest Culman about life in Germany before his family's escape to Shanghai, is put together from seven separate places in our interview. My reordering of events as told into events as experienced may obscure some of the speaker's own purposes in telling. But the result is a set of narrative streams that reveal the larger flow of history.

I have not put these narratives into the form of rehearsed speeches or published memoirs. Some of the meandering quality of spontaneous storytelling is still here, opening windows into the minds, and not just the experiences, of our narrators. Nor have I removed every hint that conversations between the narrators and myself are the source of these stories. Those references locate the telling of these memories in times and spaces far from their origin.

History can rarely do better than provide some true pieces of a much more complex reality. Every selection of narrators offers a truncated view of life in Shanghai. Because Shanghai stories were rarely told publically until the 1990s, either orally or in writing, much of our information comes from the generation of young adults, not from the generation who took leadership roles during their Chinese exile. The selection of narrators here reflects the demography of those former refugees who have talked or written about their lives: the oldest, Lotte Schwarz, was born in 1910 and arrived in Shanghai at age 28; most were under 20 when they arrived. Although stories about other family members are central to these narratives, we meet older generations indirectly, from an inevitably less mature perspective.

A larger gap in these stories reflects the distance of Shanghai Jews from understanding Chinese culture and society. Few learned to speak Chinese or absorbed Chinese habits and ways of thinking. The role of

Shanghai in modern Chinese political and economic history is significant, but it does not appear in the narrators' words.[14] Because of Shanghai's colonial history and unique international governance, it was possible for Europeans to get along with a few words of Shanghainese, the local dialect. Instead, Germans and Austrians learned English to function in Shanghai. The whole Shanghai refugee community was extraordinarily isolated, first forcibly from their fellow citizens in Greater Germany, then culturally and socially from the Asians among whom they lived in China. The narrators rarely directly address this isolation, but it is apparent in their words and in their silences.

Every interview contains reminders of how fragile memory is. They may be expressed directly, as Heinz Grünberg did in his ironic, Viennese way at the beginning of our interview: "*I have to say one thing right away, my knowledge consists mainly of gaps.*"[15] In my interview with Herbert and Ilse Greening excerpted in this book, they smoothly filled in each other's lapses of memory after 60 years of marriage. In most of my interviews, however, the narrator had to rely solely on his or her own fallible memory.

A few well-publicized cases of invented Holocaust tales have recently created skepticism about survivors' stories.[16] Anyone knowledgeable about the Holocaust realizes that the extraordinary narratives told by survivors can barely communicate unimaginable experiences. But historians sometimes worry that processes of remembering and forgetting, especially for aged survivors, may distort the accuracy of memories half a century later.[17]

My interviews showed me that powerful experiences leave indelible traces.[18] Rita Opitz, who now lives in Berlin, remembered the words of the Sturmabteilung (SA) men who came to arrest her father in 1938 in two versions in our interview:

> "*Is your Papa at home? . . . here's a penny, go buy yourself in the mean-time some candy.*"
> "*Is the Father here? Here's five cents, go buy yourself some candy.*"[19]

I see these slightly differing versions not as a problem, but as proof of how powerful and accurate these memories are. After 56 years, Opitz recalled some of the words she had heard as a six-year-old. There is no significant difference between the two versions. She says, "*I see them still today standing in front of me . . . that I will never forget.*" I believe her and the narrators I quote in this book.

Narrators do make mistakes, especially when they talk about government policies or faraway events that they heard about from others. It is often instructive to see how information from the wider world penetrates the everyday understanding of refugees. I have noted those places where a narrator's words need explanation or correction. There are very few.

I bring up these features of *Exodus to Shanghai* at the outset so the reader can more easily use the story lines to understand the many minds that formulated them. This is a book of history, not fiction. There is much imagination within these stories, but they are not imaginary.

I have not, however, simply allowed the narrators to tell their stories. I have also used their words to tell a bigger story, the history of a whole community. I have not added ideas that they did not bring up, but I have emphasized some themes and not others, and made some shifts in placement and structure, so that some stories I wished to tell become more prominent. Although I have held back from writing my own words, except in the brief introductions to each chapter, I have acted as a historian in my selection, ordering, and editing of these stories.

Escape from the Third Reich and survival in Shanghai were rarely individual achievements; they represented the collective success of family units in which stronger and weaker members pooled some resources. Refugee life shifted family dynamics: men lost their jobs and often their status as household heads, women made crucial decisions while their husbands suffered in concentration camps, and parents lost power over children. One person might notice the mother making decisions in the father's absence without realizing that relationship shifted similarly in other families. I have deliberately included such stories and given them a greater prominence than the narrators did.[20] I pressed them for details about the preparations for leaving, because they are so revealing about the specifics of the Nazi plunder of Jews.

More often our story-telling intentions, as eyewitnesses and historian, run together. Holocaust narratives are family tragedies about mothers and fathers, children and siblings, aunts and uncles, and distant cousins. In our interviews, I heard survivors tell their own lives in the form of stories about family, and that is what I have tried to reproduce.

The family stories of refugees cross the globe in all directions. Alfred Kohn showed me how he had transmuted grief into a story that he must tell often, but cannot fully control.

Two of my mother's sisters married two brothers, and the brothers looked like twins. I told this story yesterday. Both of them wore glasses. One brother worked in an underground factory for the Germans as a slave laborer, and one day he broke his glasses, couldn't work anymore, so they shot him. The older brother went to Argentina, and he's walking in the street [emotional voice] and a man comes over and says to him, "Are you Mr. Mondschein?" He said, "Yes." And he says, "I can't believe this, I saw how they shot you. I saw how they dragged you out from the underground." He said, "That's my brother."

During some of my interviews, the most difficult moments came at the separation from relatives, usually the oldest, who were never seen again.

Family tragedies are never forgotten. But they do not always appear in interviews. Every interview leaves out significant events. Even the conversational spontaneity that opens memories is affected by the tape recorder and the formality of an interview. Lisbeth Loewenberg said the words "my father" nine times before she added this, late in our interview: *"Oh, I forgot to mention that my father died. My father died in February '42."* That was the final mention of her father.

Interviews are truncated representations of refugee experiences. As in every diary, letter, interview, memoir, or official report that tells of personal disaster and family crisis, the stories here are human constructions, shaped by conscious and unconscious purposes. What may be missing from this book is not easily found anywhere else.

This work took place within my much larger project of interviewing eyewitnesses, reading their memoirs, doing research in archives, and exchanging ideas and information about Shanghai with other historians. It fits into a professional lifetime of studying and writing about German history, especially the history of the Holocaust.

I grew up with the exodus to Shanghai on my mind. My father and his family were hounded out of Vienna by the Nazis; my father came to the United States, but his parents fled to Shanghai. In this way, I am not merely a mirror or a loudspeaker for the narrators, I am a Shanghai storyteller myself. Rather than taking up a place in front of these narrators, I wish to stand beside them. All of us tell our family stories in our own way, with our own purposes, conscious and unconscious. I think of this book as our collaboration.

CHAPTER I

In the Third Reich

During the first five years of Nazi persecution, from 1933 to 1938, about 130,000 of the 525,000 Jews living in Germany left the country. No nation welcomed Jewish refugees; antisemitism was a worldwide disease. Except for a handful of famous people, like Albert Einstein, each escape was a triumph of luck and determination. Every year it became more difficult to find refuge.

Many German Jews hoped they could continue their lives in their homeland, because they were veterans of World War I, because they owned businesses or real estate, or because they just felt themselves to be German. Many others wanted to leave but found their way blocked by governments that did not want any more Jews and that refused to acknowledge the Nazis' deadly intentions.

The national quotas in the U.S. Immigration Act of 1924 theoretically allowed over 50,000 Germans to enter the United States each year. Because most Germans who wanted to enter the United States after 1933 were Jews, the U.S. government employed restrictive procedures to allow fewer than 100,000 Jews to enter the country between 1933 and 1939. The Austrian quota was tiny, limiting Austrian immigration to the United States to 785 people per year, from a Jewish population of over 200,000. Other countries used other methods of limiting Jewish immigration; national self-interest was defined by white, Christian elites as keeping the Jewish presence to a minimum.[1]

Few Europeans knew that no papers or permission were required to enter Shanghai, and even fewer cared. Through the end of 1937, only about 300 Jewish refugees arrived in Shanghai.[2]

For those unable to escape to Western democracies and for those who thought they could survive Nazi persecution, 1938 was a series of rude shocks. On March

12, the German armed forces marched into Austria, and the Austrian population responded with an orgy of violence against Jews, especially in Vienna. On June 9, the official demolition of the Munich synagogue began. A week later, 1,500 Jews were arrested and sent to concentration camps, the first mass arrest of Jews. Behind the barbed wire, the Holocaust began.

On that same day, the Evian Conference of 32 nations ended without taking any action to increase opportunities for Jews to emigrate. In fact, doors to the most obvious destinations were closing that year. The Polish government began depriving Polish Jews living abroad of their citizenship. The Swiss Bundesrat adopted more restrictive measures against Jewish refugees. Britain imposed a visa requirement on refugees with explicit restrictions for Jews.

Suddenly, Shanghai became an acceptable choice. Austrian Jews began anxious attempts to leave soon after the March Anschluss. After June 1938, Jewish organizations started to advise German Jews that Shanghai was a possible destination.

Kristallnacht, as most of our narrators call the days of November 9 and 10, 1938, was a carefully organized national pogrom against synagogues, businesses, and people. Every Jewish family's life was threatened by this sudden escalation of violence. Thirty thousand men were taken to Dachau, Sachsenhausen, and Buchenwald. Only with great difficulty did family members discover that a ticket out of the country could get their men released from concentration camps. The illusion that Jews could somehow find an accommodation with the Nazi government was destroyed by the end of 1938. German Jews left the country in 1939 at four times the rate of previous years.

Nazi policy appeared to encourage, even force, immediate departure. Adolf Eichmann set up the Central Office for Jewish Emigration in Vienna to promote the rapid expulsion of Austrian Jews, a model later copied in Berlin. Jews still argued about whether it was better to go to unknown Shanghai right away or to wait a little longer. In early 1939, Dr. Julius Seligsohn, a leader in the German Jewish community, wrote a report stressing how undesirable Shanghai was as a destination, comparing it to a transit camp.[3] As the stories of those who did leave demonstrate, however, the Nazis' determination to frighten and humiliate Jews and to plunder their property also made it more difficult for many to escape. After being robbed of their assets, the expensive round-trip tickets to Shanghai were a significant obstacle for newly impoverished Jewish families.

Of nearly 600,000 Jews in the enlarged Third Reich in March 1938, more than half were still there when war broke out in September 1939. Our narrators belong to the minority able to leave during these 18 months. Their families overcame a long series of obstacles to get some of their members out of danger.

In few instances was any significant help provided by non-Jews. The unwillingness of ordinary Germans and Austrians, public officials, business colleagues, and former friends to offer assistance, and their willingness to accommodate or participate in Nazi persecution, represent crucial silent spaces in these testimonies to which we must also pay attention. In a country whose official policy was to get rid of Jews, warning a Jewish family that they should escape right away barely counts as a gesture of solidarity.

The world's governments were not merely passive observers as the Nazis deliberately excluded Jewish citizens from German society, systematically robbed them, destroyed their synagogues, and threatened their lives: individual citizens from Western democracies were actively discouraged from helping Jews escape the Nazis.[4] A few foreign diplomats stationed in Europe offered extraordinary assistance in the face of their own governments' policies. Chinese Consul-General Feng-Shan Ho, stationed in Vienna since 1937, made the greatest contribution to saving Jewish lives in the Third Reich. In 1938 and 1939, he issued thousands of Chinese visas to Jews who lined up at his office. These documents were not needed to enter China but were very useful in getting the Nazis to issue passports, in convincing third countries to allow entry, or in buying tickets out of Germany, as described below by Eric Reisman.[5]

Who are these families? They were Europeans of the urban middle class, as were most German-speaking Jews. They had Jewish backgrounds but were not especially observant, again like the larger Jewish population. Many families were mixed: perhaps 20 percent of Jews had married non-Jews during the Weimar years. They were German or Austrian and proud of their patriotism, proven by their men who had fought in World War I. They spoke German and had absorbed German culture. They felt their persecution keenly, as both the state and their fellow citizens lashed out brutally.

Those who went to Shanghai were ordinary Jews. The wealthy and famous were considered desirable immigrants in Great Britain or the United States and could use international connections to procure necessary visas and affidavits. The masses of anonymous Jews had nobody to vouch for them in the United States, were unable to bring significant financial resources out of the Third Reich, and had no especially desirable skills. They were families of salesmen, doctors, and store owners. Shanghai was an exile of the little people.

Nobody has written biographies of these narrators. Few outside of their families asked them about their lives before these interviews. Their stories therefore reflect the typical experiences of the majority who fled the Third Reich in all directions, rather than the famous few whose lives have often been retold. Until they got to Shanghai, that is, where they became a unique community that lasted nearly a decade and then dispersed again over the globe.

Lotte Schwarz (born 1910) worked for the Hilfsverein der deutschen Juden, the Aid Association of German Jews, which helped prospective refugees with advice and sometimes money for passage. As in many Jewish families who had not yet left Germany, the arrest of her husband precipitated an intensive search for refuge. Her story shows how wives were galvanized into unfamiliar action. When she and her husband fled to Shanghai, the Hilfsverein paid for their tickets.

I come from a little town in Germany, it's in the Sachsen-Thüringen area. Nordhausen is the name of the town, had about 32,000 inhabitants that time, but many Jewish people. Most were wealthy, we were not.

I come from an Orthodox German Jewish house. It was Orthodox as long as my grandmother lived. She lived with us all my mother's married life. They called her the *rebetsin* in Nordhausen.[6]

My father was very young, he was 44 years old when he died. And my grandmother said, I never forget that, she was over 80 already, and she said, "Why couldn't I die?" She died the year after my father died. He died of a lung disease, you know. He was in World War I, and he came home sick. But he didn't stop smoking. He smoked secretly and openly, and he smoked more and more. We all were there and saw it. There wasn't anything you could do. He died in '24. And there my mother was with three kids, 12, 13 and 14. She made it, too. We had a good education, my mother saw to it.

My brother Heinz, the older one, was already working, apprentice in a *Kaufhaus* [department store], which he hated. He was smarter than we did. He worked in a little town on the Weser in Germany, and already in 1933 they arrested quite some people there. So he left his job, and he went to Lithuania. He went *Hachsharah*, that means they learn how to farm. For one year, he went there. And when he came back, he came home to us for a few days and packed the few little things he had. I remember our landlord, a Jewish man too, he was a butcher, and he had those big, high boots, and he gave him a pair of those boots. He said the best what he brought with him were these boots. And he left to Israel.

I finished school, and I even finished college two years in Nordhausen. I learned English, French, and Spanish.

I worked in 1933 for a large lawyer firm in Hannover, a very famous firm, and I worked till first of April '33, and that was the time when no Jew could work with a non-Jewish place anymore. So I had to quit. And then I met the secretary from Dr. Schleisner, a former lawyer, who couldn't go to the courts anymore. You know they didn't let the Jews go into court anymore. He was a very good man. He had a family with three little kids. She said, "You know, I'm going to get married. Why don't you take my job?" So I got her job. We didn't have any business, with another lawyer with us, too.

After a little while, that office for the Hilfsverein der deutschen Juden gave Dr. Schleisner the job, he was a representative for the Hilfsverein for the different provinces around Hannover. Hilfsverein was in Berlin, and we were a branch, and got all the regulations from them. And I was his secretary for the province Hannover, Westfalen, Hessen-Kassel, different provinces. But he was so depressed that he couldn't go to court anymore. So I did most of the work. That was around 1934.

Right away, people start coming to us. Like for instance, you had a cousin or an uncle somewhere in Brazil or in Argentina or in Uruguay, so we told him what they needed to immigrate there. They went to their government, and you get the papers, and you had the money to go, or we provided the money through the Hilfsverein, then they could go. We had a full house, yeah. Everybody came. Either they didn't have the immigration laws or no papers to go somewhere, or they didn't have any money to go.

In the beginning, they could still go to England or France, if they had people there. But that was out later, I mean, you had to go overseas, like I did. And mostly they came to apply for the money to get overseas. Many people had somebody in America. They got the affidavit to go to America, but they didn't have the money to go. So we made some research, of course, if the people had money. We tried to get some money wherever they want to go.

There were in Germany wealthy Jewish people, big Jewish organizations, I think, they gave that money to the Hilfsverein. Nobody ever thought about that, where the Hilfsverein got the money. There was never a question, when they filled all the others' conditions, that they wouldn't get the money, at least not as long as I was there. Other people had some money, but didn't have anybody to go overseas, so we tried to a find a place for them.

Later on, the last few years, they didn't have anything. Then there wasn't anything open anymore. Nobody could go to America anymore, you know. And when you didn't have anybody in the United States, the only way to go was Shanghai. And that's when we sent everybody to Shanghai, which was terrible. When I started, I didn't know anybody who was in China. The Hilfsverein had no information about China or Shanghai, that anybody had gone to China before. Later on, of course, we all went to China.

I went on a vacation in the Schwarzwald during my time for the Hilfsverein, because I was so overworked and my mother was living with me. She always saved some money from every paycheck, and she said, "You have to go." And there was only one place which still took Jews. It was in the Black Forest. And I went there.

I met my husband in the Black Forest. First I met a young man there, Benger, who was from Hannover, too. He wanted to marry me [laughs] too. Benger said, "Fräulein Cohn, when you don't marry that Mr. Schwarz, would you marry me?" [laughs] But I married that Mr. Schwarz.

I left the Hilfsverein when I got married in February '38. My husband was an insurance person, but he really didn't have a job anymore. We went to Berlin, but it was hard for him to get new insurance. We had part of a large apartment from a Jewish couple on Kaiserdamm, beautiful neighborhood. After just about three months, somebody knocked at the door. And the lady who belonged that apartment, she went out and she came and said, "There's somebody who want to talk to you." There were two men outside. They said, "Herrn Schwarz?" He said, "Yes?" "Go with us." It was the Nazis, you know.

They arrested everybody on that fourteenth of June.[7] They took all the Jewish people, I don't know how many there were, and they brought them to Buchenwald. They were [laughs] a danger to the public or something, they said. My husband was no danger, he was a very quiet man, you know, no danger.

It took me about a week till I knew where he was. I had no idea that something like that could happen. I called my boss, Dr. Schleisner, in Hannover. And he was nice enough to come to Berlin where I was, but he couldn't do anything, he just explained to me how the situation was, you know, he couldn't do anything.

My husband was very neat and very clean. When he wasn't shaved, he wasn't dressed, okay, that was impossible for him. So I packed his little razor stuff and other toilet articles that he needed, and I went to the police department. At least, I wanted him to have his stuff. And when I came there, that whole police department, that room was full of people. Later on, I met some in Shanghai too. The Nazis said, "Why don't you divorce him?" I said, "I don't want to be without him always."

And the only way what I heard then was, when you show them a ship's ticket to overseas, then you would get him out. I think they told me that at the Hilfsverein. My husband had some relatives in America with a very famous name, but when we wrote to them, they just didn't want to do anything, you know. So I tried real hard, and I worked for the Hilfsverein, and I couldn't do it. So that's why we went to Shanghai.

He was gone three months until we get the tickets from Hilfsverein. They sent it to us without even asking much. The Hilfsverein had the money, and they paid for us, too, for my husband. Then he came home after three months, and we had to leave within two weeks, I think.

My mother, she collected stuff for years and years and years. My mother had a beautiful home in Germany, and I took all that beautiful china with me. I made a list. I still have the list. I typed it, always had a typewriter, or my husband had the typewriter, and I wrote down that everything was from my mother and it was 10 and 20 and 30 years old, you know. I could take everything, they did not open those boxes or anything.

My brother Berthold lived where I come from. My brother worked in a non-Jewish big men's clothing shop there. And when we left, he laughed, it couldn't happen to him. But a few weeks later all the Jewish people left in Nordhausen were sent to concentration camp. He was three months in Buchenwald, too, not quite three months. So we got him a ticket to overseas, we helped with getting that. He came right with the next ship, I think.

We wanted my mother to come before, and she said, she is not going before all her kids are out, that means my younger brother in Nordhausen. Then it was too late for her. She couldn't get out, you know. My mother stayed in Germany, and died there. It was terrible.

Ernest Culman *(born 1929) was forced to change schools, his family had to give up their apartment, and his father, a doctor, was forbidden to have Christian patients. The Gestapo arrested his father the day after Kristallnacht, but the local police chief arranged his release after a few days. His brother celebrated his Bar Mitzvah just before the family left for Shanghai.*

My father's family actually has lived in Germany for centuries, and he felt very much a German patriot. He served in the military as a doctor in World War I. He settled in a little town in Silesia called Liegnitz, roughly 70,000 inhabitants. Now it's called Legnica, because it became a part of Poland. He was not an observant Jew by any means. My father had a seat in the synagogue, but basically he considered himself a German.

My mother was born in Breslau, and her parents lived there and her sister and brother. My mother came from a more observant family, but in our house we didn't keep kosher or anything like that. We went to temple. We had lived in a very large apartment, which had been two apartments and my parents broke through the walls. Half of it roughly was my father's offices and the other our living quarters.

School didn't start until you were six. So I got enrolled in this nursery school, 1935, maybe '36. The lady in charge was a Miss Schröder. My brother had been there before, and she knew my family very well. And one day the doorbell rang. I opened the door, there is Miss Schröder, in tears with a big bouquet of flowers in her arm, wants to talk to my mother. What happened was that one of the kids' parents, also a doctor, objected to having a Jew in the class with his boy, so she came over to tell us that I had to leave. That was my first touch of antisemitism on a personal level.

The following year when I got enrolled in the public school, my mother took me to school, of course, and go into the class and she sees that kid in the same classroom as I. So she went back to the principal, whom she also knew, I mean, my father had lived there for 30 years, everybody knew us. Explained the situation and he put me into a different class where this Mr. Thiel was my teacher.

I didn't really know what was going on. But I always was aware that I was different from everybody else. Military parades used to go down the street in front of our house, it's one of the main streets in a little town, and you know, kids love a parade. And I used to run out there with the other kids watching the parade go by. But I knew I'm not supposed to hold up my hand like the others did.

We went on many trips. We were not too far from the Czech border and frequently went to Czechoslovakia for the weekend. One time going someplace, the car broke, the axle, whatever. Big bang, there was a big part of the car sitting in the back, it was raining. Next thing we know there's a big military convoy coming up, and the guy in charge comes over, "Can we help you?" Then the German *Wehrmacht* helped us move the car and get us to a train station and everything. At other times, we'd go through a little town with big signs, "This town is *judenfrei* [free of Jews]." And sometimes when we saw a parade or something coming by, my father said, "Just hold your hand up to the ceiling, hold up the ceiling, like that, so they think that we are saluting."

Things started bad in 1935 after the Nuremberg laws came into effect. I think it was 1935 or maybe 1936, I don't remember the exact year, my parents wanted to go for a summer vacation to a resort along a lake. We heard of a Jewish bed-and-breakfast, and we wrote to them and got the reservation. This was not too far from Berlin. My father asked, can we swim in the lake, because so many places had signs, "No Jews allowed." "Oh sure, it's no problem here." So we went up there and sure enough all around the lake, "No Jews permitted." We said to the landlord, "What goes on, you told us we could." "Nobody pays any attention to that, just go ahead." So we went swimming, next thing we know there's a guy with a big German shepherd dog yelling at us, we don't come out at once, he's going to chase the dog in after us. So we came out, my parents were very annoyed at the person that was running the inn. We went to another place, also a Jewish resort, but they had their own lake, and spent the rest of the vacation there.

Sometime in 1938, my father lost the right to practice. His practice had been primarily in the working area. He had very few Jewish patients. They took away his right to practice for Gentiles, for Aryans, if you will. He was appointed the health official for the Jewish community in Liegnitz, something to that effect. And he decided we don't need that big apartment anymore. We knew a family by name of Braun, who had sent their three children off to different parts of the world, so they had empty rooms. Their place was on the first floor. On the second floor was a Jewish old age home. So we moved in there.

On November 10th, I went to school. I was the only Jewish kid in the whole school, not just in my class. The kids were all excited about what happened during the night, and I couldn't understand what was going on. When I came home, my mother said, "Did you hear anything?" I said, "Yeah, the synagogue was burned or something." My mother was there in tears. She told me that one of the guys in the old age home had gone, was very observant, he went to synagogue every morning, and he stuttered. He came back and tried to tell her that the synagogue was burning. Her initial thought was somebody had left a lamp on or a candle on and got thrown over, whatever. Nobody thought that it was done deliberately. Then my father got called to a patient who had been taken by the Gestapo during the night, beaten up. While he was there, the Gestapo came to our house looking for my father and my brother. My brother all of almost thirteen. And she said, "Dr. Culman isn't here." "Well, where is he?" "Well, he got called to a patient." "Where?" So they went over to that person's house and picked my father up there and took him to jail from there. My brother was attending school in Breslau, he was born in 1925, there was a Jewish high school there, which we didn't have in Liegnitz. My brother eventually came home from Breslau, and my uncles in Breslau got warned somehow, I don't know the details, and they left by train to Dresden, where we also had relatives, and somehow escaped being taken prisoner.

My father was in jail. Everybody else was in a large dormitory type room, he was in a room by himself. Everybody knew my father, he'd been there for 30 years. So my mother said to the jail keeper, "How come he is solitary confinement, so to speak?" "It's not solitary confinement, Mrs. Culman, we can't put Dr. Culman in the same group as the others." They thought they had special privileges. Solitary confinement is horrible, have nobody to talk to, nothing to do.

After November 10th, I went back to school. And my teacher, Mr. Thiel, came and sat down on the bench next to me every day, "Is your father home yet? Is your father home yet?" The chief of police of Liegnitz took it upon himself not to send anybody to the concentration camp who had been an officer in the German army, so after five days he came home. And when he finally was released was one of the few times in my life that I saw my father crying. [sighs] It was horrible to see my father cry, to try to understand what was going on.

After he came home, we heard on the radio that Jewish children can't go to public schools anymore, so I didn't go the following day. My teacher comes to our house to bring all my books and all that, he was very nice. He said he was so glad that I didn't show up that day, because the principal sent somebody over to him, "You have the only Jewish kid in the whole school, make sure he gets out of here." And he was able to tell him, "Well, he didn't show up today in the first place."

I met Mr. Thiel on the street, he was riding on his bike, a number of times, he always stopped to talk to me to see how I'm doing. He came and brought the report cards to me. Many, many years later during the Korean War I had been drafted and was back in Austria actually, I was stationed in Salzburg, and I made contact with him through the mail. I never did get to see him, but we corresponded for a few months. He remembered me. He was very, very nice.

Almost as long as I can remember, there was always the thought in everybody's mind about emigrating. Even before Crystal Night, my parents were planning to go to Palestine. Some of the furniture my parents had redone for tropical climates. Big heavy bookshelves were put on legs, some pieces were cut shorter, and a lot of clothing was bought. Double soles were put on the shoes, so that when the soles wore out, you tear them off and you had another set of soles in there.

They had pretty much everything in order to get to Palestine, but at Crystal Night the Palestine office in Berlin or wherever it happened to be got burned down, so those papers got lost. And then right after Crystal Night, my father was still in jail, is when my mother found these relatives in Cincinnati and we were thinking of coming to the United States. So we knew we need to learn English.

Couldn't go back to school, and I loved school, always had. And then I had a tutor come to the house to teach me a little bit, including the beginning of English. It was a teenager, maybe early twenties, she wasn't really a trained teacher.

My brother was Bar Mitzvah in Germany a month after Kristallnacht. Our synagogue was burned down. There was no Torah in Liegnitz left for him to be Bar Mitzvahed with. In Breslau, 40 miles away where he had attended the Jewish school, there were little *shuls* [synagogues] that were part of buildings that didn't get burned down, and there were some Torahs there. He had to carry a Torah on the train from Breslau to Liegnitz to be Bar Mitzvahed. The Bar Mitzvah was in a Jewish old age home. People had come back out of the concentration camp, like our rabbi, and it was quite emotional to have a Bar Mitzvah at that time.

We had made contact with some relatives back in Cincinnati, and they sent us an affidavit, but we had to wait like everybody else.[8] One day we had a dinner party at the house. One person said, "I'm not staying here any longer, I'm going to Shanghai." The next person said, "I'll go with you," and my father said, "I'll join you, too." So there were about three families. My brother and I were the only children. One couple had sent their children to England, Holland, and Argentina respectively. The other one had two children that went to Palestine. And the third one was a single man. He had been married to a non-Jewish woman who wouldn't go with him, so they divorced. His wife and his son stayed behind. I think that his son actually went into the German army. After the war, he went back to her, lived in East Germany. These nine or ten people that we were, got together, we booked passage on a Dutch liner out of Genoa.

When it actually came time for packing, all our belongings were packed into a gigantic box, they called it a *Lift*, which was basically the size of a room. A Gestapo agent was there to supervise what you put in there. The silver and gold had already been turned in for pennies, they paid you by weight. But we were allowed to take out two sets of silverware per person, which in our case was eight pairs. I have a few years ago given that to my daughter, she still had that. I had, as toy money, some aluminum coins from when Germany had this tremendous inflation. They were absolutely worthless. My mother was getting ready to pack them, and they stopped her. She said, "Look, let it go," she finally talked them into that it's toy money. I said to her later on, "Why didn't you just let them have it?" I didn't care about my own things as much. But they watched everything that was in there. My parents had some fun glasses, you know, it looked like the glass was filled with wine, but when you drank it, nothing came out. They were fascinated by it, and my mother gave it to them and then they relaxed a little bit and the packing proceeded faster. However, my father would not think of doing anything illegal, he didn't want to take any chances.

We had special clothing made. My uncle had a haberdashery place and clothing made to order. I think the whole family wore the same material, suits for my father, suit for my mother, Henry and I had a lot of clothing that we took along, some suitcases were specially designed to hold a lot of dresses, for example. We took a lot of clothing with us. My mother did take along a fur coat, my father a microscope and all that, and much of this we eventually sold in Shanghai.

As a boy, I was very excited about all this, you know, just like a big adventure for me. Everybody get out of Germany to go to Shanghai, I mean, I had no idea where Shanghai is and neither did I have any idea what fears my parents had. What they must have gone through I have no idea, because I never got a chance to talk to my father about that after everything was over. He died too soon.

When we finally left for Shanghai, some of my father's Gentile friends came in the middle of the night to say good-bye to him. The outside of the building had a big sign, *Israelitisches Altersheim*, Jewish Old Age Home. People were afraid to come in there, be seen. And I remember the one man saying to him, "In some respects you have it easier than we do. You can say what you want in front of your children. We have to watch our tongue in front of our kids, because they could turn us in, and they would turn us in." That stuck with me. I was nine.

*A Christian neighbor in Berlin helped hide **Alfred Kohn's** father when the Gestapo came for him. When Kohn (born 1927), his brother, and his parents had to leave in late 1939 as antisemitic violence increased, there was no place they could go but Shanghai.*

My father was a prisoner in the First World War in Russia, fighting on the German side, and he spent five years in Siberia on a farm. One day a Russian soldier comes by and says, "My God, the war's over already three years, why don't you go home?" So he and a guy from Hamburg went back to Germany, and they arrived, I would say, '21, '22, something like that. Then my father started work in the fur business.

He worked for a company where my uncle was a big furrier, and he met my mother there. He got married and opened up his own business. I was born in Berlin in '27, and so was my brother, I was born in January, he was born in December 1927. We had a nice business, everything was going fine.

In 1933, I started school. I went to a Jewish school, my brother went to a Jewish school which is still in existence today in Berlin. And then my first taste of antisemitism came. I came home from school one day, and I saw the Nazis marching. They had a big camera set up on a piece of wood, they were taking movies. Suddenly they were yelling, *"Haut die Juden,"* hit the Jews. So they grabbed a couple of people who were standing there around, and the people were yelling, "We're not Jews, we're not Jews," and they were beating them [laughs], and the camera kept on rolling. So I ran home. I said, "This is not for me." I told my father. My father instructed that when you were standing in the street, you had to salute. When we saw the Nazis marching, we always hid somewhere.

There was a resort place where you went in the summer time. My father closed up the fur business, and we usually went there four, six weeks in the summer, because my father needed the health, he was very sick from the fur business, the asthma. We were going second class in the train from Berlin to Munich, it's a long trip. This must have been '37, maybe even '38. My father, my mother, my brother, and I, second class in

Photo 1 A German family: Alfred Kohn at left, his parents, and younger brother, Ingolf

Germany, you have a compartment, there are six seats. The door opens up and a very high SS officer walks in and sits down, starts a nice conversation, and we have a wonderful time together. My brother, when he was a young boy, blue eyes, blonde, typical German-looking kid.

And the conversation is going good, and suddenly the guy takes out his card and he says to my father, "Your son looks so typical German, when he eventually goes into the Hitler Youth, I want you to tell the people that you are the friend of Obersturmbannführer whatever-his-name-was." And my father says, "I don't think my son will go into the Hitler Youth." The guy said, "Why not?" And my father said, "We're Jewish." He got up, took his suitcase, walked out. The train was crowded, he stood outside, he never came back into the compartment. This is German logic.

We had a high German Air Force officer in our building where we lived, and about '38 he came to see my father. He warned my father, "Mr. Kohn, I want you to leave Europe, not stay in Europe, because we Germans are going to take up all of Europe."

But we also had good experience in Germany. In Kristallnacht, we were very lucky, the building that we lived in, there were many Jewish families. The guy who was in charge of the building stood in front and says, "No Jews live here," and they passed us by. We were not touched by Kristallnacht. Later on we took a relative, lived with us for six weeks until they went to England.

There was a family on our street by the name of Gabriel, Germans. Mr. Gabriel would call up and say, "Mr. Kohn, why don't you come over tonight for an evening, we want to play some cards." My father didn't play cards. We knew the Gestapo was looking for Jews, so my father spent the night there. When the Gestapo came, my mother, "I don't know, my husband went out to play cards, I don't know where he is," that's it. This thing broke off in '39. One day they were looking for Jews, so we went over there, and as we walked into the house somebody said, "Oh, here the Jews are coming again." We were afraid to go to them, because it would be giving them away. But when the rationing came in, for butter, for milk and things, we always got from them, you know. They were good people, good Catholics. If there is such a thing, but they were.

We once tried to go across the border. We wanted to go to Belgium, Switzerland. We had relatives in this country who came here in 1848 already. But because of the quota system, we couldn't leave. Everything tried, nothing worked. And there was no place in the world to go except Shanghai at the very end.

Eric Reisman (born 1926) describes beatings from other youngsters in Vienna, the takeover of his father's business by an employee, and the agonizing search for a way out of the Third Reich. His brother witnessed the murder of a schoolmate. Reisman's family escaped just after Kristallnacht with help from the Chinese Consul, Feng-Shan Ho, after all other efforts failed.

I'm Eric Reisman. My family originated in Czechoslovakia, in Theben-Neudorf, where my father and mother were born. After World War I, my father and mother immigrated to Vienna, where my father went into business. That business broke up, and he went into a rather strange but different type of business of citrus fruit import in wholesale, with another person, and they did very well. He had a truck and he had a place on the *Naschmarkt* [open-air food market], where he sold to the wholesalers. My mother, being a very business-minded person, opened up a delicatessen store not far from where we lived in the eighth district in Vienna, Josefstadt, and pursued her own business career.

I was born in Vienna on April 26, 1926. My brother is three years older than I. My brother and I went to school, we had friends, we had playgrounds in the area. We played the normal soccer, and we had a very comfortable life with few worries of anything. We joined the Boy Scouts, which kept us active. During the summer vacation, my father would rent a room in a farmhouse outside of Vienna, where my brother and I and my mother would spend the summer months out of the city.

Antisemitism was already felt way before the annexation of Austria to Germany, and as a youngster, you had to bear with it. You bent with the wind and you couldn't do very much about it. We were of course geared and directed toward preserving the regime, which was under Schuschnigg at that time, and we were very pro-Schuschnigg and against the elements of the Nazi regime.[9]

We had a Friday night meeting in the Boy Scouts, which was walking distance away from where we lived. Already there were outbreaks of violence, where Nazi underground youths would storm into a Boy Scout meeting and beat the youngsters up and destroy whatever was there, because they knew that the Boy Scouts were against their theories. So consequently, when we were in there, the door was locked.

Suddenly there was a knock on the door and shouts from a person outside, we didn't know who it was, that Hitler had crossed the borders and for us all to go home. It was one of the members of the troop's mother

Photo 2   Jews scrubbing the streets in Vienna, 3rd District, March 1938

that was at the door, and she told us to go home through side streets. We were in uniform, and we had these swatches on the sleeve with the insignia of the Austrian patriotic flag. My brother being older, he had the foresight, "Let's go down through side streets back to our residence." We tore off these swatches and made our shirts just look brown, rather than have any kind of identity on there. We ran home through side streets, and we weren't gathered up to be made a spectacle of by the howling masses.

I got home, and my father closed the windows and he says, "Don't illuminate the light, show that there's anybody in the residence." I asked my father, "Where is mother?" He says my mother is downstairs on the street, she was taken to clean the street. I looked out the window, saw my mother being surrounded, there were about 20 Jewish people there cleaning the sidewalk.

What they were doing actually with scrub brushes and water and soap, whatever they had, trying to get the propaganda slogans that were with oil paint put on the sidewalks, voting propaganda, vote for this party or for that party. They were trying to erase any traces that showed that there was propaganda for the Schuschnigg regime.

Unbeknown to my father, I ran outside. I got down there, and I got myself by the storm troopers, and one of the guys said to me, "What are you doing here?" I says, "I'm going to help my mother, she's down there."

So he grabbed me by the seat of my pants and up in the air, right in the middle of everybody. [laughs] I kneeled and scooted over toward my mother, and my mother was surprised to see me. I was helping. We were there a while. Every minute lasted like an hour, the howling masses and the dirty water being spilled on us. We were on our knees scrubbing the sidewalk when I heard our superintendent of the house that we lived in say to one of the storm troopers, "That woman over there with the child, you don't need to show them what work is, she's a hard worker." That somehow weakened that storm trooper and said, "You with the child, go home." And so after a few hours we were able to go home. The next morning when I looked out the window, those same people were still there scrubbing. So we were fortunate to be able to get away sooner.

My brother went to the *Maschinenbauschule* [machine-building school] in Vienna. One day when he came into school, there's a hullabaloo, a whole ruckus. One of his classmates, a Jewish youngster, was carried up a winding staircase to the top flight. They threw him over, and he was killed. My brother ran home, and he had a nervous breakdown from that experience. That was very difficult for us, we didn't know which doctor to go to, other than the doctor that we knew, who happened to be a Jewish doctor, very good doctor. He started treating my brother, and lucky enough the treatment that he prescribed cured him basically.

This doctor, Dr. Schäfer, his two children were schoolmates and playmates of ours. One day we found out that he had committed suicide and took his family with him. The Christian population, I would say the antisemitic population, wanted to better themselves, so they knocked on Jewish people's doors, threw the occupants out, and moved in. And if the people said, "Where should I go?" "There's the Danube, go into the Danube." Meaning, "Kill yourself, go drown yourself, do whatever you want, but you're not human. We are now the master race, and we want that apartment, or that house, or that residence, whatever it is." That happened time and again.

The eighth district, the area we lived in, had Jewish people, but in a very great minority. The friends that we used to play football with, tag, hide-and-seek, whatever young people played, they didn't want to know you anymore. Suddenly you were an outcast. People that you used to eat ice cream with, you used to drink a glass of milk with, you had a snack with, and you used to chat, suddenly either they walked away or clammed up when you approached them, so it was a very peculiar feeling.

I went to school in my district, and that was out of the question, we couldn't go there anymore. We all had to go to a school in the seventh district. We lived in the eighth district, and that was a very long way. I couldn't use public transportation, you weren't permitted to do it, so it meant walking. You got up an hour and a half earlier to get to the school. However, you got to school, and there were Jewish children from all around the area, several districts combined into one school that they all had to attend. The classes were over-filled. There was one teacher for two or three classes in various grades.

Learning in itself was difficult, because your mind was also set, now you had to go home. Not so much when you entered the school, but when you exited, there was crowds outside waiting with bottles, stones, and swinging chains. You were exposed to other children and the hatred that was either instilled by them or unfortunately they were born into. They would attack in groups. And you had no choice, they'd surround you and gave you a good shellacking. Anybody walking by got hit by rocks and bottles thrown at him, whether they were girls or boys. You took your life in your hands trying to get out of this school.

So then we walked back about a good hour's walk, and I had my lederhosen on. I didn't know that the lederhosen was considered a part of the Hitler Youth uniform, which was either a black velvet pants or lederhosen. As I was walking with my school satchel on my back, I got held up by several youngsters from the Hitler Youth demanding my lederhosen. So I gave it to them, I could not resist. Fortunately I had gym pants underneath, and I walked home in my gym pants. But it left me with an impression. I got home and I told that to my mother and father. I wouldn't wear lederhosen anymore, because that would antagonize them and that was the one thing I didn't want to do.

To live as a youngster, it was not easy. It was all these antisemitic slogans, made me as a youngster of 11 years at that time grow up practically overnight. You had to think very rational and do everything with a great deal of thought and caution. Your youth was stolen from you. That's one thing that I can never regain, the free thinking, the carelessness of a youngster. As you got older, you had to help your parents in the struggle for survival.

On my own, my parents did not force me, I said to my parents, as young as I was, that learning is an impossibility. I told my mother that I wasn't prepared to go to school, I wasn't going to learn anything.

I always liked woodwork and the smell of wood. It so happened that I had tradesmen in the house, downstairs in the basement they had a *Tischlerei* [cabinetmaker's shop]. I got to know the guy who worked there, and he was a nice fellow. I always helped him carry lumber or do things, so whenever I came, he put me to work. Surprising enough, he had contracts with various SS organizations, and they built a new office building for the local gendarmerie. He would take me along. As a youngster I didn't look too Jewish. He said, "Call me Father," and so I worked with him wherever we went. We laid parquet floorings and so forth, and I helped him carry the heavy sacks of hardwood flooring pieces, parquet slabs, up the stairs, and I handed him tools. So that's what kept me busy. And I stayed out of trouble that way.

The day that Hitler's troops entered Austria, my father went into his place of business, and the driver who drove the truck said, "Reisman, go home. This business is mine, it's no longer your business." My father couldn't do anything, so he went home. The banks were closed to us, everything was not accessible to us, so what we had in the house was all we had. My father, sensing the situation, he said, "I can't wait for the regime to change. I have to feed my family, I have to support my family." He immediately, the second day, pursued the emigration out of Austria.

We wrote letters to family members, nephews that my father had that I never knew lived in Argentina. We didn't have anyone in the United States at that time. And we tried to dig through registries to find someone that we possibly may have known, and tried to write letters to get an affidavit of some sort. Vienna being the capital, it had the embassies there. We went to countless consulates and embassies trying to get an entry visa into any country. My father, my brother, and I, we took turns to stand in line in front of a consulate. We'd stand in line from the evening before until the morning, nine o'clock when the consulate opened.

On every consulate, there was a policeman out front, sometimes there was a storm trooper out front, sometimes it was a government official out there quote unquote "guarding" the consulate. He had acquired or assumed the responsibility of telling how many people could go in. Sometimes the first ten would only go in, sometimes only the first 15 would go in. If you were lucky, be among the first 15, you could go in. That luck enabled you to get an application or meet somebody, an ambassador or a consul from that country, to talk to him and plead with him, "May we have an exit visa? I would like to immigrate to your country. I have a family, whatever know-how I have that I could impart to that country, and thus be of value to your country." Well, those experiences were countless. They would give you the application, the application would require you to have your copy of a translated birth certificate to that country's language, your marriage certificate, countless documents translated, which was costly and time consuming. And that would have to accompany the application. That gave you at least encouragement that maybe it would develop into some-thing. That basically happened from one consulate to the next consulate to the next consulate, regardless of what country it was.

Until one day we stumbled on the Chinese consulate. The Chinese consulate said, "Yes, I give you a visa, if you can give me a document where to give the visa into, a passport." Well, okay, we got an assurance that we could get to China. But now came the question, where are you going to get a passport? They wouldn't give you a passport, unless you had a visa. They couldn't give you the visa, unless you had a passport. So where are you going to go? I don't know whose idea it was, but the people that were trying to immigrate to China were able to convince the Chinese ambassador that he would provide us with a promissory note saying that if we had a passport, he would stamp the visa into that passport. That promissory note he was able to give to those interested to go to China. We were able to get that.

With that promissory note we had to now convince the German Austrian authorities to issue us a passport. Again it was the process of standing in line, waiting countless hours, countless days, to try and get in to see the authorities to convince them to give us a passport. First, you have to get what they called a *Steuerunbedenklichkeitserklärung*, which means that you didn't owe any taxes to the government, the previous government or this government. Secondly, you would have to go to the police authorities and give them proof that you had not been convicted of any minor or major crime, that you had never served in prison for any wrongdoings. You had to get from your local authorities that there were no outstanding traffic violations or pedestrian violations, whatever vio-lations, that you were in the clear there. Basically countless documents to include in the application for a passport. Overcoming that hurdle, we finally got our passport with the red letter "J" in there.

Okay. Now that you had the passport, we had to get a booking to go to China. My father had bought my mother Persian rugs. I have a special liking for them, because those Oriental rugs basically saved our lives. We didn't have any money, so my father was able to sell these Oriental rugs for a fraction of their value, but it gave us sufficient funds to buy a ship's passage to China. In September, we got our tickets and got the visas and so forth, and were able to leave in November.

We were trying to get these big steamer trunks. Those were very much in demand. We were able to find through an ad in the paper a person that was selling steamer trunks, and it was a far distance away from where we lived. I was working for a cabinetmaker, and he had one of these large hand carts, so I asked him if we could borrow the hand cart, my brother and I. And we went from one end of Vienna to the other pushing that hand cart through the streets, to pick up these steamer trunks which my father bought from that person. The school that I went to had its sport grounds in that very same area, and I knew there were antisemitic gangs always lurking out in front of the school for any Jewish kid, or anyone that looked Jewish. So I said to my brother, "We should avoid that section because I know, I've been there before. That's a very bad area, we don't want to go through that." He said, "I'll go with you." My brother was blond, didn't have a trace of Jewish looks. So he says, "I'll push the rear of the wagon and you steer the front, we're going to go through there." Lo and behold, just as I predicted, these kids spotted me as looking more Jewish than him. He got up to them, and he defended me. Anyhow, we got into a big beating there, we couldn't fight the masses, but we got the trunks and we went back. That was one beating that I couldn't escape.

Funds we did not have. First of all, you could not exit with any funds. But we didn't have any, because my father didn't have any source of income. We had a safe in the house. My father had some money in there from the business that was not deposited in the bank account for normal payment of bills, but that was used up very rapidly. The source of income we had was to sell whatever we had for practically nothing, because there was so much of it on the market that you gave things away. But it gave you enough income to be able to buy the milk, to buy the bread, to buy the potatoes. And so we didn't have the problem of worrying about how to transfer funds.

My uncle, he was one of my father's brothers that came to Vienna later from Czechoslovakia, and he had a hat factory in Vienna. He was doing fairly well. He had connections, and so he got a visa to Australia, and he transferred money with someone that had a way of getting the money out to Australia. Before his ship docked in Sydney, Australia, the fellow sent word up that he couldn't get the money out. A lot of our own people cheated the rest of them, one way or another. My uncle had a stroke and died on the spot, he never set foot into Australia.

Valuables we were able to hide. You knew you were permitted one set of earrings, one ring, one chain around your neck, one of each, but not more than one. Some of the heirlooms that my mother and father were able to save from the family were priceless to them, they were treasures, so my father was able to hide it and hoping they would not detect it.

My uncle, for instance, he took a rubber heel off a shoe and hollowed that portion out. People cut out books and made them into hiding places.

People put false bottoms in valises. They would hide things in cameras, tell people that there's film in there and don't open it.

I don't know how we escaped, but we were very fortunate. We lived in a very nice apartment in a very reputable area, and the *Gauleiter* [Nazi district leader] of that district wanted our apartment. For some reason he had pity on us. He knew about the Kristallnacht before the date it was set for. We had a knock on the door, and there was an SS man standing there. I said, "Now it's our turn to move out, he wants the apartment." The *Gauleiter* sent a letter, telling us to paste that letter on our door. It said, "This apartment should not be touched. It belongs to me when the people move." We were left alone, because he wanted the apartment and he didn't want damage to the interior of the apartment, because it was his. So that saved us there. The next day, when we heard about all the damage, my brother went to the Neudegger Temple, where he was Bar Mitzvahed, and he saw it was burnt out. All the Jewish stores were smashed, the windows were smashed, everything was robbed. These are the things that we endured during that time, but we were fortunate, very fortunate.

We left after Kristallnacht, we left the end of November of 1938, so we had a considerable amount of time under the thumbs of the Nazis and under duress there, we were exposed. I don't know whether I had nerve or I had guts or I had gumption or whatever I had, but when there were parades I went to see the parade. When Hitler drove along the Ringstrasse, on his first visit to Vienna, I was there with all the crowds. I wasn't yelling "Heil Hitler," but I was there looking, just like anybody else was looking. And I saw a lot, and I wasn't molested too much, other than that incident of the lederhosen.

We stayed together. My mother and father had the opportunity at the time, the mothers could go to England as housekeepers and take one child along, that was permitted, and the English would give visas to housekeepers. And my father said, "No, we're going to stay together. Together we can bear the hardships much easier than if we were separated from each other." So we stayed together, and we were able to get out as a family, and that was my father's doing. My mother, in turn, was able to care for us and nurture us, including my father, because he sometimes came home very disillusioned, and my mother was able to give him the strength in order to bear through those kind of turmoils in our life.

What I am very grateful to my father and mother for is one thing, that my father recognized the situation immediately, and he also knew that the family should stay together. We could bear all kind of hardships as long as we were a family.

I guess I was very, very fortunate.

Ruth Sumner *(born 1927) lived with her father and sister in eastern Germany. Their cleaning lady was the only Christian who offered real help. After her uncle's murder in Buchenwald, her father realized his wealth could not protect them. They left in January 1939, on a Japanese ship. Sumner's older sister, alone in the family, was able to get a visa for the United States.*

I was born in Silesia, Beuthen, which is part of Poland now. We lived in that small town called Bobrek. I was raised with a maid, nurse, chauffeur, all this kind of stuff. My parents went to Switzerland and shipped us off to children's camps, the best and the finest. My father was wealthy. He operated a kind of a bar right across the street from smelters, it was like Pennsylvania, and you know how many pubs they had. I have one sister, Eva, four years older than I.

When I was six my mother was killed. She was shot by a drunken intruder. He shot at my dad and put him in a hospital, killed her. He fled. It was one of those bizarre cases. Later on I found out that she had been pregnant at the time. I didn't know it. My sister told me.

My aunt, who was my grandmother's youngest sister, came to live with us. I guess I must have been about eight or nine years old when Papa sold the business. He sold because of Hitler, and we moved to Beuthen, which was the closest town, about '37, I don't know for sure. We lived about a year or two before we left Germany in '39.

My father lived off his money, retired. He owned the huge apartment complex that we were living in. My sister told me that. He had no intentions of leaving Germany. Most of this that I'm telling now is retold, because I was too young to remember. All the memories I have of Germany was that we were no longer allowed to go to the school anymore. I went to a private school, I believe. I was not a particularly good student. We were asked to leave. And I had to go the last year or so to a Jewish school. But my memories are very weak on that. We couldn't go to movies anymore, the persecution started. That didn't feel good that I couldn't go to a Shirley Temple movie.

I think you might be interested in a story. We weren't allowed to have a live-in maid anymore that we had for eight or ten years. She had to leave. And we were the type of people that always had servants. Then we got a Christian woman that cleaned house for us, Mrs. Deckert, I remember that lady fondly. Why do I know she was Christian? Because her sons were Matthew, Mark, Luke, and John. That old lady, she might have been in her fifties, I don't remember. At that time, it was very dangerous to be friends with Jewish people. She took us to her home, which was on the outskirts of the city. It was a little house, like we see more in the United States than in Europe, with a garden around it and a fence. She took us in there, and she had a root cellar. She lifted up the rug and opened that up and said, "If you ever have any problems, we'll hide you." That's unheard of in those days, because everyone was afraid for their own lives, not that we blame them.

I remember when they shipped all the Polish Jews out of Germany. Beuthen was close on the Polish border. I remember my sister going to the *Bahnhof* [train station] to have food and stuff for the people that came through by train. That was before Hitler took over Poland. And then I remember Kristallnight, the night they burned the synagogue down, going to see the rubble.

Just shortly after that, it might have been a week, my daddy got a notice that his brother had been arrested, sent to Buchenwald and they had sent him back. They said he tried to escape. He was all chewed up by the dogs, he died from the wounds. I was nine years old, ten years old, I was very young.

My daddy had planned to get us kids out of Germany, and he figured he was retired, he had money, and he wasn't that old. He was in his middle forties at that time. He had made arrangements for my sister to come to the United States. My grandfather's brother lived in Bell, California, and he was going to take my sister, who was 13, 14 at the time. And then if it worked out, they were going to take me. But when this situation occurred with my dad's brother, he said, "We're getting out of Germany."

He went to Berlin and came back and said, "The only place you can go to without any papers was Shanghai. We're leaving." And within three weeks, we were gone. All of our possessions, we just left with suitcases. We left in January, I think. We left my sister behind, and my sister left that spring for the United States.

It's hard for Americans to realize that when the front doorbell rang, my daddy went out the back door. We were living in that much fear towards the end, just before we left. After we left Germany, my sister said the doorbell rang and a couple of SS soldiers were at the door. They asked for my papa, and she said he wasn't there. And they asked her some questions, and she said, "For the first time in my life, I was frightened. I knew they were looking me over, from one end to the other. He was making questions and kind of backing me up against the wall." She was 14, a young lady. Mrs. Deckert came out and said, "She is not alone! I'm here and I'm responsible for her." And they backed up. She was okay. That I didn't know until recently, you see, some of the holes in my early life, my sister consequently remembers more than I do.

What else do I remember of Germany? Germany, I was growing up. Then we got out before it got bad. But that's all the memories I have, because I was too young.

Gérard Kohbieter (born 1922) decided to go to Shanghai at age 16. Neither his father nor his mother were ready to leave, so he went alone, hoping to support himself as a magician.

I was born in Berlin, May 30th, '22. I went to school there, the last two years in a Jewish school. My parents had a big healthy business, distribution of electrical stuff and lighters and so on. I lived alone with my mother. My mother was an intellectual. She was politically very interested on the left, although she did have money, which is a good combination, because those people can do things. Interesting woman, laughed a lot, had a great humor, social graces. Man, she was the kind of woman that in another time would have had a salon. She always had interesting people around, creative people. Papa had left earlier. But we saw him under good terms. It just wasn't enough to stay together, I guess. It happens. By then it was '38, and I had been thinking about emigrating and we had written to relatives in the States, distant, distant relatives, who didn't really care very much.

They had loudspeakers in Berlin. Not everybody had a radio in those days, and they had loudspeakers, I guess, to get a better listening rate for Hitler's speeches, or for whatever propaganda was coming through there. But when nobody was speaking, they were playing march music, which up to this day I can't stand.

I heard the grown-ups talking, man, and what was happening and what happened, this one got busted, that one got busted, and businesses were closing. Meanwhile the jokes were going, how this can't last forever, you know. There was a significant joke about how two Jews meet on the *Kurfürstendamm* in 1960 and one says to the other, "Six months I give him." But I wasn't taken in by that. I felt danger. It was like a cat reacts to people who are real nervous, cats stay away from them, they don't hop in their lap. It felt dangerous, all those clowns walking around, man, with this super-masculinity, this marching, this macho thing, God in heaven, and it was directed at us. I wasn't particularly a religious Jew or anything like that. I felt unsafe.

And then happened November 9th. I mean, nobody bothered us. But on my way to school I saw the Jewish stores, I heard the stories. And the guy across the street that had the biggest car on the block and a factory, a very civilized and cultured and powerful man, got busted, came back shaved, and packed his suitcases and left without saying anything. I realized, I gotta go. I wasn't ready for this. My mother had been feeding me pacifist literature from the time I started reading, so that I had perhaps not a political view, but certainly developed a feeling for the dangers that can befall man in our society.

I was 16. I started working on my mother. It took many, many evenings of persuasion. And she let me go. She said, "Okay. If that's what you want to do." My father brought up arguments like, "My God, what are you going to do in Shanghai? We don't know anybody in Shanghai, and you don't know the language, and my God, how dangerous. How can you? It's quite an adventure that you're doing this." And I said, "Well, yeah. But look how dangerous it is to stay here. This is an adventure, too. I'd rather." But the decision was with my mother anyway. She was the stronger personality.

We had a connection in Shanghai, a doctor that lived across the street that lived there already for quite a few years. Excellent doctor, woman doctor. My mother wrote her a letter and said, "Listen. Perhaps you can help in this somehow."

My mother had a love affair with somebody. I don't know exactly what her motivation was. She said, "Listen, you go. We'll fix everything up for you, and then I'll come a little later." Well, there wasn't time. Shanghai was closed, at one point you couldn't come in anymore. And that was it.

You couldn't take money. I left the country with four bucks, ten Marks. There was a death penalty on smuggling money. And, man, I wasn't about to risk that. I've never been able to risk jail, no matter how attractive the proposition may be. Never. Don't have the temperament for it. There was fear then. The money was there. I could have, but other people managed.

But you could take things. So I got myself all fitted out, I got a whole bunch of good clothes. I got myself a tuxedo, and I got more magic tricks from the magic store. And photos, because I knew I was going to need photos if I start a career as a magician. Man, I was 16. I had never done this, but I had a magic teacher, who also showed up in Shanghai, who had showed me the business, how you need photos and how you approach agents. So I had a little bit of a theoretical background. And the rest was taken care of magically by the parents. That's the beauty of being a child. I would sometimes think it wasn't really worth the trouble of growing up. They got the ticket, they did all the paperwork for me and that was that.

The ticket had to be purchased in Hamburg. My mother's boyfriend had to fly to Hamburg, man, to nail it down. Berlin was sold out, but in Hamburg there were some dealers. They bought up the tickets and then sold them for twice the price. He paid, I don't know, 1,300 Marks for a ticket to Shanghai that should have cost 650 or something like that. I don't know who the dealers were. I know that Lloyd Triestino, the line that a lot of the guys came on, that whole blocks of tickets showed up on a black market, which you knew because you heard so-and-so and so-and-so got tickets. Somebody was making money.

Those were the preparations. That was in '39, in March, about six months before the invasion of Poland, before the whole thing started. So I packed up, and I went to Shanghai.

Herbert and Ilse Greening (born *1912 and 1919), among the oldest of our narrators, were married right after Kristallnacht. Herbert's medical school fraternity life shows the growing tension Jews felt in their German Jewish identity. Their marriage preparations combined traditional customs with the collapse of normal life for Jews. The Greenings tell their Shanghai stories together.*

Ilse Greening: I was born in Hannover, Germany, and had a pretty ordinary life, a very easy life. My mother's father was well-to-do. Her father emigrated from Poland to evade the draft and came to northern Germany and became very successful. My mother had a traditional upbringing. She went to finishing school, and she married my father. We had a very big house in Hannover, and servants, a chauffeur and a governess and a cook and a maid.

My father served in the First World War. He came from a religious, very Jewish home, and we were observant to a certain extent, but we were Germans first, and we really were brought up German. My father had a family tree made, and his family lived in this area in Germany since 1600. I remember my grandfather had the papers to prove those things, which unfortunately do not survive.

We moved to a small town, Peine, which is half an hour from Hannover, where my father bought a business. I was a kid. There was already anti-Jewish feelings, and people were told not to buy from Jewish merchants.

Because we were so German, he was deeply hurt. But my father put all his medals from the war on a board, and he put that in the shop window. It says, *"Der Dank des Vaterlandes ist Euch gewiss."* [The gratitude of the Fatherland to you is certain.]

My father killed himself in 1933, because it was just too much for him. So then we moved back to Hannover. After my father died, the teacher in school told the other kids that they have to be especially nice to me.

My mother and my sister and I were alone. I went to a commercial high school in order to have a job. I worked for a lawyer. I started when I was 16 years old, which was very uncommon in those days, but I wanted to be independent.

My mother's sister had a husband who was a traveling salesman in the Far East already before the First World War. He traveled by boat and by Trans-Siberian Railway. Not only to China, he traveled all over.

In 1932, I think it was, he decided to settle permanently in Shanghai, because it had seasons. He was selling piece goods, he thought it would be better if there was a season for his business. His wife and daughter finally also went to live in Shanghai, where the foreigners lived a very luxurious life with servants. Since they were making money in foreign currencies, the exchange rate was very favorable, and there was nothing they couldn't have.

Herbert Greening: I was born in Königshütte, Upper Silesia, in 1912. When this part of Upper Silesia became Polish in 1922, my parents moved to Hindenburg, which is also Upper Silesia. I went to high school there, graduated in '31, and went to Bonn Medical School.

Medicine was not my first choice. In high school I wanted to go into theology. I studied Talmud, and I really enjoyed it. But after a while, I went to the rabbi, "Rabbi, I don't think I can become a rabbi." "Why not?" "I don't have the faith." He said, "Don't worry, don't worry. You just keep the tradition, the faith will come." I said, "Not for me."

I didn't think I had it for medicine, but in my fraternity I saw kids who were much more stupid than I was. So I said, "If they can do it, I sure can do it, too." So I switched to medicine, and it came very, very easy to me. I was a good student, a good learner without studying too much, and was happy ever after. That's the story.

We had a real fraternity after the German model. It's a national group founded in 1896, *Kartell-Convent deutscher Studenten jüdischen Glaubens* [Union of German Students of the Jewish Faith]. It accepted both Jews and non-Jews, but the Jews were in the majority. We had to pay a fee for being a member, and that was adjusted according to the money we got from our parents. We had a house where we had lunch every day, we paid for that extra.

In the fraternity, we had one guy who was telling us about discipline, another guy who was telling us about religion, another guy about physical activities. We had to learn boxing, we had to learn fencing, we fenced three times a week. That was important, being in good physical shape, being well dressed. We met every Saturday night at the house of the fraternity and had a "drinkfest," we drunk plenty, beer mostly.

They were a close-knit club, actually. A little bit conceited, very aware of their Germanism, but good Jews, religious Jews mostly, I would say on the liberal side. Still, many of them went to Israel, many of them became good Zionists. I am one of them who did not become a Zionist.

In Germany, there was so-called academic freedom, you could change university any time you wanted. So I first stayed for two semesters in Bonn, and went to Berlin to meet a girlfriend. In Berlin we already had, how shall I say, protest parades against the Nazis. Didn't help much. Then I went back to Bonn and did my *Physikum*.[10] I was told two weeks prior to the *Physikum* that all Jews had to get out of school. But there was a special legislation in Upper Silesia called the Geneva Convention, according to which we were treated like political minorities, the Jews, so I could keep on going to Bonn. I finished my *Physikum,* and after that it became sort of difficult for us. I moved to Breslau in '34, which was closer to my parents. I wanted to be closer to them.

In Breslau, we noticed antisemitism in school. We were not allowed to sit in the lecture halls, we had to stand at the back, behind the seats. We were not allowed to touch German women and men, which made it difficult in obstetrics. In obstetrics we had to pass a seven-day in-school test, but we only had the theoretical part. We saw a delivery, but we never took part in it.

There were only oral examinations. There were 40 students and one professor, and he grilled you for about three to four hours. I finished school Christmas '36 with very, very good marks, except in bacteriology, where the director of bacteriology was a top Nazi and he made it difficult. I was the last Jewish student to graduate in Breslau. In January, I got a job as an intern at the Jewish hospital in Hannover, a small hospital, 60 beds. After finishing my internship, I became assistant at the same hospital.

In the morning of November 9, I was in the operating room, we were doing a breast. The Nazis came into the hospital, and the nurse in charge of the operating room said, "You can't go in there. They're operating, and you are not sterile." So they never came to the operating room. That night I hid in the basement, and in the evening, I got a call from my medical chief, I have to make a house call for him. The first house call in my life. How can I go? I couldn't say no, there was a sick guy, and I had to go and see him. So I put a hat on, put it over my eyes as deep as I could, and took the streetcar and made a house call. Everything went well. In the morning we heard about the synagogues and the destruction. My 9th of November.

I wanted to emigrate, and I wrote to our former family doctor, who in the meantime had emigrated to America. Never got an answer. Another patient of mine, who thinks I saved his life, promised to do something for me, but also an empty promise.

Ilse Greening: After the Kristallnacht, we sent a telegram to Shanghai to my uncle, whether we would come, because there was a lot of pressure then on the Jews to leave the country. And he wrote a telegram back, "Welcome." Everything was sudden, and we knew we had to go, so we went in a hurry. We did not have any other choice.

People like Herbert's father or my boss, who was a lawyer, never expected Hitler to last. Even in November after Kristallnacht, my boss, who was a very intelligent, well-informed person, said, "It's a pity you have to leave so soon, because Hitler is not going to last." So did Herbert's father and many, many people. People were very innocent, and I have to say that I personally never, never suffered any discrimination. Never a single remark ever about Jews and antisemitism.

I told my mother that Herbert did not have any chance to leave the country. He didn't know anybody, the few people he contacted never answered. So I said to my mother, "What's going to happen to Herbert? He has to stay here." And then she said, "He can come." She asked me whether we intended to get married, and I never had given it any thought. We were friends, but not serious friends.

My mother thought it would be better if we got married, so we finally decided to get married in December 1938. There were no rabbis available, and we just had a registry wedding. Much later, when our son was six months old, we had a religious. That's it.

Herbert Greening: We were going steady, and Ilse came one day and asked would I go with them to China. I said, "Of course I will, I'll go anywhere." So we got engaged in November of '38. In December 1938, on Christmas time, I took Ilse to Hindenburg to meet my parents. They had to leave their own apartment, they lived in the apartment of my sister's in-laws.

Ilse Greening: Because their apartment was destroyed and the store also. Herbert's father thought I was an heiress.

Herbert Greening: She wasn't. But they liked Ilse, or they said they liked Ilse, and that was that. And then came the preparation for going to China. My mother gave me as a present an electrocardiograph, which I was not allowed to take along. The Nazis said, "You want to go from house to house with your electrocardiograph and show off with our German science," so that was out. But a retired physician gave me all his office equipment, which I took to China, which I used all those years, and I still have those.

I had my instruments, I had an examining chair. I had a complete office outfit and nowhere to go.

Ilse Greening: When we finally were packing a *Lift,* someone came from the authorities to check what we were putting in, but he had been in Shanghai a long time ago, and he didn't really care what we put in. He was very lenient. My mother had some jewelry, we had expensive china and silverware and all that.

I think we did not take advantage of the freedom. For instance, we only took one sofa for four people. You did not think rationally in those days. I don't know, you cannot explain. People were in a daze. Lots of people came to Shanghai with lots of money, but we were innocents abroad. We only had the four dollars. The sewing machine we took. When we got to Shanghai, they wanted duty because they thought it was a new machine, but my mother had had it forever.

Otto Schnepp (born 1925) was 12 when the Nazis marched into Austria. Although his father was a doctor, the Nazi policy of systematically confiscating Jewish property made it difficult for Schnepp's family to buy the expensive tickets to Shanghai. As in most Jewish families, family needs kept some members behind, and they were eventually murdered.

I lived in Vienna. My father was a physician in the 20th district, Brigittenau, which was a relatively poor district, and he was not a good businessman ever. He was interested more in the medicine, so money had always been difficult in our family. I knew that. The Germans moved in in March '38. At that time, the information I absorbed from the surrounding environment as a boy of 12 was that it was depressing. There was fear as Jews were pulled out to clean some inscriptions on the streets that had been the result of patriotic Austrian demonstrations before the annexation. There were arrests, there were fears spread, pressure spread, then of course came the Kristallnacht that made it clear that there had to be some move to get out of there.

My father was never arrested, fortunately. There were people who protected him, and then we moved to my grandmother's house. I remember a piano was sold, probably furniture also, because we didn't take any furniture to my grandmother's house that I remember. Nobody knew basically that he was there. There was a point where he didn't go out, he stayed at home. That must have been very hard on him. During Kristallnacht, we went somewhere. I was actually out on the street at that time. I saw people breaking windows of shops and so forth, and we were lucky as hell, because we were in a taxi. A sister of my father's came to warn what was going on and that my father should go somewhere. She was a very tough woman. Some friends that my parents had, he was an Italian non-Jew, and we went to his house and I didn't want to be left behind. Then my mother and I came back, and my father stayed there. But to my knowledge nobody came.

So eventually this idea of Shanghai surfaced somewhere, the information spread that there was a place one could go to, there was no need for a visa or for permission. Having passports was not a regular thing, that everybody had passports like nowadays. We had passports relatively early on, because I know that they had to be taken back. They had this big red "J" on the passports of Jews, and I remember that suddenly my father or my mother or both had to go back to get that stamped in. We did get a visa, nevertheless, in our passports, from a Chinese Embassy, but it was completely meaningless. However, the problem was to get money together to buy a ticket. That's really what it amounted to as far as Shanghai was concerned.

Not everybody tried that hard. Some of the people I knew, my friends' parents, I suppose, clearly said, well, there's no place they have to go to, and it was very difficult to find any place to go to.

I always had the feeling that basically my father pushed for the decision to leave, and I think it was made before Kristallnacht, but I cannot be sure of that point. Certainly that gave it a great push and determination. I think he was just perceptive. I always thought my father was not a realist in many ways, and yet in this case he was clearly a realist who pushed.

My mother's father had been reasonably well-to-do. My grandfather had died of natural causes, and my grandmother then had the money. She had funds from which our fares to Shanghai were paid. My parents talked about obtaining some money from the Society of Friends, the Quaker society, that gave money to Jews who wanted to emigrate. Lloyd Triestino was the shipping company through which we got these tickets.

My father said that my grandmother should come to Shanghai, and there were some family circumstances why that never happened. A younger brother of my mother's didn't go to Shanghai. He first wanted to go to Australia, but he went to England eventually somehow. He survived the war in England. My mother also had an older brother, he stayed there. His wife was quite ill, and he didn't want to leave, she was not Jewish, it was complicated. It was probably to a great part because my grandmother did not want to leave that son there, that she didn't leave. So neither of them ever got out. I get sad, because that grandmother played an important part in my life. She was killed somewhere.

 *The father of **Melitta Colland** (born 1917) thought the Nazis would not last. Her mother's insistence that all the children leave was the key to her survival. Love almost kept her in Europe.*

My parents are from eastern Europe. We lived in Vienna. I came from a family who was observant, who kept a kosher household, who had relatives who went to Palestine already. I remember when I was yea high, to talk about it, that so-and-so is leaving and so-and-so is leaving. My father, even though he was a very good Jew and a very observant Jew, used to laugh about these people. He would say, "What are they going to do there?" He thought that only the Jew with the beard and *peyes* [sidelocks] and caftan would go to Palestine, but not an assimilated, halfway educated Jew. But even the assimilated Jew, like my father, looked down very much on a Jew who converted. That was taboo. You stayed what you were born, and that's it. And I knew a lot of Jews in Vienna who tried to get away from it simply by converting.

My father was in the Persian rug business, let's say comfortable middle class. I had two older brothers, I was the youngest. The oldest brother, Paul, had finished medical school. He finished his internship at the Jewish Hospital in Vienna and was looking to get away. It was 1938, in March, Vienna was occupied by Hitler. And from that moment on we started thinking of leaving.

My brother Henry, who was 14 months younger than the oldest, the doctor, he had a good friend who had connections to Panama and was offered a job in Panama. But that young man didn't want to go. He felt that Panama is not a climate that he would like. And my brother came home one day and said to mother and father that Heine Tillinger was offered that job and doesn't want to go. "How would you think of my applying for that job, if Heine has no objection to it?" Mother said, "Anything. Just get out as quickly as you can." And Henry went to Heine Tillinger and asked him, and Heine said, "If you want to go to Panama, that's fine with me, go ahead." So Henry was really the first of the three of us, the middle son, who went to Panama.

My mother was the brightest woman you ever want to know in that respect, really. Because she already, long before Hitler came to Austria, kept saying, "I want you kids out of here. I want you kids out of here." And nobody could really understand how a mother could push her son to go into Panama, because in those days, from Vienna into Panama, or Vienna into China, was like sending your own children into Siberia. You know? It was unheard of. And her friends used to say, "How can you even think of sending your son to China? How can you even think to send him into the tropics, into Panama?" She said, "I don't care. Anywhere else but here." And we really owed her an awful lot in that respect.

My father refused to leave Vienna. He said, "In six months this whole misery will be over, and you will all come back. But you have to take the young people out."

Then it got worse and worse in Vienna. My brother Paul had to hide in the hospital November 10th night, Kristallnacht, because they were going from door to door and looked for young Jewish men to take them to the concentration camps. In those days, we didn't know that there were concentration camps. We only knew that they're taking them to the police station. But he stayed hidden in the hospital, and they came to our door in the middle of the night. Mother and I were rather frightened of it. But we said he had left already. And that's how he got away.

Paul became one of a group of nine young doctors who tried to get out as quickly as possible. Nine Jewish doctors, all different. One was a dentist, one was a psychiatrist, and so on. My brother was a chest physician. In those days they didn't have families, they were single young men. They decided the only place they can go and stay together is China. They were able to get passage to China in December of '38.

I had a very close friend in Belgium, and he was able to get me into Belgium and got me even a job in a department store in Liège. From Vienna, I left one day before Hitler's birthday, April 19th, '39. But I had my ticket to China in my bag.

I was young, I was a little bit in love with this young man who got me into Belgium. He was only half Jewish, his mother wasn't Jewish. He wanted me to stay. He worked in Belgium for a German auto firm. He was an auto car racer, and he sold the cars and so on. And for Hitler's birthday he had to show his face for the party. He said, "I'm only going to show my face. I'll be back in less than an hour." As we hugged, and I said good-bye to him, his lapel by accident turned over and he had the swastika underneath. Which was one of the major reasons why I left Belgium. This little incident made me realize, "What am I doing here? I don't belong."

I went to the man who gave me the job, and I said very honestly to him, "I appreciate your giving me this opportunity to work for you, but what would you do if you were in my shoes? I have a ticket for China in June. I can leave from Trieste with my mother, or I can stay here and work for you. What would you do if you were me?" He said, "Young lady, I'm not Jewish. And if I wouldn't be totally tied down here, with everything I own, I would leave tomorrow, because pretty soon we'll have the war, and there won't be any getting out anymore." I owe this man my life, really, [laughs] because I probably would not have had sense enough to leave.

Of course, my father didn't want me, as a young girl, to go alone to China, so Mother had to go with me. My mother said, "If you are going to China, I'm going with you. If you decide to stay in Belgium, then I stay in Vienna." So I decided to leave.

The Viennese family of **Lisbeth Loewenberg** *(born 1922) went to Shanghai in pieces, first her father, because at that point Jewish men were the most threatened, then Lisbeth and her mother, much later in 1940. By that time, the open door was almost closed, and they needed special permission to join Lisbeth's father.*

There was the *Anschluss.* My father lost his job, because all Jews were dismissed immediately. He didn't have anybody in the United States who we could ask for an affidavit. My father was born in Czechoslovakia, he had a sister in Prague. Czechoslovakia at that time was not involved in the Nazi catastrophe yet. So he went to Prague to see if life in Czechoslovakia could possibly continue. There was nothing for him to do there, no possibility for him, and nothing else was open. My mother wrote to him, "How about Shanghai?"

Rumors were going on that people did go to Shanghai, that this was supposed to be where one could go without any visa, without anything. At that point my father turned around, sold his diamond ring, got the ticket for Shanghai, and went. And my mother said, "Well, I wasn't that serious! All I did was say, 'How about Shanghai?'"

You have to know that in Vienna, we were every day already afraid of our lives, because so many people got picked up and brought, not women at this point, to concentration camps. Most of the males that were still around that we knew didn't sleep at home, slept every night somewhere else, from one friend to another. If they would come to their home to pick them up, which they did, they just knocked at the door to pick up the people, so they weren't home. It was true, they were someplace else. And so you'd shiver every minute for your life.

Jews were allowed to go shopping in grocery stores only at certain hours. When people were standing in line, everybody knew that they were Jews, because they were the only ones who went shopping in that hour. People came by at this time, and they made nasty remarks, "dirty Jews," and this and that.

Then my mother and I tried to get to Shanghai. That was later already. It turned out that one had to have somebody guarantee one thing or another even to come to Shanghai. When my father first came, he did live in Hongkou, like everybody else. And it was difficult for him to get that paper, to ask us to come. We heard if you do not live in Hongkou, but live in the International Settlement, it might be easier to get that guarantee, so we did write him again. He moved out from Hongkou into the International Settlement, and from there he sent us the necessary papers.

The difficulty was to get a passage, a ticket on a ship, because there was only one ship a month leaving from Italy, either Trieste or Genoa. I can still see us waiting in line for tickets, tickets, and people bought tickets just before us, last ticket sold, everyone went back home without tickets. That was very late, the first transports to Poland were already going.[11]

There was an organization in Vienna that was called "Jewish Cultural Community." This was really the place where all Jews had to register. They issued birth certificates for Jews, and they registered all marriages and everything. We had told them, if they could help us in any way to get a ticket or tickets to Shanghai, because my father was already there and they had this guarantee, all they needed were tickets. So one day they called us and said, "If you give us all the cash that you have, we have two tickets for you."

Of course we did, there was nothing we could do, we couldn't take it out anyway. It didn't make any difference to us, because all you could take out was ten Marks, to start your new life on a different continent.

You couldn't take out any jewelry, not anything of value, nothing. And ten Marks. We got the tickets in January 1940, after the war had started.

*The family of **Ralph Hirsch** (born 1930) was uncertain about whether they should leave Berlin, as were many Jews. Although they decided to get out soon after Kristallnacht, they were not able to escape until 1940. By that time, a ship's passage was so difficult to find that the Hirsch family took the Trans-Siberian Railroad eastward to China.*

I was born on December 2, 1930, in Berlin. My father had been born in Berlin. His parents had been born in Berlin, and, although his mother's side of the family is Dutch, he felt very German. He was Jewish, he and all of his siblings were very assimilated, as was the household in which they grew up, although I didn't know either of my father's parents. My father had been decorated on the Western Front in World War I.

My father spoke English and French and Spanish, my mother spoke tolerable French, but little English. My father had studied law and was working as an economic consultant to several large Jewish-owned textile firms in Berlin and often traveled on their business abroad.

My father couldn't believe that the various measures, the successive deprivations and limitations of the right to work and so on, were aimed at him, and he ignored them all. For instance, Jews were not supposed to have a shortwave radio, and we had big shortwave Telefunken receiver and listened to it frequently. He frequented the same restaurants and clubs that he always did, although there were signs by that time on the doors, *"Juden unerwünscht"* [Jews not wanted]. In fact, he was never challenged, he was never arrested, he never, so far as I know, had any kind of direct unpleasantness because he was a Jew. Perhaps he was not recognized. He was certainly not recognizable by the *Stürmer* image or anything like that,[12] and somehow he was able to carry this off until the time we left Germany.

I went to school for the first two years in the *Volksschule*, the public elementary school, and the last year I went to a Jewish school. I very much disliked the physical plant of the new school, which was dark and dingy and had only a small playground. It was not very welcome to me to be forced to change schools in that way. That came sometime after Kristallnacht.

There never were any incidents that I remember at the *Volksschule* nor outside on the streets of Berlin that involved racial epithets or anything like that. I must have entered that school in the spring of '39, because I recall that I was there for about a year.

One incident that I remember, it must have been prior to Kristallnacht. I probably was about seven at the time. My father was at work, and my brother and I were both at home. The bell rang sometime in the morning, and my mother went to the door of the apartment. There were two men in leather coats there. I walked out there with my mother, and they said, *"Heil Hitler! Gestapo, Geheime Staatspolizei. Haben Sie ein Rundfunkgerät?"* "Do you have a radio?" And my mother said, "No." They said, *"Danke. Heil Hitler!"* turned and went down the stairs. About two minutes later, my mother went into hysteria, because it was illegal for us to have the radio, and if they had walked to the door of the living room, they could have seen it, because it stood there in plain view. But she controlled herself until they were out of earshot, before she started crying, and then she sort of collected herself. I know she called my father at his office and told him what had happened. After that we covered up the radio. It may be that for a while after that also we put it into a cupboard. But we continued to listen to broadcasts from England and just generally from other countries.

There were many friends and colleagues who were suffering in various ways, whose businesses had been wrecked or whose practices, if they were doctors and lawyers, had been ransacked. I think for a long time until then, my parents and their circle thought that either that Hitler was sort of a temporary phenomenon or that the good Germans would put a stop to this kind of excesses. My immediate family were not affected, but we were affected through what had happened to other members of the family and various friends and colleagues.

I think the decision was precipitated immediately after Kristallnacht. That was sort of a turning point, because it shocked the family very considerably. And it started my mother pressing my father to find ways of getting us out of Germany. At the time I was almost eight. I remember it was a time of great stress, and people coming in and going out, and a lot of talking in ways that were meant not to be understood by us children. In part it had to do with the fact that one of my father's sisters and her husband were very despondent after Kristallnacht and finally committed suicide. I only found out about that quite a lot later, I don't remember when.

My mother, who was not raised as a Jew, but converted to Judaism when she married my father, and whose family spent the whole war in Berlin, pressed my father and said, "With two small children we can't risk staying here." He then went seriously about the task of finding countries that would issue a visa to us. I know that my father, who had in his work traveled extensively, spent a great deal of time going to consulates and steamship companies and information bureaus, and whatever else was necessary to put the package together, that would enable us to get out, including various offices of the German government. I remember seeing visas from the Dominican Republic, from Bolivia, possibly from Cuba, and from several other countries, but not from the United States. He actually managed to assemble a whole slew of visas, but for one reason or another having to do with external circumstances, either of war or of the governmental situation in those countries, we couldn't use them. A couple of the visas, certainly I remember the Bolivian one, became invalid because of a change of government between the time that it was issued and the time he could book passage.

As near as I can tell, the plan was to go to Shanghai and to try to have some money available there, so we could use that as a kind of a staging area for the long trip across the Pacific to the Americas somewhere, depending on where we then could get access.

So it came down to going eastward instead of westward, to Shanghai, and using Shanghai as the jumping-off point instead of Berlin. That decision then had to wait for the period after the signing of the Non-Aggression Pact between the Nazis and the Soviets.[13] And a few months after the pact went into effect, we left Germany.

Doris Grey *(born 1912) fled Berlin with her husband. Because they left so late in 1940, they also had to pay for special permission to enter Shanghai. She describes the growing fear about whom to trust and the bureaucratic complications of packing. An underlying theme of her story is the mother she left behind.*

I was born in 1912 in Hindenburg, Upper Silesia, and I lived there until I finished school. I wanted to be pediatrician, but Hitler came and it was out of question. So I choose first to be a baby nurse, and I worked towards my degree. After two years in Breslau at the *Städtisches Säuglingsheim* [City Nursery], I went back home.

In the meantime, my brother was a full-fledged lawyer in Berlin. That's my only brother, he's eight and a half years older than I am. For him, I'm still his little sister. January 1933, he was there for three years already and had a very, very successful practice. Under Hitler, he had to stop as a lawyer, and he became a car dealer, of all things. Of course he didn't like it, he played more tennis.

My mother always said to me, "As much as I love you, but you go to a bigger place and see that you can stay there." I visited my brother in Berlin. It was close to the first of April '33, we went first to a hospital which was run by the city, very well-known, Virchow Hospital. There was a Red matron, she refused me right away. She asked for the name, "Where are you born, what's your religion?" So I knew already. Well, everyone at that time refused Jews. She didn't know what was coming to her, you know, under Hitler. My sister and I said, "You know what, we try with the Jews," *Krankenhaus der Jüdischen Gemeinde* [Jewish Community Hospital].

Then I worked myself up, I was first the charge nurse, and then assistant head nurse, head nurse, and then I was in charge of the medical floor, 120 beds.

We got married '38. Willy knew about art, he studied art in Berlin. Most of the time we were married, he was not allowed to work in his profession, not in Germany officially, not since '33. Willy always said, "I marry you, if you promise me that you see to it that we leave Germany." I said, "I will try."

In summer '38, they made it a law that all Jewish people who had money had to go to the *Finanzamt* [tax office], and they had to declare how much money they had.[14] We had about not quite 10,000 Mark. I had a cousin who was bank director. He said, "Under no circumstances, don't say anything, don't declare anything, because they wouldn't think you have any," due to the fact that Willy was forbidden to work. And that saved us, because they went into the apartments to all the people who were in higher positions and took them to the concentration camp. And the hospital too. They took all the people who were in charge of departments, they took them all.

The Kristallnacht? Well, I tell you, we were living in Berlin, in a very nice neighborhood. I went to work with tram to the hospital and I noticed, first of all, they painted everywhere, *"Jude,"* so they knew already which store has a Jewish owner. You just saw glass, and nothing, not burning, but everything demolished. And then I came to the hospital, and they said, "Did you see anything? They say the synagogues are burning." They interned Jewish people in the streets. So I called up my husband and said, "Stay home, don't leave." At that time, he knew something already, but I didn't know that they come to the apartments, too, to look for people.

My husband had a brother who was a psychoanalyst in New York, but he didn't do anything for us. He sent us affidavit when it was too late. He could have done it right after we got married.

My brother emigrated to South Africa, Durban, where he lived for 27 years. I knew my brother was working to get my mother out, and we didn't have any other connection. My mother had everything ready in '39 to go to South Africa, and it was very difficult for my brother to get into South Africa. But she didn't go.

At the beginning of '39, we moved to the hospital, and I was in charge there. I took it so my husband could live there, too. That was included in my salary, you know, I had two rooms on the medical floor and, of course, everything free. He was fed like the hospital employee, while I was fed on the hospital floor.

Slowly, I start to remember things. Because for a time, I didn't want to remember. We had a lot of Gentile people who were employed at the hospital in the kitchen and all over, they became the worst. We had a *Luftschutz* watch [air raid warden], you know, everything was dark on account of the war. Every night she wanted to take me to the police, because you could see just a little light through the window at night. Every night I had the trouble. Later on, I was dreaming about this. "I take you to the Gestapo! I take you to the Gestapo!"

We had several people who worked with the Gestapo, too. We had one nurse, she was sitting on their lap and patting them and pretending being good friend and finding out who was on the next list. She did it the other way around, she told the people before, so they could get away somehow. I have a good friend, she lives in Florida now, she and her husband were hiding in a private place during the war with some Gentile people, and so did other people, too. You were afraid, because you couldn't trust the Jewish people, either. You didn't trust the next one, Jew or non-Jew.

We had an affidavit, but we had a very high registration number, so we couldn't wait for it, because we would end up in the concentration camp. Then we heard about Shanghai. It was war, and we thought, we go to Shanghai and wait for our for affidavit there.

I tell you, Shanghai was the last place to go. They always said, only people who have been in prison, the worst people go to Shanghai. That was known, *"Verbrecher gehen nach Shanghai"* [criminals go to Shanghai], so to speak. Even though it was war, even as we said, we only go to Shanghai to wait for our affidavits, then we go to America, which was our intention. We didn't know we would stay. You were almost ashamed to say you go to Shanghai. It's unbelievable today, you know. But there was no other possibility, and the Chinese saved our lives, no matter how, they saved our lives.

So, now, how do we get the passage to go? Hilfsverein in Berlin said to get in touch with the Italian Lloyd Triestino. I went to the Lloyd Triestino. Everywhere I went, I went in my nursing uniform. And I was told, you have to give them some money under the table. You know, I was so bashful, I was so ashamed to do. I had an envelope, which was, I think, 60 Mark, which was a lot of money. And he saw already, you know, so he said to me, "Oh, leave that envelope there, that's all right, that's all right." And then somehow I managed to get the passages, that money we had. I don't recall how much it was. It must have been, at least, I think, 1,600 Mark or so, something like that.

To get out, you had to make all those lists of what you take along and most of it was crossed out. You were not allowed to take any money, ten Mark, and most of the things you couldn't take. And of course you had to pay *Auswanderung* [emigration] tax.

My mother came to say good-bye to us and to help us with the packing. That was 1940, May. The packers were sent by the government. We had a date with the packers on Monday. They came on Saturday, but we had the order from Gestapo to get our passes and the permit to pack ourselves for Monday. The Gestapo was in one of the former Jewish community houses. And so I went in my nurse's uniform, and we were standing there, didn't say anything. Luckily there was an older gentleman who was working there and he came to me, "Oh little nurse, what are you waiting for?" So I told him my story. He said, "What do you need?" And I told him that we actually have an appointment for Monday, but the packers are there. So he said, "Wait here, wait here. Don't get upset. It will take some time." He brought me the papers. That was lucky.

When we came home, my mother said, "They are still waiting." They wanted to go already, because we didn't have the permit. So my mother had some beer there for them. Where she got it from, I don't know, but we gave them whatever we had to eat. My best crystal I gave the packer. They packed everything. One of them was a supervisor, and he saw to it that you don't take anything you're not allowed. For instance, they had the lists there already, and what they didn't allow you they crossed off and you couldn't take. The most important books, art books my husband wanted to take along, crossed off altogether.

And then he put down the prints. We were good friends with Käthe Kollwitz, my husband was very friendly with her. We had a lot of her early, early originals and, really, all the Kollwitzes you see in America come from us. That they didn't cross off, so we took them. That was a big, big thing. Then they packed and, you see, they tried, "Don't you have anything else you want?" We said, "No, we don't have anything." Most of the things we packed, we got back.

That went to the *Packhof,* they called it. They controlled it again, and they took out what they wanted to. I was fully equipped to do private nursing, from rubber glove to enema can and instruments and everything. Part of that they stole. And a few other things.

We had to have, each of us, $400 to be allowed to get into the French Settlement. My husband had very good Gentile friends from Switzerland who were art experts too and had an art colony. My husband was in business with him. He could do it, yeah, *er hat für uns geburgt* [he vouched for them]. The $400 were sent from Switzerland to Shanghai, it had to be there. He even sent us $100 when we arrived in Genoa.

When Hitler came to power, my mother said, "Oh, he will not last long, it's impossible, it couldn't be." Many people thought, that can't go on, you know. My mother could have gone, but she didn't. We couldn't take my mother along, because we just didn't have the money, you know. So we thought when we arrive, we put $400 down for her and she will come. She ended up in Auschwitz.

CHAPTER 2

Leaving Home

Families who had been divided in their reactions to unprecedented persecution, often along generational fault lines, became united behind the idea of escape through the sudden Nazi takeover in Austria, unexpected arrests, and the planned riot on Kristallnacht. Virtually all of the hundreds of thousands of Jews in the Greater Reich wanted to leave.[1] They were now forced into the arms of a Nazi bureaucracy determined to rob and humiliate them. By late 1938, the Nazis had stolen the financial resources needed for international travel, while the rest of the world raised bureaucratic walls, which were often also motivated by antisemitism.

Preparations for the trip to Shanghai were collaborative reactions to a hostile world repeated throughout Jewish communities in Berlin, Vienna, and many other cities. Family crises intensified the memories of our narrators, compressing meaning into normally mundane activities.

The task of organizing the trip often fell to wives and mothers, particularly when fathers had been sent to a concentration camp. Women had to find out from the Gestapo where their husbands had been taken and how to get them out. They arranged for passports and prepared the pile of documents the Nazis demanded of Jews. By late 1938, the few regular ships on cruises from Europe to China were already sold out, so getting tickets for a family meant bribing a travel agent or anxiously waiting for a cancellation.

Packing was a nightmare of hurried choices, often made in vain. Nazi regulations forbade bringing most valuables out of the country and limited cash to 10 Marks or $4 per person. Customs officials watched while families packed to ensure they took no forbidden valuables. Just as the choice to leave for Shanghai was wrenching, families had to decide whether to risk smuggling bits of gold or jewelry in their clothing or inside a child's toy. Many refugees tell of filling crates with necessary belongings that they never saw again.

In contrast to the bullying treatment of government officials, the worldwide community of German-speaking Jews smoothed, and often financed, this journey. The Hilfsverein der deutschen Juden in Germany and the American Jewish Joint Distribution Committee in New York had been founded in the early twentieth century to help threatened Jewish communities in eastern Europe and Palestine. Now they cooperated to offer broad assistance to Jews in Nazi Germany, including tickets to Shanghai for the poorest families.

Our narrators tell us the consequences of such distant political decisions. Leaving Germany meant personal suffering and familial upheaval. We read here about successful escape plans, but those successes were embedded in larger family dramas with deadly endings for others.

Once out of Germany, some of these narratives of global journeys evoke the retelling of dreams: the warmth of Italy just across the border, unimagined vistas of the Indian Ocean or the Siberian forest. The trip was hardly preparation for life in Shanghai. Many refugees had been forced to buy first-class tickets. They were treated well by the ship's staff and had no responsibilities. Although the Nazis forbade taking cash out of the country, ticket holders could put funds into "board money" to be spent only on the ship. They had succeeded in escaping after harrowing experiences. The unknown Orient was still far away.

Since anti-Jewish violence was first applied by the Nazis on a broad basis in Austria during the Anschluss, Viennese Jews, such as Eric Reisman, were the first to seek out Shanghai as a destination for mass flight. During 1938, perhaps 1,500 refugees arrived in Shanghai, two-thirds of whom were Austrian. When the families of men arrested during Kristallnacht in November 1938 began to arrive in Shanghai in large numbers in early 1939, the proportion changed to more than two-thirds from Germany, in line with the relative sizes of the Jewish populations of Germany and Austria. By that time, the ships of the Italian Lloyd Triestino Line, along with ships from Japan, Germany, France, and Holland, carried over 1,000 refugees a month.[2] Nobody realized that few among the relatives and friends unable to leave would survive.

Shanghai had already offered an open door to refugees for nearly a century when Jews started arriving in large numbers at the end of 1938. Then suddenly, a more restrictive immigration policy was demanded by the American, British, and French businessmen who ran the international zones of settlement through the Shanghai Municipal Council (SMC).[3] Economic self-interest and traditional antisemitism determined the hostile reaction of Shanghai's Western economic elite to the refugees. In late December, the North China Herald reported: "The growing influx of Jewish refugees...is already giving rise to considerable *anxiety in local authoritative circles."* That month, the SMC voted to prevent the arrival of any further Jewish refugees; the Japanese, who by then controlled the port, refused to comply. Soon, Washington and London, continuing to prioritize the economic advantage of their citizens in Shanghai over the lives of foreign Jews, officially requested the Nazis not to allow any further Jews to leave for Shanghai.[4]

The Japanese, although allies of the Nazis, were much more accommodating to the refugees. Since their war with Russia in 1905, when the American Jewish banker Jacob Schiff had helped finance the Japanese military effort, the official Japanese attitude toward Jews was extremely positive. Believing that international Jewry possessed wide powers, government policy was designed not to antagonize Jews. Even as the Western community in Shanghai complained about the influx of refugees, a conference of the top five ministers in Japan on December 6, 1938, decided to erect no hurdles to further immigration. This policy served the increasingly close diplomatic relationship with Germany, because the Nazis were clearly interested in maximizing the flight of Jews out of Germany. The Japanese Foreign Ministry told its representatives in Shanghai to reject the request of the SMC to restrict Jewish arrivals in December 1938. Foreign Minister Arita stood by this policy publically several times in the first half of 1939.[5]

The official Japanese position changed only when German and Japanese officials and business owners in Shanghai joined their Western counterparts in complaints about the economic impact of the growing Jewish refugee stream. The German Consulate alerted the Foreign Ministry in Berlin in February 1939 to the dangers that Jews presented to German economic and political interests. In March, a report of the consulate expressed "the greatest objections to any further immigration of Jews to Shanghai." In particular, they disliked the heavy presence of Jewish doctors and dentists. In May and June 1939, by which time 2,000 Jews were arriving every month, Japanese Consul Ishiguro repeatedly complained that Jews were taking business away from Japanese residents of Shanghai and asked what the German reaction would be if the Japanese restricted Jewish entry.[6]

When the Berlin government responded positively, the Japanese moved quickly to restrict entry. On August 9, 1939, the Naval Landing Party, the highest Japanese military authority in Shanghai, announced that no further refugees would be admitted to Hongkou after August 21. The SMC followed immediately with a similar decree that European refugees would no longer be permitted to enter the International Settlement. Over the next few days, steamship companies and Jewish agencies in Europe and the United States were notified that all emigration to Shanghai must end. Although none of these new regulations specifically mentioned Jews, it was clear that only refugees with a "J" stamped into their passports would be affected.

Both the Japanese and the SMC soon revised the complete prohibition of further entry. First, those who had embarked before August 21 were allowed to land. Then in October, the SMC announced new regulations, allowing immigration to those who could fulfill any of the following conditions: they had an immediate relative or intended to marry someone already in Shanghai, held a contract for a job in Shanghai, or possessed $400 U.S. as so-called "guarantee money." Only a handful of refugees managed to get Japanese permission to land directly in Hongkou. Most who entered Shanghai after the restrictions went into effect were parents of residents who received an entry permit from the SMC. A much smaller number could show $400 U.S., as some of the narrators describe. The Jewish relief agency Hebrew Immigrant Aid Society (HIAS) supplied some refugees with checks to cover this amount. Both Jewish and non-Jewish businesses in Shanghai offered fictitious job contracts to refugees to help them get out of Europe.

After August 21, 1939, about 1,100 more refugees arrived on boats that were already underway or about to leave, as Alfred Kohn describes. But the Shanghai door had been effectively closed for the hundreds of thousands of Jews remaining in the Third Reich. The flow then dwindled to several hundred over the whole next year. The new restrictions, as well as the German invasion of Poland in September and the beginning of World War II, made leaving Germany even more difficult.

The trickle of successful applicants for entry permits dried up after June 1940, when Italy entered the war and the British closed the Suez Canal to Italian ships. After that, it was possible to reach Shanghai only by crossing the Soviet Union. Ralph Hirsch's family was one of the few who made that journey.

Later, one more sizable group of eastern European Jews reached Shanghai. After the German and Soviet armies divided up Poland in 1939 and the Soviets began to move into the small Baltic countries, Jews in Lithuania discovered that the Japanese Consul, Chiune Sugihara, and the Dutch Consul, Jan Zwartendijk, would issue visas for Japan and Curacao. Brandishing these papers, over 2,000 Jews, mostly from Poland and Lithuania, crossed the Soviet Union in 1940 and 1941 on the Trans-Siberian Railroad and landed in Kobe, Japan.[7] Eventually, the Japanese sent them to Shanghai and allowed them to settle in Hongkou, at the same time as German soldiers were shooting every Jew they could find on the Eastern Front.

The German invasion of the Soviet Union in June 1941 cut off this final means of escape. About 18,000 Jews had managed to get to Shanghai from Nazi-controlled central and eastern Europe. Millions were left with no place to go.

Because **Lotte Schwarz**'s husband was sent to Buchenwald in the first mass arrest of June 1938, they were among the first to leave, well before Kristallnacht.

As in most refugee stories, even small amounts of money become significant. The Italian liner "Conte Verde" regularly oscillated between Trieste and Shanghai.

We left Germany by train to Trieste, it was a beautiful trip. I left in '38 in summer, I think in August. It was the last beautiful thing I saw, because we went through the Austrian Alps by train to Trieste. Then from there the "Conte Verde" left. Everybody was in the same condition, same situation, you know. It was nice, because it was an Italian ship and we were in the tourist class, so it wasn't too bad.

My husband's mother, she had died already at that time, but she had a very wealthy brother who was a French citizen in Paris. And when we were on the ship, he sent us a few hundred dollars. We didn't ask for, but he did. But it was a good feeling, you know.

On the ship, we were all together German people. And we called it *Umschichten,* you know, you changed whatever you did. We met another German, Bayer was his name, that man went in a restaurant and learned how to cook. And he was very good in it. He talked to my husband on the ship, he was a very nice guy. Later on, we found out he was an alcoholic, but we didn't know that before, and when he was sober, he was the nicest guy. He was with his wife, too. Anyway, he talked to my husband and my husband said, "How about I do the business part and you do the cooking for our German refugees?" Because we knew another ship was coming and nobody liked to eat Chinese. I still don't eat Chinese, not after ten years in Shanghai.

*On the trip to Shanghai, **Eric Reisman** and his family experienced the generosity of Jewish communities along the Red Sea and the Indian Ocean, as well as the hostile suspicion of the British imperial governments in the ports they visited.*

We left by train November of 1938. It was a funny sensation, leaving by train, because you were on a German Austrian train, you were basically on Austrian ground going to Italy. Italy was part of the Axis power, so you never really could breathe freely, that it's behind me, it's a thing of the past, because you were still under that fear. Approaching the border, you heard from other sources that Jews were taken off the train, because they had more than one ring on their fingers.

We then went across the border, and we came to Naples, Italy, and there again we came on an Italian ship. Now we were basically on Italian ground, so we had to refrain from any celebration of any sort that we were finally free. We had to simmer everything down, calm everything down, not to show whoever the crew members may be, that it may be detrimental to you, that you could get yourself endangered.

That was a 28-day trip from Naples to Shanghai. On board the ship, my mother would wash out little things and hang them up in the cabin that we occupied. The cabin was just big enough for one person to stand, the others would have to jump in bed [laughs] or leave the cabin.

The first port that we were able to get off ship was Aden on the Red Sea. One of the large stores along the waterfront dockside was evidently owned by an Arab Jew. We walked in, we had no money to spend, so we just looked around at all the beautiful things, they were mostly tropical things. We had winter suits on. So the fellow came up to me and he says, "Have you got a hat?" And I says, "No, I don't have a hat." "You need a tropical helmet." He gave me a tropical helmet, and I said, "I can't pay you." He says, "I don't want any money." And it was the first time in my life that I experienced the emotions of accepting a gift from a stranger. It made me realize that it is much easier to give than to gracefully accept a gift. Taught me a lesson. I wore that helmet during the tropical heat and exposure in China until I couldn't force it on my head anymore, [laughs] but I was very proud of that hat. It saved me probably a lot of heat strokes and so forth.

Other ports of call, we weren't allowed to get off the ship for fear that some people would stay unauthorized. They came up with an idea, that one part of the family had to stay aboard, only one part could go off ship. So that's what we did. My father and mother took turns of going on land and looking at the various cities that we stopped in and took either my brother or I with them and one had to stay behind.

The difficulty of getting tickets on the few ships to Shanghai, combined with great anxiety about the safety of Jewish men, forced **Otto Schnepp**'s *parents to send him separately with strangers a month after they left. Only years later did he realize how much this decision upset him. Lloyd Triestino liners from Genoa and Trieste eventually carried more than half of the refugees to China.*

We had reservations for January 1939. However, there were circumstances that arose in December of '38 that brought about a switch. I was left behind and left only with some other people in January at the original date, this couple my parents met in the course of making these reservations. He had been arrested and had been in detention following Kristallnacht, I believe, and he got out and it was too late for them to get their papers for leaving. They had a reservation for early December, and there was a lot of maneuvering and reasons. My father was the most important one to get out, because men were threatened by arrest and detention and concentration camps, but there were reasons why they couldn't arrange formally for me and my father to be sent out. So the other alternative was only my mother and father. They made a switch with those people, and the result was that I had to wait there. I had met them, but I didn't know them. They were strangers.

It was quite a traumatic experience for me in the sense that I felt endangered, abandoned. There was, of course, a real fear that had gotten to me, the fear of being physically insecure in the street. I was assaulted once by a bunch of guys, and I did have the awareness at some level that somebody could just kill me in the street and nobody would lift a finger. There wasn't any defense or any resources to draw on. So that feeling had gotten deep into me at that point.

I didn't deal with that, I didn't deal with a hell of a lot for many years until, starting about 1970, I got into some therapy here. Many of those things I've sort of explored, but that doesn't mean I've resolved them completely. I don't think I'll ever resolve them. It was a time of very deep feelings of fear, of abandonment, that were very, very strongly repressed, that did a lot to me in my personality. So it was a difficult experience.

I then left with those people by train and went to Genoa. We stayed a night in Genoa at a hotel, and then we left the next day on the "Conte Biancamano," that's the name of the ship. I was 13 at the time that we left Vienna for Shanghai.

Ruth Sumner *and her extended family left Germany in January 1939. About 10 percent of the refugees who escaped the Third Reich to Shanghai sailed on the many ships of the Japanese line Nippon Yusen Kaisha from Naples. Each ship carried from 50 to 100 refugees.*

We left for Shanghai, we went by train. My dad, my aunt Tante Erna, her only son Gerry, and myself. We spent a day in Rome, I think. We went to Naples, yeah, spent a day there, and then we took a Japanese ship, "S.S. Hakone Maru." We had first-class cabins, everything.

The majority was filled with Jews. A Japanese befriended me, he must have been the age of my daddy, that seems a little bit funny. He even wrote me some letters, you know, a ten-year-old gets attention, it means a lot to her. But they were mostly Jewish refugees on that ship. It took us about three weeks, we went sightseeing, we came to Shanghai.

We left with suitcases, and my father's lawyer shipped our personal belongings over later on. That's how I got my bicycle and our furniture and stuff. They came later, just before World War II broke out. I mean, within weeks before the war started, our personal belongings were shipped to us. You didn't want to have any papers, as far as I know. I was too young to realize all these things.

*Like most of those who fled to Shanghai, **Gérard Kohbieter** sailed from Italy in 1939. At 16, outfitted with his new gear, he put on his first magic show. Kohbieter also keenly observed his fellow refugees of different classes, values, and experiences coping with the shock of violence and expulsion.*

I took the train to Genoa in March in '39 and then 29 days, adventurous days. It was a strange atmosphere, you know. When you are on a boat, that sort of feels like vacation, but on the other hand, you were really sailing into a black hole. You didn't know what in God's name awaits you there. There were reports. There were whole lists of things you should bring for the climate, because it's so different from here, and a wee bit of stuff, also, I think, how to get along with the natives. But all in all, you didn't know much about what you were getting into. But you knew what you were getting out of. And that to me, that was a panda bear. I didn't care.

The fear that people had was probably pushed back, you know. You could tell who it had hit particularly hard. There were people that were pacing the deck all night, couldn't sleep, people that came out of the concentration camp, wasted, wasted. The people that were psychically so terribly hurt that they walked like animals, like the freedom-loving animals in the zoo, like the fox. You can't put a fox in a cage. The fox paces back and forth. Every time he goes to the wall, he puts his paw up, just touches it. And the fox reminded me of some of those guys on board. They weren't walking as fast. They were walking slowly, like ghosts. I didn't sit there and watch them for a long time. I just happened to see them, every time you go out, there were those guys walking.

People tried to put up a good front. Though it seems to be in the Jewish nature to *kvetch*, you know, to complain and so forth. The *kvetchers*, they were aboard too. But mostly people were sort of wondering and exchanging stories, what they'd done at home.

You really had a spectrum of society there. You had people that came from very poor neighborhoods and talked *Milieu* [slang]. The interesting people were the middle-class little businessmen that were enlarging their achievements enormously. When you're very young, you know when people are sort of putting you on. I still do, actually, most of the time. I was attracted to the Viennese. The Berliners didn't like the Viennese, they were too polite for them, too gracious. They thought, *"Sie sind falsch. Sie schmieren. Dir Rotz um die Backe."* They put honey around your cheeks. I figure everybody does that, only they do it more charmingly.

I had 130 Marks board money. I put on my tux. I knew how to get into the first class, and sat down at the bar, drank my first scotch. My God, I thought I'd die. At 16 you don't drink scotch, you know? I immediately developed a relationship with the bartender. I bought cigarettes. How did that go? I got cigarettes, and I sold them to the crew or something, and that way I got cash. I did a magic show on the ship to ingratiate myself, and made a little money, and I arrived in Shanghai with 150 bucks or something. Lost my virginity aboard, and that was pretty exciting. And I got the first whiff of emigrant talk.

It was like a Bar Mitzvah. It was my entry into adulthood. It was the first time that I was independent. That part of it had a certain charm, charm in the magical sense. I was a grown-up. All decisions were made by me, though I had no trouble with decisions in the home. I had a very groovy mother. But I didn't feel lonely. I didn't feel, "Here I'm all alone, and they are all together." That came later. And I had the confidence that young people seem to have, the overconfidence, that I'm going to knock everybody flat on their feet with my magic. Well, I did make a living there for a while, on and off.

I got off everywhere where they let you off the boat. It was a leisurely way of traveling in those days, the proverbial slow boat to China. In Colombo, I got off and took my photos and went to a hotel in the foolish hope that they might say, "Ah, you are a magician. Good God, you're just the man we're looking for. Get off the boat and stay here." Of course, it doesn't happen that way. But I met a dance team there, Dutch people, that asked me where I'm from. When we parted, the guy gave me 20 pounds. Twenty pounds was a reasonable amount of money, it was, hell, probably like a couple hundred bucks today. It embarrassed me, and I said, "Oh, no, no." He said, "Go ahead, son. Now take it. You're going to need it." And he was very natural about it. It was cool.

That's how I got to Shanghai.

A few refugees, like **Ilse Greening**, *found passage on German freighters leaving Hamburg in the north. Their trip was longer, possibly encouraging some passengers to transgress normal social boundaries.*

We started in Hamburg with a small Hapag freighter, "Oldenburg." My mother came from Oldenburg. There were quite a number of Germans. There were several German women who had been evacuated from the Far East, from Singapore and Colombo, but also from Shanghai especially. 1937 was the war between the Japanese, and the German government had forced them to evacuate with their children. On this boat, they were coming back.

One of the German officers was very friendly towards us, he was fantastic. We had a little window towards the gangplank, and every morning he came and we discussed everything. This officer came to me once and he says, "Just be on your guard, because so-and-so is a Party member, and he is a Gestapo man." Yes, he was pro-Jewish. The captain, too.

It was a small boat, we were only 35 passengers, so nothing was hidden. This officer said, "Wait until we get past the Suez Canal. The people change. Oh, my job is much harder, because for reasons I cannot explain to you, people get out of hand." Once they leave Europe, he said, not only passengers, but also the officers and the crew, they all go wild. It must be the climate or something. The married women used to go to the cabins of the doctor or the officers, and they went wild. He said he has no explanation, it happens on every trip. And of course all those middle-class people, European people, they were horrified, but it happened. Must be the climate.

For people my mother's age, it was very hard to get used to those situations. For us it was interesting. We were young, I was 19. So, it was a different life from Hannover, believe me. And that's what happened in Shanghai, too. People sort of, their lives went out of bound. Many. That's what prepared us.

Ernest Culman and his family sailed on a Dutch liner, where some of the staff found ways to help them save money. Dutch Jews in Batavia, now Jakarta, the capital of Indonesia, like all the Jewish communities from Italy to China, helped the refugees on their way.

When we finally left Germany, we traveled by train to say good-bye to the other relatives that were still there. And we came to the Brenner Pass, the border into Italy, middle of the night, I was asleep, but everybody had to get out for customs inspection. My mother said to the guy, "Can't I leave my kid here, he's fast asleep?" He said, "Sure you can, but I don't guarantee that you'll be back on the train before the train leaves." So obviously I had to be woken up.

The Germans only allowed a certain amount of dollars and cents, or marks actually, to take out as cash. What my father had over and beyond that when we got to the Brenner Pass, he wired the balance to his brother.

Then we came to Italy, to Genoa. My mother's sister had gone to Italy from Germany before that, and she came to see us off in Genoa, at the boat. It was very emotional to have her wave good-bye to us when we boarded the ship.

First of all, on the ship, being a Dutch ship, we had all the freedom that we wanted. It wasn't like the other refugees, who often went on Italian ships. We did pay a lot into the board money, which is money to be used on board the ship. They had to keep a record of what we spend it for, but they just wrote anything down. Like my father would go to the purser, the purser would say, "Well, didn't you lose a hundred dollars in gambling last night, and didn't you buy some good cigars?" and they wrote all that down, and so we got all the board money in cash for us.

The Dutch had a regulation that kids under ten could not be in the same dining room with the adults. So I had to eat with the little kids. I got very upset about that. And I got seasick the first time when you could still see land.

My parents thought that on the way to Shanghai they might be able to get off in some other place, like Singapore, Manila, Hong Kong. But obviously we couldn't get off. We had to transfer in what is now Jakarta, at that time it was called Batavia, where we had a one week layover. In Batavia, the Dutch Jewish community welcomed us, and they put all of us up in nice hotels. My father and his family, we were taken in by a major in the Dutch army, a Jewish doctor, and we lived like kings, you know, like the typical colonial British and Dutch people lived. We had a car for our disposal with a chauffeur, I mean, it was wonderful. A week later we went on board on this other ship that eventually got us into Shanghai.

Melitta Colland and many other refugees tell how their carefully packed belongings for their new lives in Chinese exile, inspected and stamped by the Nazis, disappeared on the way out. Because they were allowed to take only a minimum amount of cash with them, those possessions could have served as capital in Shanghai. Colland's family had to pay for first-class tickets to China, but she and her mother arrived in June 1939 with five Marks and a couple of suitcases.

My mother made what would have been the equivalent of a trousseau for me and packed it all up into a big overseas trunk. There were all my school reports in there, and everything that I learned and made in the *Schneiderakademie* that I went to.[8] The young man in Belgium, since he could travel freely still from Vienna to Belgium, he took it out into Belgium for me. Then I was supposed to take it to the ship. I was going from Brussels to Trieste by train, via Paris. I left without any money in my pocket really. And when I came to Paris, they told me I hadn't paid enough for the transportation of that overseas trunk. I mean, this young man helped me. He didn't know that he had to pay more for it. I was ashamed to ask him for money. Do I have more money? I said, "No, I don't have any money." So that overseas trunk was lost, because I had absolutely no means and didn't know anybody, in the middle of the night, to ask for help to pay for that overseas trunk to go to China. Never seen it again. And that was it.

My mother packed up a large *Lift* [crate]. There was an enormous amount of valuable things in there, silver and Persian rugs and furniture and fine linens and whatever we had was in there. It went as far as Italy, and then Mussolini didn't let anything go out that belonged to Jews. And that's where it was lost and never seen again. Had that *Lift* arrived, we could have been living from what we sold for ten years.

I met Mother in Trieste. We were allowed five Reichsmarks each to leave the country. That was all the cash we were allowed. We were fortunate to be able to get first-class transportation on the "Conte Verde," which was an Italian line, to China. But we also needed money for tips. And the Italians were not very friendly, already, to the Jewish refugees. When my mother was very ill one night on the ship, because she was suffering a great deal with gallstones, I asked for a special diet food. One of the waiters, very gruff, said to me, "When you get to Shanghai, you'll be glad you can afford to buy any food." And he was right, [laughs] unfortunately. He was very right, but it wasn't very nice. But anyhow, the reason I mention this is that five Reichsmarks went for tips on the ship. So we arrived, between the two of us, with five Reichsmarks, July of '39.

This is how I came to China.

Alfred Kohn and his family were among the last to come into Shanghai. By the time they left Germany in late August 1939, the Japanese were restricting entry. Then Germany attacked Poland, war broke out in Europe, and all aspects of the journey became less reliable.

We finally bought a ticket to go to China. At the last minute, the Italian company said, "We don't accept German Marks, you have to pay in dollars." So quickly my father made arrangements through relatives in America, they paid the thing again in dollars. Eventually after the war, my parents got the money back from the German government for the tickets.

When we left in 1939, there were people already in Shanghai a year or two or three, so we knew already what to take. So you bought some medication in Germany, because we still had money. We couldn't take the money out of Germany anyway, so we had medication, and my father sold some medication to buy food and things like that. I had malaria in China, and it was good for us my father took along some malaria pills.

The problem only was that my parents had made application to leave with all the things that we had and jewelry, and then a law was passed, you had to hand in your jewelry, and my parents lost all of that.

We left Germany on the train, and we were in Italy when the war broke out on September 1st. We didn't know if the ship is going to leave.

But Italy didn't enter the war immediately, so that's why Italian ships could still go through the Suez Canal to China. The stuff that was sent to us in Shanghai went on a German ship. The German ships always went around Africa, so that's why the stuff that we had never got there, it went on a German ship, it went back to Germany.

We went through the Suez Canal, hoping maybe to leave the ship in Port Said and go to Palestine. When we got to Port Said, the war was on already, couldn't get off the ship. The ship eventually was interned in Dutch East Indies. We were supposed to be 32 days on the ship. God knows how many, it must have been much, much more, I don't remember the dates. We finally arrived in Shanghai in 1939 in October, November. And all we had is each ten Marks in our pocket, and each a suitcase, hoping that the stuff from Germany would come, but the war was on, it never came.

Lisbeth Loewenberg and her mother went to Shanghai well after the new immigration restrictions were implemented. The most significant exception to the bar on entry was to join a relative, in this case her father. She was a teenager, like Gérard Kohbieter, and the behavior of the adults remained in her memory all her life. Loewenberg's appreciation of the beauties of the trip reveal the emotional release that escape from the Nazis could bring.

We went by train from Vienna to Trieste in January 1940. When I left Vienna, it was winter. The streets were full of snow, completely white. I remember the cab drive from our house to the train station. It was early in the morning, the city was completely quiet. Vienna was a beautiful city, covered in snow, and we didn't see a person.

I remember that train journey so well, every detail of it. First of all, you sit there and you shiver and you are afraid. We are still in Germany. We were so afraid of the control at the border. Of course, we hadn't taken anything that we were not allowed to take, because you said, whatever you can take, your life is more important. If they find something that you are not supposed to take, it isn't worth it. We got to the border of Italy, the German control opened the door and said, "Have a good trip," and didn't look at anything. There was a human being by mistake.

When we got to Trieste, I thought it was the most beautiful place in the world. Because you could breathe freely, you were not afraid for your life anymore as of this moment. And Trieste is beautiful. There is this huge piazza directly at the Mediterranean, you see the ships lying out there. It's just gorgeous. But it probably wasn't as beautiful as it seemed to me at that time. Just me and my mother.

We came one day, and our ship left the next day. An Italian committee gave us a place to sleep for that night, because of course we had no money, and the next day we went on the ship. That is the strangest thing in the world, you know, it was like a luxury liner. My mother and I had a cabin together. You could barely get any food in Vienna anymore, and Jews didn't get anything. All of a sudden, you were on the ship and you had three meals a day served to you in the dining room of the ship. For me it was a fantastic experience.

The trip is absolutely gorgeous. It takes four weeks from Trieste, first through the Mediterranean and then through the Red Sea, Aden, Bombay, Singapore, Manila, Hong Kong, Shanghai. Of course, we were not allowed to get off the ship at any of those places. I was everywhere, but only in the harbor, didn't see anything. But still it was an outstanding experience. The nights on the ship you see the flying fish, you know. And you are free.

I remember particularly one thing. At this time, people could still get out of concentration camps when they had tickets to go to someplace. There were two young men on the ship who had come out from the concentration camp. They were playing the piano and singing in the evening, you know, light songs, popular music, like "Mack the Knife." I said to my mother, "How is it possible that people when they come out from the concentration camp are able to enjoy themselves and sing and be so happy? It seems like a contradiction to me." And my mother said, "Well, it's because they came out of the concentration camp that they are happy." Yeah, there were any number of refugees and other people on the ship. It was a great experience.

Many refugees say they got on the last ship to Shanghai. There were many last ships, such as the last ship before the Shanghai door was slammed shut in August 1939, or the last ship that was already on the seas when this order was announced. **Doris Grey** *and her husband, Willy, were on one of the last Italian ships that left Europe for Shanghai. Exactly a month later, Italy entered the war and the route through the Suez Canal was closed.*

We left on the fifth of May 1940. We went to Munich, and in Munich at the station, somebody was waiting for all the people who go to Shanghai. They just say Jewish *Centralverein*, so we knew already. We were about 33 people. So they collected us and brought us to a place, a kind of *Vereinshaus*, and gave us to eat.[9]

All we had was ten Mark, and a little bit, you know, in case we need something on the train. But before we came to the border at Innsbruck, we gave what we had over to the conductor. So the train arrives in Innsbruck during the night at two or three o'clock in the morning. The Gestapo men, "Everybody who wants to go to Shanghai, out. 'Conte Verde' doesn't go." Here we were stateless, you know. Innsbruck was *Judenrein,* no Jews.

There was an older man who worked at the station He said, "Come on," and he put us all in the waiting room for fourth class. My husband went to him, if we could make a phone call, a collect phone call. My husband's best friends was the doctor in our hospital, and he called him and told him what happened. So he said we should give him the number and he will see what he can do. They got in touch with the Hilfsverein in Munich. The Hilfsverein ordered an extra *Waggon* for the next train, and we went back from Innsbruck to Munich. So again the *Centralverein* sent somebody to pick us up, and we were there the next evening. They said to us, "You will try again, you will go again."

So next night, we went again and we made it. We went right near the Brenner to Innsbruck. We had to stop at the border, and then to Genoa. And on the tenth of May, we made it in the boat, "Conte Verde." We were on the way four weeks.

Our boat, that was the last boat, took soldiers to Ethiopia and also Italian officers. This boat had a mission. When we came to Naples, they were exercising, they prepared for war. Young boys, 12, 14 years old in uniform, everybody.

Of course, we didn't have a cabin together. I went with three other ladies, and Willy had a cabin with somebody else. [laughs] It's funny to talk about, but I remember there was one couple who had a single, a cabin to themselves, so they let us use it. [laughs] We had certain days, you know. That's the way it was, and today you laugh about it.

So we started out in Genoa, then the first stop was Naples, then we went through the Strait of Messina, then we went through the Suez Canal, then we went to Bombay, Ceylon. It was beautiful. We were not allowed to get out, because we were Germans, you know, for the English we were the enemies. But people came to the boat from the committee there.

And then we went to Singapore. We had one lady who got off in Singapore because her daughter lived there. We had good friends, they emigrated before us to England, they had a brother in Singapore. His relatives wrote to him, and he came to the boat.

We went to Manila, and in Manila we were allowed to get out, because it was American. I never forget it. It was so hot and it was so humid. It was beginning of June, and I guess they assigned families to take care of so-and-so many people. We didn't see anything of Manila. We spent most of the day in an air-conditioned restaurant and were drinking Pepsi-Cola.

I never touched it until lately. I was so sick when we came back to the boat. You know the change of climate and the cold and restaurant and the humidity and the heat.

And then from Manila, we went to Hong Kong and Shanghai. Willy called me, "You know what? There is the Bund. We are in Shanghai."

Ralph Hirsch was among the last German Jews to escape to Shanghai.[10] Since the sea route was closed, the only path was directly eastward through the Soviet Union. Most Jews still in Germany at that time were murdered in ghettos and concentration camps.

We left sometime in October 1940, and arrived I believe it was November 1st of that year in Shanghai. We went by train from Berlin to Moscow, a German train that took, I think, two days. We spent a day or two in Moscow at the Hotel Metropol and did some sightseeing in Moscow. I remember distinctly being very impressed with the world-famous subway. We were amazed at how deep it was and how lavishly the walls were covered in marble and how clean it was. We visited Red Square and just looked around the city.

And I remember enjoying the hotel. I can't remember having stayed in a hotel up to that point. I think it was considered one of the two best hotels in Moscow. My father had spent quite a lot of money on the trip. I believe the most of it, at least to the extent he could obtain it, was by first class, including the hotel. So it was very lavish. For a little kid taking a long trip for the first time, it was a very exciting period.

Or the start of a very exciting period and became even more exciting, when we got on the Trans-Siberian Railway a couple of days later, because that was sort of a little world in itself. We were on that train for just about two weeks, with many stops in many places and days and days where we went through deep green forests. I remember thinking, crossing on the south shore of Lake Baikal, which seemed to take forever, we rode there for hours and hours and hours, it was like a riding along the ocean, except that it was so wonderfully covered with trees, that it was the most beautiful thing I'd ever seen. We stopped in several cities. I remember Omsk and Tomsk, and we made one stop in Novosibirsk, which was remarkable, because there seemed to be no city there. There were just some temporary shacks, they were very large, but no real city. I think the city was in the process of construction then, and I was surprised at that.

But then a lot of the things about that trip surprised me, including the fact that most of the passengers in that train were Russian soldiers. My brother and I had a wonderful time. As soon after breakfast as possible, we escaped from my parents' compartment and spent the time with the soldiers. We learned Russian words for cheese and tea and sausage and a few other things, and they sort of adopted us and taught us to swear in Russian, which I can still do to this day. And tried to, you know, show us how their guns worked and various other things that appalled my mother. Every evening when dinnertime came, she had to go through many cars on the train searching for us. We, of course, tried to make that a game.

That leg of the trip came to an end in a little border town in Manchukuo called Manchouli, which was a very primitive place and was the transfer point to the Japanese train. And I remember being very excited by Manchouli, because it seemed like a village out of one of those adventure stories that Karl May wrote, and I was particularly glad because my Karl May books had been sealed up by the Russians. I had brought a whole batch of them, which my parents had bought me for the trip, but the Russians sealed up all of our German books at the border, presumably because they thought that it would contaminate Marxist doctrine or something.[11] Anyway, there was a village right out of Karl May, with camels on the streets and tribesmen with guns slung over their shoulders riding shaggy ponies and wearing fur caps and so on. But the downside was the flea bag of a hotel, that was, I guess, the only accommodation in town. My mother took one look at the bedding and said, "I'm not going to sleep on that!" [laughs] I guess somehow after a few hours she decided that it was that or nothing. So we did sleep there, we survived it.

And got onto a train that was extremely different from the Russian train. Where the Russian train had been very open and friendly and a lot of fun, the Japanese train was very regimented. All the windows were sealed, they had tape over the windows, and we were instructed that on pain of being shot by the sentry, there was a sentry of each car, we were not allowed to look out. And so of course my brother and I looked out. We peeled tape away from the bottom of the windows. One of us was the lookout, the other one was the peekout, and whenever the sentry came, put the tape back and whistled so-and-so. There wasn't a whole lot to see. The scenery was not so different from what we'd seen in Russia, but it was an interesting game. We knew the adults were not allowed to do that, to be able to look out.

There was a rather mixed batch of passengers, quite a lot of the people from the Trans-Siberian and various other mostly Japanese people. There were quite a few Japanese soldiers, and we were not allowed to move so freely on that train. So I don't really know for sure who was there, because if we got too far from our car, the guards would shoo us back. It wasn't nearly as much fun, so my brother and I were glad when we got to the port city of Dairen, which was the end of the train journey.

I don't think we stayed there overnight. There was a big hassle, because the steamship company which my father had booked cabins for us wouldn't accept those tickets, and so we just got some deck space between decks, plain flooring and not very clean. There were various people who looked Asian huddled there in little family groups, and my mother said, "Absolutely not, I'm not going to travel this way!" So my father went back and, I guess, slipped some money to one of the officers. So we spent the two nights in the officers' mess and slept on the benches in the officers' mess.

We had good weather for those two days that we were at sea. Mostly we played on deck, we tossed a ball or ran around. It was pretty crowded, and the thing about that trip that sticks most in my mind is that, while my brother and I were tossing a tennis ball back and forth, I almost hit a Chinese man who was walking between us. I pulled back just in time and didn't hit him. Then when he was past, I said to my brother sort of loudly, "Some people just can't watch where they're going!" in German. And this Chinese man turned around and dressed me down in flawless German and said something like, "You rude little boy. Why aren't you careful about how you throw the ball!" I was absolutely thunderstruck to hear this beautiful German coming out of this strange looking face. I had never met a Chinese up to that point. I had seen some, but of course they had spoken a very strange language, and I don't think I had ever spoken to one before. This was a shocking experience for me. My mother said I said hardly anything the whole day after that. I remember it more clearly than anything else about the trip.

CHAPTER 3

Culture Shock and Community Creation in Shanghai

As European luxury liners steamed up the Huangpu River, their Jewish refugee passengers were on the verge of unimaginably new lives. Arrival in Shanghai was a shock. Loaded onto trucks like so much baggage, they were driven across the Garden Bridge to a barracks outfitted with bunk beds. Two hallmarks of European domestic life, privacy and cleanliness, were suddenly replaced by tropical heat, bedbugs, and shared toilets. The Nazis had stolen their possessions in Europe, but the reality of refugee poverty struck them first in China.

Shanghai itself was stunning. Few Europeans knew anything about Shanghai beyond prejudices about Chinese and stories of lawlessness. One of the largest and most cosmopolitan cities in the world, Shanghai in the 1930s was an international banking city and the gun-running capital of Asia, a center for trade in textiles and opium, and an open port where Chinese Nationalists and Communists, organized gangsters, Western capitalists, and the Japanese military competed for authority. Extremes of wealth and poverty jostled in the crowded streets.

Shanghai was a capitalist paradise. After the British navy defeated Chinese forces in the Opium War of 1842, two large sections of central Shanghai became autonomous foreign entities: the International Settlement, dominated by British and American business interests and governed by the Shanghai Municipal Council (SMC), and the French Concession, run by the French government through its Consul General. The extraterritorial governments controlled police, customs, and judicial matters. The SMC was elected by the tiny proportion of foreigners who owned substantial property. Chinese only won the right to vote for the SMC in 1927, when Chiang Kai-shek and the Nationalists came to power.

Some of the earliest British subjects in Shanghai were Jews whose families emigrated from the Middle East. In the early twentieth century, poorer Baghdadi Jewish families fled from conscription into the Ottoman Turkish army. By the 1930s, the Baghdadi community numbered nearly 1,000. They practiced Sephardic Judaism and created their own school, the Shanghai Jewish School, on the grounds of their lovely synagogue in the International Settlement. A few families amassed enormous wealth and joined the financial elite in Shanghai, including the Sassoons, Kadoories, and Hardoons.[1]

The other Jewish community in Shanghai came from Russia as refugees from Tsarist antisemitism, revolutionary upheaval, and Stalinist terror. They were Ashkenazi, and more numerous, numbering about 5,000, but not as well off as the Baghdadi Jews.[2]

During the early twentieth century, the Japanese became the largest foreign colony in the city. In the 1930s, Japanese military pressure on China, especially the occupation of Manchuria in 1931 and 1932, coincided with the increasing Japanese presence in the Hongkou District of Shanghai. In 1937 through February

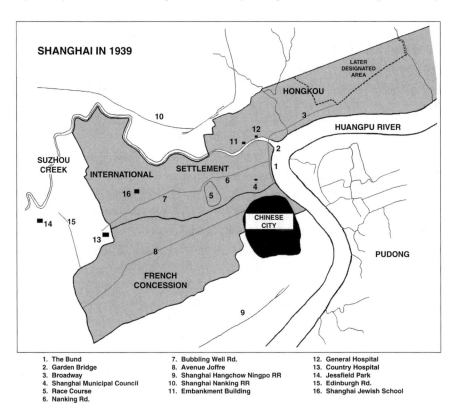

1. The Bund	7. Bubbling Well Rd.	12. General Hospital
2. Garden Bridge	8. Avenue Joffre	13. Country Hospital
3. Broadway	9. Shanghai Hangchow Ningpo RR	14. Jessfield Park
4. Shanghai Municipal Council	10. Shanghai Nanking RR	15. Edinburgh Rd.
5. Race Course	11. Embankment Building	16. Shanghai Jewish School
6. Nanking Rd.		

Map 1   Shanghai in 1939

1938, Japanese forces battled the Chinese army in Shanghai for several months, destroying large parts of Hongkou. The Japanese became the dominant military power in Shanghai. They controlled customs, post, and telegraph, and took over police powers in Hongkou, officially part of the International Settlement. They demanded a greater voice in the SMC and its police forces. Unwilling, however, to antagonize the Western powers, the Japanese did not challenge other extraterritorial privileges within the International Settlement. They also made no effort to restrict the massive Jewish refugee immigration that began in 1938.

The national and ethnic communities in Shanghai responded quite differently to the newly arrived refugees. Even before any significant number of refugees arrived, the Baghdadi Jewish community created in August 1938 a relief committee headed by Paul Komor, the Honorary Consul General for Hungary, to greet the refugees, provide temporary housing, and integrate them into the Shanghai economy. The Sassoon and Kadoorie families used their wealth and influence to smooth the descent of these Europeans into refugee status. Many in the Russian Jewish community offered assistance, but on a less organized, more individual basis. Our narrators talk individually of the wide variety of services provided to them. Collectively their stories show how the level of help decreased as the number of arriving refugees soared. Soon, thousands were housed in barracks, called Heime, created from unused buildings to accommodate those without sufficient funds to rent their own rooms. The Kitchen Fund offered meals to any refugee family who needed them.

Although help from both Russian and Baghdadi Jews was indispensable to the survival of the refugees, the central Europeans remained socially isolated. Nearly everyone named by the narrators in these interviews came from the refugee community itself; contacts with the two other Jewish communities tended to be sporadic and formalized. Only a few refugees, such as the Greenings, bridged the deep cultural differences that separated central European Jews from everyone else in Shanghai.

Much less welcoming was the Western business elite. There is no evidence that the Western business community provided any financial assistance to the refugees, although some, like Eric Reisman, describe important individual contacts they made with generous Westerners.

Life in Hongkou brought out two powerful strands of refugee culture. Although many families had put little energy into being Jewish in Europe, the Nazis forced them to consider their Jewishness. The particular form of cultured, secular, and patriotic Ashkenazi Judaism that developed in central Europe during the nineteenth and early twentieth centuries, often called the German-Jewish symbiosis, was now recreated in an Asian port city. Jewish institutions and forms of self-governance were developed by refugees. The founded a

Jüdische Gemeinde *[Jewish Community] patterned on similar organizations in Germany, uniting the whole spectrum of religious observance.*

These refugees saw no contradiction between Jewish and German culture. Within a few months of landing, the Austrians created a café life on the streets of Hongkou. It took only a bit longer to develop cultural institutions sophisticated enough to provide regular entertainment and edification. With few stars from Berlin or Vienna, the experienced theatrical professionals gathered over 200 artists and organized dramatic ensembles and artistic societies. By late 1939, theater productions appeared monthly. They produced Lessing's "Nathan der Weise" in January 1940, and many newly written pieces developed out of refugee life.[3] Gérard Kohbieter describes the less exalted productions of Shanghai's nightlife. Newspapers emerged, notably the Shanghai Jewish Chronicle, *published by Ossi Lewin.*

Probably the most ambitious and successful creation was the Shanghai Jewish Youth Association School, informally named the Kadoorie School. Providing young people with a good education was a central Jewish value, but creating a functioning school in wartime Shanghai was a colossal achievement. When refugee children overwhelmed the existing Shanghai Jewish School, the community leased a vacant building in Hongkou from the SMC. In November 1939, the SJYA School began classes financed by the Baghdadi community, especially Sir Horace Kadoorie. About 600 students attended a mixture of religious and secular courses taught in English by refugees and modeled after Jewish schools in Germany. In January 1942, the Kadoorie School moved to a better site, a building that is fondly remembered by its former students.

The shock of expulsion from Europe and flight to China soon sorted the 16,000 German-speaking refugees into three broad economic classes. Those who managed to bring a few dollars or some valuables to Shanghai rented apartments in the International Settlement. The early arrivals could still find jobs or open businesses. A second group of families fell into poverty, each squeezing into one rented room in Hongkou. They survived by selling their possessions and eating the one free meal a day provided by the Baghdadi-supported welfare committee. A third group had nothing and lived in the Heime, *supported by Jewish charity.*

Gradually, families slipped down this scale after selling their possessions, losing their jobs, or receiving less charitable support. Meanwhile, prices in Shanghai spiraled upward as a result of the war with Japan. Most of our narrators trace their gradual downward mobility after arrival. Poverty altered the internal dynamics of formerly middle-class families.

The development of the war into a worldwide conflict had a direct impact on the refugee community. At the same time that Japanese warplanes bombed American ships in Pearl Harbor in December 1941, the Japanese military marched into the Western enclaves of Shanghai and took complete control of the city. For the rest of the war, Shanghai was under military occupation by the Japanese, allies of the Nazis.

The American and British businessmen who had enjoyed the benefits of colonial domination lost their jobs and eventually their freedom. The Japanese set up internment camps for enemy aliens. But the refugees were not considered enemies by the Japanese. Many were forced to move, like Eric Reisman and Lotte Schwarz, yet most Jews from the Third Reich could continue their lives unimpeded, as long as they acknowledged Japanese dominance.

Survival dominated the present. Nobody could predict the future. Meanwhile, in Europe, mass murder was in full swing.

*When **Eric Reisman** arrived at the end of 1938, the Shanghai Jewish community could still offer remarkable assistance to refugees through its relief committee. Ensuring that children were well taken care of was a high priority for the committee. Reisman and his brother were boarded with and taught English by local middle-class families until their parents were more settled. In this way, individual members of the Western expatriate community demonstrated considerable generosity. But it did not last beyond Pearl Harbor.*

We basically came penniless. We arrived in December of 1938 on a very, very dreary day. It was cold, raining. We were loaded on trucks. The Komor Committee, made up of local Jews, tried to settle the new arrivals. It was a marvelous thing they did for us, for us and anyone else that came. They settled us in Hongkou, which was basically the worst part of Shanghai at the time.

The meager belongings that we had we put into that room that they gave us. It was Ward Road, number 24, I'll never forget. It was wintertime, and that was the rainy period in Shanghai. It came down in buckets, and we took our shoes off and went to bed that night. In the morning, I'm getting out of bed, and I can't find my shoes, they're floating. The room was flooded. So the little we had with us was soaking wet [laughs] the following day. My father was able to get us a room on the first floor subsequently.

Where we lived had a fireplace, an open hearth where you burned briquets, and being cold and damp, that was the only means of warming up. When I was still in Vienna, I had scarlet fever, and the side effects of that scarlet fever was a punctured ear drum. Due to the cold in China on arrival, my ear started to bother me.

And so the first thing on the agenda was to try and get me to a doctor who could relieve that terrible earache that I had. Not speaking the language, it was rather difficult to pursue that endeavor, but my father was able to find a doctor for me and I was being treated. One of the things that relieved the earache was to get me some heat. I had no thermos and no heating pad, nothing, so my parents bedded me close to the fire and kept the fire going and that would help me. That was the room that we lived in.

When we came there, 1938, now we're going into 1939, a family of four could easily live on 15 dollars a month, that was paying for the rent, paying for everything, you could eat very well. Things were dirt cheap.

After we arrived there, the Komor Committee placed young kids into families that lived there, whether they be Jewish or not, and it so happened that I was placed in a childless family, husband and wife. Pyle was their name. He was the assistant principal of an English school in Shanghai, and he got me enrolled in that school.[4]

So I learned English with a British accent. I had to learn it overnight, and I seem to have gotten along fairly well with the kids there. I lived with the Pyles for about six months, maybe a little longer, and they were very good to me, and they gave me a place to live, and they fed me. He had a car, and I drove with him to school every day and came home with him. And I tried very hard to learn the language, it was either swim or sink. In six months, I was basically fluent in English. I had to learn English, and I learned it, and I made good grades then, grades enough to keep me in school.

My brother was taken in by a Methodist missionary family that had two sons, both of the sons I still visit occasionally. We became very close friends to the Berckmans. They never tried to convert us to their thinking or their belief, they respected our religion, but they were very, very good to us. And I considered Mr. and Mrs. Berckman as my second parents. My brother didn't stay in contact with them, yet I did, and I found them loving, caring people. My brother lived with the Berckmans about as long as I did, and then he went to work for the bus company, and I went to the Kadoorie School.

We were one of the early immigrants that came to Shanghai. The war remnants were very, very visible, to the point where you saw carcasses of people that the Japanese executed still hanging on the ropes in doorways, that the Japanese in their cruel way of conquering certain parts of the world displayed. It was a rude awakening to see that.

We saw the Chinese living in cardboard boxes, in ruins, and dead people laying on the streets when we arrived there. It was terrible. The population was very poor, undernourished, and there was a lot of infant mortalities. The people living there had no means of burying the young children that were born. You would walk, and suddenly you'd see a package laying there, and as you looked closer onto that package wrapped in either a straw mat or a piece of newspaper, you saw a small leg sticking out. It was dead children that the parents laid out on the sidewalk.

There was an organization from the municipality, like you have here, people collecting garbage, their responsibility was to go around continuously every morning and picking up dead bodies. And they would take them to a crematorium and burn them, which was also in Hongkou not very far from where we all lived.

Those were some of the impressions that were shocking to a lot of people, but made you after a while very callous, to the point where you didn't even walk around that package. If it was laying right on the sidewalk, you would step over it. The Chinese would walk on the street, they would make a circle.

When we got to China, we all started to work. My mother had the foresight to go through ORT, the organization, she learned how to make leather gloves in Vienna, before we left. And she also went with ORT through a confectionery baking school.[5] Unfortunately, the majority of our Jewish population in Vienna were not tradesmen. They were businessmen, doctors, lawyers, but trade? There were very, very few, a handful of tradesmen. A Jewish shoemaker was unheard of. So my mother knew that if she learned a trade, she would be able to do something with it. And the first thing she did when we came to China was make gloves. My mother made hand-sewed gloves, she had blisters on her fingers in doing it. And my father, being a businessman and being able to talk to people the right way, was able to sell them. They accumulated a nice bit of change.

We as children helped as much as we can. My brother was learning to be an automobile mechanic, and he worked in the bus company. I was 12 years old at that time, I was going on 13, and in April I was the first child to be Bar Mitzvahed in the temple in Hongkou. I knew very little about the Jewish religion, somehow I knew the *brucha* [blessing] of the Torah, and knew a little bit of reading, then they bestowed the Bar Mitzvah on me.

As we were able to make a little bit of money, we moved out of that one room into a larger room that had a balcony, and we lived on Chusan Road. All by herself, my mother was working, my father was selling these gloves, vendoring from door to door, and it was all word of mouth. "Could you recommend another family that they may want to buy a pair of gloves from me?" I don't know what he got for a pair of gloves, but it was adequate enough for us to live on and save some, and we accumulated enough money to buy a small home. You didn't go to the bank to get a loan, you bought the house, and that house belonged to us.

We bought a home in Kinchow Road, the same road that the Kadoorie School was on, and it was a very nice house. It even had a WC, which was very rare, because the honey buckets were the common denominator.[6] We were able to buy that house and have tenants in it, so that we had a small side income from the renting out the rooms. All families lived in one room, that was the luxury living, compared to the less fortunate ones that had to live in the camps, Ward Road Camp, Chaoufoong Road Camp, where families lived in bunk beds, and curtains or sheets would give them a little bit of privacy.

In Hongkou itself, our Jewish people knew that they had to do something, so soup kitchens were built in the camps, and you were able to get at least one hot meal a day, meager as it be, but they baked bread and people worked in the soup kitchens, and the volunteers, some of them would get paid. Where the funds came for the payment was primarily from the United States, donations, or the local Jews that were in business over there. Some of them were very wealthy, they were the Jewish aristocrats. But they were very, very, very helpful to us, as they did magnificent things. Without their help and aid given to us, I don't think that the European immigrants would have fared as well as they did.

Pearl Harbor came and, lo and behold, the house that had the WC was a place that the Japanese liked very much and they confiscated it. I spoke English, my father's English was very poor, and he took me along to talk to the Japanese authorities to try and find out if we could possibly stay in the house or get some compensation for it. We met up with the Japanese authorities, I remember, and all I would get is a nodding of the head and a big smile and nothing. And that was it. We couldn't get anything, no compensation for the house, that was it. Here we were, we started out from scratch all over again. We moved then into another room.

Right after Pearl Harbor, the British, the Americans, were put in internment camp. First in house arrest, they couldn't leave the houses, and then they picked them up and put them in camps. The family that I went with, Pyle, was in camp, and I was able to get food to them to show my appreciation for what they did for us. Mr. Berckman was interned in an internment camp. The family were able to get out before the war, because the American Consulate evacuated nonessential personnel from China before the war, but he stayed on and he was interned.

I was very helpful to him, he trusted me a great deal and he trusted my judgment. When he was under house arrest, before he was put in internment camp, he gave me the key to his office, and he said, "Eric, I need you to go to the office and get certain things." And I bicycled to the office and opened the safe, got those things, put them in my leather schoolbag. As I came out, I heard the Japanese coming. On their shoes the Japanese had steel caps, and I could hear these caps shuffling up the front steps. I ran down the back steps, and I took my bicycle and pedaled away. [laughs] So I got that stuff out for him. He was forever grateful for me. To this day, I don't know what was in there, whether it was money or documents or shares or valuables, I don't know.

That was after Pearl Harbor. We were still able to move around.

Lotte Schwarz and her husband were able to get a loan from the Komor Committee to start a coffee shop. Some elements of a normal life emerged as friendships were made, children were born, and religious holidays were celebrated. They did business with a non-Jewish German and with Japanese soldiers. The Japanese takeover of Shanghai after Pearl Harbor coincided with the impoverishment of the refugee community by 1942.

We got there '38. We only lived in Hongkou. Where the Bund ends, there's a Garden Bridge, and then Hongkou starts. Only rich people who came with their own money, they went across the Garden Bridge. And most those people, when the Japanese took over when the war broke out, they came over to us, too.

Photo 3 Garden Bridge to Hongkou: from left, Broadway Mansions, Astor House Hotel, Russian Consulate

By the Garden Bridge were all those little houses. And all those little houses belonged to Sassoon. Sassoon must have been very wealthy. He was a tall, beautiful-looking man. Those houses were empty. Before we came in, the Chinese and Japanese fought, and the Chinese had to leave or run away out of all those houses. And they were in a terrible, terrible situation. We got a loan, I don't know how much it was, from Sassoon.

With the little money we had, we fixed up one of those little houses. We slept in there, and we cooked in there, if we had anything to cook, you know. We had the Chinese oven, the rooms had a little balcony, so till I got that thing going and not having all the smoke in the house, I did it on the balcony. But most we didn't have anything to eat. Every month, Mr. Goldberg, or Goldenberg, I think was his name, came and got the rent. We paid it, mostly we didn't have it, you know, and he was real rough. That was a time.

Downstairs there was a refugee dentist. Our room was upstairs in that little house there. The stairs were so narrow. In the back was another room. We divided the room, and we had the front and Bayer and his wife, they had the back.

We had a coffee shop in the beginning for our refugee people called "Esplanade." We found a Chinese carpenter, and he fixed up our little place. It was terrible, but it looked nice after we renovated it. Bayer cooked, and his wife and I, we did the service. It was good food. There was a butcher, one of our German people, and he made very good salami and hot dogs and everything, sold it at our market. And we sold that, too. So that was in the beginning.

We had a boy, our cookboy, his name was Hans. There were many German people in Shanghai, not Jews. They had big businesses, import and export and everything, and that Hans was a servant or cook in one of those families there. One of the rich German people, he came in the store. He had the German beer, import or export, and he wanted us to have beer. He gave us that Hans. And he said, "If you had beer and you could sell beer, you would get other people in and you would make some business." He was a nice German man. And then we took the beer in and that was when Japanese came, you know.

See the port was right down that street, the end of the Broadway where all the Japanese soldiers came. So they came in, and they drank a beer, and so we made a little better business. They came in the store and they liked to eat steak. Of course, we didn't have any money to stock up. So Hans did the cooking, and every time we needed a steak, he'd run over to the butcher and bought a steak, you know, and we made it for a while.

When we came, they still had the houses. But then there weren't any more. People came, they didn't have money either for anything anymore. So they stayed in the *Heim.*

My brother Berthold came very few months after we did, I think three months later. He lived, I think, in the Seward Heim. He had even a good job in Shanghai. He was in men's clothing. He wasn't married when he came to Shanghai. He married a woman from the *Heim* there.

I remember one time, it was still in the good times, because we still had the first place, the coffee shop. I walked the street, and I looked down, there was a five yen. And five yen was enormously much money. And I run to my husband and said, "Boy, I just found five yen." And he said, "You know what you do with it, you go right next door and buy you a dress." I think it was the only dress I ever bought in Shanghai.

So we had a little room, and the Bayers had a little room, and we were very glad. And then we both got children. They got twins, and I got my daughter in February '40.

When I got pregnant with my daughter in Shanghai, we didn't know how our doctors were. And I didn't want to have the baby in one of our *Heims* there. In the French part was the St. Marie's Hospital, all Catholic with Catholic sisters. And I said I would like to go there.

I came there, and the nurses spoke only French. And they weren't even nice to us. I had fever like anything. I was burning up, I was so hot, and I said, "There must be something wrong." I called the nurses so many times. One of the sisters who was there said, "The sisters are busy in the first class." And I never forget that. Took a long time till they came. But anyway, then finally they brought me out. And I don't know if I had Caesarean, it was very complicated. I had a baby. I got hotter and hotter, and they took the baby away, Heia, she was five and a half pounds, I think, so not a big baby. They finally took my temperature, and it came out later on that at that time in Shanghai was a scarlet epidemic, and I had scarlet fever. I got it during I had the baby.

So my husband took the baby home, and we took a lady, one of our refugees, who knew how to handle *Kinder,* and she stayed with the baby all the time, with Heia. And I was a few days at that hospital, and they only spoke French to me. I thought I could speak French, but I couldn't, when you speak with people like that, anyway. And I said, "I want to go to the Chaoufoong Heim, to our people."

Then one of those ambulances came and took me, a Chinese ambulance. They stopped about three or four times and put new people in and took people out, and it took forever. And when we came to Chaoufoong

Heim, where our hospital was, they had the doors open, they had my bed ready, they had everything ready, and they said, "My goodness, where have you been?" When they checked me, my breasts were infected like anything.

The doctor who came, a surgeon, he said, "Where are you from?" I said, "From Nordhausen am Harz." He said, "That's where I am from." And he was Dr. Erich Marcuse, who lived right around the corner from us. I knew that he was a fantastic surgeon, and he was in Berlin at the famous West End Hospital already. He operated on me right away and cut open the breast. He came and treated me, and it healed wonderful and was okay. He even came later on, when I was still home and checked. By then, everything was all right and my husband had taken Heia home, you know. Can you imagine, in comes a doctor and operates on you and he is from Nordhausen, from that little city. Isn't that something?

And I remember, I was alone in the hospital room in the Chaoufoong Heim, in the morning they had to come in and light the stove. Because we didn't have anything else than an old stove there. When they lit that stove, the smoke came out, when you were sick and everything. But they were good, and they had good nurses, our people, you know, because they put a little heart in.

I stayed there six weeks, I think. And when I came home, you know, those little houses there, the staircases are so narrow, and of course they are steep up, and our room was in the second story. So it was impossible for me to go up those, one took my hands and pulled me and my husband pushed me till I got up to bed, you know. But from then on everything went okay.

Her name was Bella. We had to take a name out of a list from Hitler, you know, because we were still German citizens. We were the only dumb ones who did that. My friends, they just took any name they wanted and didn't even go to the German Consulate and registered her. So we registered her with the name Bella, but we never called her Bella. My husband called her Häschen, Häsie, you know *Häsie* is a little rabbit. So she couldn't say that. And she said, "Heia," when you ask her, "How's your name?" So we call her Heia. And she's fifty years old now. And George is forty.

We went to the High Holidays. We even closed the little coffee shop. We never went, of course, where the rich people had the synagogue. We had a room in one of our *Heims,* or there was a movie house which was empty, and during the High Holidays we went in there. We had a rabbi and a cantor from our own people. There was no regular synagogue in Hongkou. Poor people don't need anything.

Bayer, he had to go later, because he drank too much, he couldn't do it anymore. They had to move out. Behind our house, you know, we called them lanes, they were narrow streets with little houses. They moved in one of those.

The Chinese, where we bought in the market, they learned German, you know. [laughs] We all spoke German. And they learned very easily. "This no good, Missy, this no good, Missy," when you want to buy that. There were many beggars. Next where our store was, was a little plaza, and there was a woman, and she had always a little baby in her cape kind of wrapped around, and she was old. But when that baby grew up, she brought another baby. And everybody gave her money once in a while. I gave her something to eat there, you know. There were very many people, very poor people there. Dying in the street like anything, laying in the street. Nobody picked them up. It was a very bad time in Shanghai for the Chinese people, too. More than for us, I say.

When the war broke out, I was outside. We heard terrible bumping, like bombs and so, and then I saw fire coming from the harbor, which was close to there, too. My husband said, "I go down and see what's going on." We had no idea. And he even got dressed. [laughs] I said, "You don't have to get dressed. Just go out and see what's going on." He said, "You never know what happen. You never know if you come back." The Bund has all the ships, very close to us, and they were all gone.

Then we just couldn't stay there anymore. Japanese took over that part, and then they took over everything. Across the street was a munitions factory. Japanese said we couldn't be on that side, they needed that side. We had to move from our restaurant, we couldn't have that place anymore.

So we moved to Wayside and opened another little coffee shop. It was just for our people, but not very long. They didn't have any money more either, they sold what they have and they couldn't come anymore. The end of the Wayside was a beautiful park, but when the Japanese took over, we could not go to the park anymore.

Gérard Kohbieter was a teenager on his own with one connection in Shanghai, a doctor who had been a friend of his mother. Without resources, he lived in the Alcock Heim *for single men. Disdaining the rigid morality of central Europe, he joined the refugee cultural scene, survived by his own magic, and observed Shanghai's night life.*

I had the doctor there and, of course, the committee that picked you up at the boat with busses. And then you were driven to a camp. Not a concentration camp, a camp with beds and a canteen. You had a place to put your head. I was 16, 17, and I very, very quickly attached myself to the creative types. I tried to, sort of, buddy up to them. And I was in some cases accepted. I mean, I was a young kid. I was interested in art. Of course, I couldn't contribute to the conversation an awful lot, but I had the ability to keep my mouth shut and listen. Those were colorful people. They weren't dead yet. They weren't *kvetching*, you know, they were doing something, drawing or painting or putting little ships in empty scotch bottles or hell knows what, but they were colorful. They laughed sometimes.

I met a guy from Berlin, an excellent painter. He was making a living singing. He had done Richard Tauber imitations in a Viennese nightclub, but he came from a wealthy home.[7] He didn't have to do that for the money, but for kicks. And he went to the Reimannschule in Berlin, and he painted over there. Had a couple of shows too. Marvelous painter. He was five years older than I, and he taught me a lot about art. Cigarettes used to have pictures in them, the Olympic games or classic cars or flowers or animals or cats. They had a series on modern art, and he had bought that, and he introduced me to the whole bunch. We got the reputation of being homosexuals, because we were always buddying around, but it was just a good friendship. It didn't really bother me all that much either. Of course, one didn't see us with girls very often, because girls were hard to come by. If a girl was good-looking, she didn't look for a poor refugee. I had a girlfriend for a long time, a Russian acrobatic dancer.

I met three guys in Shanghai, three Germans, Hamburgers all. One was a burglar, one was a chemist, the third one didn't do anything. The burglar bridged the hard winters. Winter is unpleasant in Shanghai. It's very, very moist. It doesn't freeze, but particularly if you are undernourished, you know, and you have a hole in your shoe, and maybe you don't have a proper coat, because one sold a lot of stuff to get eating money, and so if you didn't gauge it right, you wound up without a coat in winter. Well, he threw a brick in the window someplace and got himself in the pokey, and the judges knew him. They knew what he was doing. English judges for the English Concession. He spent the winter in jail. I visited him a couple of times. He had no status problems with that, because that was his life. Jail to him was just a place that you simply have to cope with once in a while, if you have that form of human endeavor. He even offered me a job once. He knew where to get something, and he needed somebody to keep an eye on things and whistle when somebody comes. I couldn't see that either.

In Shanghai I went to cafés. Sometimes it was a toss-up whether I'm going to buy myself a bowl of noodles for the rest of my capital that I had in my pocket or whether I go to a café. In the café you could sit, it was warm. Usually there were people that you knew. And the main thing was they had a radio and you could hear music, and that was a big attraction. I was starved for music.

People didn't have money, but people had things. I mean, there were clubs where one knew that those two had started with a couple of cameras. Small, small. But everything was cheap, the band, the entertainers, you know, few bottles. Bars that had two kinds of whiskey and a case of beer, that's how they started. Then worked themselves up, the profit is good on these things.

The nightlife was interesting. In the beginning, the clientele was English and American, the foreign businessmen, and of course the successful Chinese. They love to go to clubs. Then when they got the camps, it was the Germans, the Japanese, and still the Chinese, of course. There was considerable contact between the German community, including the official guys from the Consulate. Prominent Nazis were seen in clubs, sitting with a Jewish bar girl and buying drinks. After the war with Japan started, after the English and the Americans and the Dutch were out, the Germans were the people that supported the nightclubs, because they had the money.

Yeah, good money was made then. You had a lot of German musicians playing in clubs, including the Joachim brothers, who were sort of known in the classical field. But they played jazz, too. Big Filipino bands that played swing charts, played Goodman charts and Glenn Miller and stuff like that. Big bands, sounded great. There was a Russian band that played really good jazz. And I was doing the silent act then, of course, because I couldn't speak Chinese, and they accompanied me. I would tell them what kind of music I wanted and had little rehearsals with the drummer when I wanted a roll.

In Hongkou, of course, most of it was in Jewish hands, the clubs, the cafés. The Viennese were very quick to open coffee houses. There was one club that was owned by French Jews. Very good club, very well-run club, good music. In the city proper, the Russians had clubs there. One nightclub was owned by an American that was known to be a fugitive from the law. He was a gangster or something, Jimmy, Jimmy's Kitchen. But he was socially acceptable. He popped up in the social columns, and society people sort of liked buddying around. They thought it was adventurous, I guess. It's a melting pot all right.

In the city, the big clubs were in Chinese hands, the big hotels with their nightclubs in the Western section, it was called the Badlands for some reason. There was gambling in the back, elegant, elegant gambling. Some refugees went to the gambling places, because they were very generous in serving food. There were always candies standing around and cigarettes, to help yourself. And if you are flat broke, that's something to be considered. So they went to these places and played very carefully, a little bit red and a little bit black, and hoping that the zero wouldn't come, or played two, black and red. That's just so to give the illusion. It was quite a hike out there, too.

The bar girls were not prostitutes. They usually had husbands, that was just the job. There were people in the community that put up their noses at these women, because they worked in a bar, because they were too bourgeois or simply too square, used to be the word, to swing with that. Not all Jews are tolerant. Bad scene. People were talking about those women sometimes in a very derogatory way. But so what? I mean, you have these people everywhere. They were my audience, too. They were the ones that were applauding nicely, they dug the playfulness of it, you know, magic is this very playful thing. Unless you go at it in a very grim way, which I don't. There were hookers, sure there were hookers. But, I mean, I didn't find it all that terrible.

Occasionally one worked together at what they called *Bunte Abend*. *Bunte Abende* is simply a mishmash of comedians, a dancer, a magician, sketches, a lot of sketches that were often written specially for the occasion. Or there were old sketches that were tried and true.

They were put on sometimes in the camps. Everybody went to the *Bunte Abende*, because it was entertainment. It was cheap. If you didn't have the money, I think you could get tickets from the committee or so. The camp where I stayed for quite a while had a stage that was used for Friday night services and Saturday services, and it was also used for a stage for plays and for *Bunte Abende*. There were entrepreneurs who would rent a theater and do the publicity and hire a bunch of people. They had an MC there, a comedian and MC, very clever, hard, hard cat, Herbert Zernik, who was with the *Kabarett der Komiker* [Cabaret of Comedians] in Berlin, he said. But he was good.

I knew Boris Sapiro, a very small, very nervous, eccentric man that ran a little theater in a café and produced Yiddish plays occasionally. But he wasn't as far out in his artistic choices as he was as a personality. He was a true madman of the old school, 18 carat. A friend of mine did backdrops for him, and he came home and had to have a couple of stiff drinks after consultations with the maestro. The rest he did was boulevard theater. What Pauline Kael called entertaining trash. Which is totally acceptable.

Why not? Especially in those times when people have *tsouris* [troubles] up to here. Anything goes.

But there were people who were pushing the drama. I've seen one guy standing on stage singing Toller songs.[8] Spread legs like this. He was singing songs about coffee being put in the ocean to keep the prices up, very revolutionary stuff, which was of course received by the audience with, you could see the split, the spectrum. Some people were saying, "Yeah, that's it. That's the way to look at things and to interpret them. We've got to do something about that." And there were other people that put their noses up at this left-wing nonsense, as they saw it. But I mean, there were never any fights or so. The next thing was a dancer, calm the waves.

The Russian Jewish community was pretty well organized. They had schools for their people. They had a Russian club. I had good contacts with Russians. It was the first time that I've seen Russians, in the after-hour joints where the musicians and the entertainers go. You didn't want to go straight home, because you're all wound up, and I've seen guys sit there and weep bitterly and drink vodka out of water glasses. It's just like in Dostoevsky, and I was deeply touched by the Russians.

It was a Russian Jew that arranged that I could travel through North China, which you ordinarily couldn't, because it was all under Japanese occupation. They got me permission to travel around there, to Peking, Tientsin, and Tsinanfoo, Tsingtao. It was a year after I got there, 1940. This school friend who lived with his family in Tsingtao had heard that I was in Shanghai, and he came visit me and asked, "How would you like to come to Tsingtao for a while?" It was a very beautiful place, and the architecture is like the Riviera, lots of little beaches. And I played clubs there, the Russian Jews arranged that for me. Well, it did a lot for my self-confidence as a performer. So there I was, pulling rabbits out of my ears, so to speak.

I performed not just in nightclubs. I worked in vaudeville houses where the audience consisted of factory workers and rickshaw coolies. Good audiences by the way. Did my magic there with music, and I started to talk a little Chinese, because my Russian girlfriend spoke Chinese. She wasn't really Russian. She always said, "I'm not Russian, I'm Estonian." It was one of these countries that had been grabbed by the Soviet Union. Four shows, four shows a day. Hard work. It was just waiting for the war to get over, and whatever came, came. Those nightclubs in Shanghai were quite posh. It looks like fairy tale, all that red and gold and the dragons, and it's an adventure. It's a trifle over-decorated by European standard, but what the hell. I mean, let's play a little.

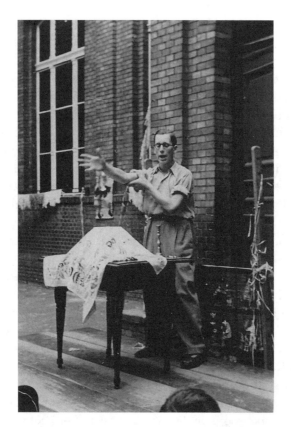

Photo 4   Gérard Kohbieter as a street magician

Lisbeth Loewenberg and her mother followed her father to Shanghai. She soon found work and later, love. Her father taught at the Kadoorie School, but he suc-cumbed to cancer. When she met her future husband, Bruno, he still suffered from his experiences in Buchenwald.

After four weeks, we arrived in Shanghai. When we got off that ship on the Bund and on Nanking Road in Shanghai, I saw these masses of people. They were all Chinese, and there was a different odor in the air. There was this smell of cooking oil or incense, and masses and masses of people. I thought that there has to be an accident or something going on, there cannot be that many people always, like ants, constantly. I thought that I would never be able to breathe again in my whole life. But you get used to it. You don't see it, you don't smell it anymore, and you don't feel the masses of people anymore.

We landed at the Bund, and then through the customs house to pick up our luggage. I remember saying to my mother, "Isn't that Papa?"

Because he had lost so much weight, and he looked so impossible, and for a moment we weren't sure it was him. He told us where he had rented a room on Weihaiwei Road in the International Settlement. He told us to take a rickshaw, and he told the rickshaw coolie the address. And I thought, how can you do that? Here in a place where we have no idea where we are, we are landing on a new continent, and how do we know this guy is going to bring us there? There is this strange Chinese character running in front of a strange vehicle, if you might call a rickshaw that. But all I can say is that he did bring us there.

He had rented one room that had a sort of a balcony. This was by the way a nice house. On Weihaiwei Road, there was something called Young Terrace, there was a lane in there, but it was not anything like the lanes in Hongkou. Those were nice houses with front yards. We had one room that had a sort of an alcove, and this was where my parents slept, and I slept on the sofa in the room, the room. And that's where we stayed. My father had a job already, that's how he could afford to rent this. He worked as a history teacher in the Kadoorie School in Hongkou.

My mother and I both tried to find jobs, too, which wasn't very easy. Before I left, I had taken a course in making gloves and belts and some things like that. There were people who manufactured gloves, so I got a job there. My mother found a job as a sort of a babysitter. A couple, they were both working and they had a daughter, so she stayed there in the afternoons.

Somehow this lady for whom my mother worked heard about a job, somebody looked for a secretary. "Can I type? Can I take shorthand?" "Yes." Another thing I had learned, took a course in before I left Vienna, was English shorthand. And I could type. So I got that job as secretary there in Cathay Mansions. Then I was big lady, because I was paid very well. Comparatively. I was paid better than the average person.

You get a job through luck, but you keep it through ability. I had this job, and I felt like a big shot. And then, unfortunately, the man died that I worked for. He had typhoid fever. You know, that was one of those things. I had typhoid fever, too, but I didn't die, obviously, otherwise I wouldn't be sitting here. But this man was much older, and when you are older, it's much more difficult to recover from things like that. So then I was desperately looking for a job.

There was this lending library, corner Moulmein Road and Bubbling Well. I applied for a job there, asking do they need somebody in the lending library. I knew the owner of that store, Bruno, we were subscribers in that library, and so I always went in there, because that was just around the corner from where we lived. And I got the job. Later on I married my boss.

He lived in the same lane, a couple of houses further down. He had rented only the balcony in one of those houses for his living quarters. One evening I met Bruno on Bubbling Well, but I didn't work for him then yet. He asked me, "Where are you going?" And I said, "I am trying to buy apricots, because my mother wants to cook apricot dumplings." That's how our acquaintance started. The famous story of the apricot dumplings. He said, "Well." And I said, "Why don't you come and try to taste some or something?" And so one day he came, but he didn't get apricot dumplings. He came and he brought coffee and he brought crackers. He says, "Oh, whenever I go somewhere I'm afraid the coffee might not be good, so I always bring my own coffee." But you must realize that coffee and everything was extremely expensive then, and we probably didn't even have any coffee at home anyway, because we never did drink coffee. My parents always drank tea, and I drank tea, too. We talked and I knew that the girl who used to work there left, and anyhow I applied and I got the job. And there we lived till the day of the Proclamation. I mean, I was working, and we were sort of getting acquainted. But we didn't get married till we moved in the Designated Area.

I remember exactly Pearl Harbor. Up to that day, the police were Sikhs, you know, Indian police with the turban. The International Settlement was really British, the police and everything. And one day there's war, the British are out and the Japanese are in. All the Sikhs and everything was gone, and the Japanese police was there. From that moment on, the situation became a little frightening again, because after all the Japanese were on the sides of the Germans. So our situation, though we didn't have to immediately move into the Designated Area, wasn't secure anymore, because we were in enemy territory again, which is what we fled from.

I remember specially one evening. The store was not only a lending library, it was also a bookstore. A Japanese customer came in, and he bought many books. We had English and German books, and Japanese were very interested in German books. As far as I remember, he bought mostly German books. And among other things, he found in stock *The Communist Manifesto* by Karl Marx. He asked Bruno, "Why do you have that book here?" And he said, "Well, it's really a historical document, and in a bookstore one doesn't ask about things like that." But he bought it, and he said, "Well, I'm going to buy it, so that it's in a safe place and other people won't see it." He bought any number of books and asked Bruno to deliver them to his house. Bruno thought it was the end of his life, that he was only asking him to immediately put him into prison or some kind of a concentration camp again. But he delivered the books to him, and this Japanese man called in his son and said, "Now this is the book you should not read," to explain to him all the horrible ideas behind the book. But everything was all right, and Bruno came back home alive. This is just an incident, you know, how one can get paranoid.

I didn't mention that Bruno had been in Buchenwald for over one year, and the way he got out, his sister got a ticket for him to Shanghai. They had picked him up in Berlin, you know, just like one day. Somebody knocks on your door, it happens to be the police, and they say, "Come with us." He asked them, "Should I take a toothbrush?" and they said to him, "I think you better do it." He had been there 13 months. So he had a complete paranoia about everything that looked like policemen or soldier or anything.

Oh, I forgot to mention that my father died in February '42, after the war started. Even at that time, the only hospital that any Jewish immigrant would go to was the one in Ward Road. I'm sure there were other hospitals in Shanghai, but nobody could afford to go into the other hospitals. But he would have died any place. He died of lung cancer a year before the Proclamation.

Otto Schnepp's parents arrived in January 1939 and still could get financial help from the Komor Committee to find housing and open a medical practice. Schnepp was one of the few refugee children able to attend the Shanghai Jewish School in the International Settlement. His excellent academic skills enabled him to support his family and later to enter the American-run St. John's University. The younger Schnepp's successes coincided with his father's difficulty in earning a living, creating uncomfortable family dynamics, which were not uncommon in the refugee community.

I arrived in Shanghai, my parents were there. When they arrived, they were received by a refugee committee that was organized by local residents. They were given some money to rent rooms and, by the time I came, that was the situation. We lived in rented rooms that were located in the so-called French Concession and International Settlement. We moved around a lot, we lived in a large number of places, the sort of room where three slept, and one shared kitchen and shared bathrooms.

My father got some subsidy from the Komor Committee. They had an office in the Sassoon House. My father opened an office in the Sassoon House, in fact, together with another physician, who was German-speaking from Prague. There were so many physicians going there, such a disproportionate number of physicians among the refugee community. That was what we lived on. That really limped along on a pretty difficult level until Pearl Harbor, when everything sort of broke up.

I myself attended the Shanghai Jewish School. I learned English, and I managed all right. There was one big family, Abraham, there that was very far-reaching, one branch of it had 11 children and were very poor. Two of the girls in that family went to school with me, Julie and Sheila. George Horowitz was a classmate of mine at the Shanghai Jewish School. He and those two Abraham girls, we were among the top students in that class.

But Jewish refugee children were not that well integrated really. It was very much a community sort of life. The Russian Jewish children, their parents belonged to the Jewish Club that was in the French Concession. They had their social life around there and at the synagogue.

The Sephardic kids lived around the school in that area and used the school as a kind of a place to meet and playground. Some refugee children also participated in that, but there was a realization there were cultural differences, and there were also levels of education, if you like, that were quite different in the background. Many of the Sephardic community were poor, and the parents obviously didn't come from professional educated background. Some of their parents were very religious, and many of them lived on Jewish charity.

Shanghai Jewish School at the time stopped at what they call Form Six. We took these examinations of the Oxford and Cambridge Overseas Examination Syndicate at the end of the Sixth Form, which for me was December 1940, and then I switched to another so-called public school, Shanghai Municipal Council had schools. This was the Public and Thomas Hanbury School for Boys near Edinburgh Road.

The only schools open to me were these Municipal Council schools. There was of course the French school, but there were a very few in that group of refugees that went to French school, because it was clear to most people that English was the language that one should learn. In addition to that, the French school was very difficult. You know, the French curriculum is more rigorous and goes to a higher level.

There were fees to be paid, got to be a complication. I started pretty early earning money by giving lessons, teaching English to refugees, doing some tutoring. I got some money from somebody at the Shanghai Jewish School who helped me, Reverend Brown, an Englishman who was kind of the power behind the organization. Reverend Brown was the Jewish Rabbi for that Sephardic synagogue. He taught us Hebrew, and he was somehow impressed by me.

I went to that school, and I finished that year, and I took those examinations, beginning first of December. And then one day, the Japanese soldiers were there with barbed wire barricades. It was sort of a big shock, this whole thing. I didn't know what was going on. From where I came, I did not have to pass these barricades to get to that school. But other people had made some arrangements, they could pass through the barricades by showing basically a ruler.

We took those examinations, and they were sent away. I got my certificate after the war. So that was my school career. And then I had nothing to do. It was impossible, I couldn't find a job. I would have liked to go with some people I knew who went to St. John's University. I had an idea that I wanted to study medicine as a career objective, but there was no way of doing that. I had to earn money. These were very difficult times also financially. Everything sort of shut down. My father didn't have any income. We sort of scraped along, and some days we sold some books of my father's.

During that period, I was 16 years old. And that's amazing really. I was very dominated by my father in Vienna, I got many, many negative messages about my being stupid and my not being capable, and so forth, which many, many fathers do. I was not the type of son that my father wanted. He was a broad-shouldered, stocky sort of person, and to him I was always narrow and sometimes more sensitive perhaps, there was lots of judgmental messages. And so I accepted that I was stupid, I guess, for a while. Fact is, I almost failed my entrance examination to the gymnasium in Vienna, and I was very poor at mathematics, which was sort of dumb! There are many interpretations one can put on those things, but my one interpretation is that, through this breakdown and through this emigration, my father simply lost power. He was no longer a figure of power. So I got out from under that, and I suddenly was very good in school.

My mother was a very nervous and a rather pessimistic sort of person. She was, I think, very frightened and very upset. I felt guilty and I felt responsible and I felt I should do something, but didn't know what to do. How it affected my father is difficult to say. He suffered, I'm sure, but he suffered more quietly. He had an internal stability. But when it came to, say, "Okay, why don't we sell this?" it was something that was put to me to do.

By that time, I was considered an important element, a strong element. And that dynamic continued further, because then in March, I got a job for a few months. That was with a British accounting firm who was doing some job for the rice office, so-called, there was rice rationing. And then that job stopped, because the company was basically closed down. I again didn't work for a while. And then I got a job through my father with this woman, Altura, who was the assistant of Komor, who opened a men's store on Avenue Joffre. I was supposed to be a salesman basically in that store, because I knew some languages. First of all I knew English, of course. By then I knew some French. I'd started studying Chinese.

I worked in this store for about a year altogether, fall of '42 till the fall of '43. But eventually I felt diminished by that. I was very underpaid by those people. I told them that I'd like to get a raise. They kind of dismissed that, and the guy who was the money man, or the boss, said, "Well, you know, better yourself if you can." So okay, that was that.

I spoke Shanghai dialect to get on on the street. But I never got to be good at Shanghai dialect. I concentrated more on Mandarin. My father motivated me to start studying Chinese, to read and write. That was with a teacher who was also a refugee. My father knew this guy, and he organized this, he had great curiosity evidently. He and I and another refugee who lived in the neighborhood, and this guy taught the three of us. He had studied Chinese, and he had a method of teaching characters that was relating it to pictures. As I know now, some of it was completely untrue, [laughs] but it helped, you know. They were sort of memory aids. There were always problems getting him paid, that I remember. But it was his initiative that got me really started. And then I just went on.

There was a man called Kahan, a teacher in the Shanghai Jewish School, a very impressive man, I thought. He was really the guy who held that school together in terms of giving it some stature and some standards. He taught mathematics and physics, a very energetic man. He became the principal, and he carried that school along during the war. I had kept up some loose connection with him.

I went to visit him one day, because I was studying Chinese and he was interested in that. He told me, basically, that I was doing the wrong thing. It's very touching really, because it was so important in my life, it was a complete switch. He said that I was just wasting my time. And of course I knew that. But I told him, financially, that was the problem. He said there was quite a lot of demand for private lessons, because children were switching from public schools to the Jewish school. He said that he could refer to me students I could tutor. I should do that and go to university. That was a very important switch in thought. Well, I did that.

A group of Chinese wanted English lessons, some of them were professionals, some of them were merchants. They wanted somebody to read and conversation and so forth. That was a very important thing for me. I worked with them on Sunday afternoons and one evening. I did that, and then quit the store. At that point they were offering me a lot more money, you see. They were very angry at me for quitting.

I was upset by the fact that my father was not supportive of my doing that, because he was worried about the loss of income. As it turned out, I earned quite a lot, and I overdid it completely, way beyond what was necessary, I'm sure. I just took on this responsibility, basically. So I became the main money earner of the family.

Transportation was very difficult. I walked all over Shanghai basically. Well, I was young. I had an enormous amount of energy obviously. I didn't study much at home. I just had relatively little time, for one. But by then I had started attending St. John's University in February, '44 and at the same time I tutored a great deal.

Fortunately at that time, we were still outside the District. I lived longer than others outside the District, because my father as a physician got extensions to stay outside the District until a certain point, when we had to move after all.[9] Eventually we moved to that District soon after I started university. We moved there something like half a year after the deadline. So I commuted by streetcar, and it was a long ride to school at the other end of town.

Alfred Kohn's life in Shanghai was much more difficult, economically and emotionally. He eventually found his own greatness in sports, especially as a boxer.

When we came to Shanghai, we were picked up at the dock by the Jewish Committee, by the refugees. We were in a camp, in the Kinchow camp. My father's brother went to Cuba, and he sent us some money, and we were able to get ourselves a small apartment on the Seward Road. My father started working in the fur business. Life in Shanghai was very hard even at that time. We had a small kitchen and one room and a little veranda.

I started going to school, my brother was going to school, and then my brother had a very bad experience. He was in a *Sportsfest*, you know, competition in the Jewish school, and he ran the 200 yards and he was very exhausted. He got an injection from the doctor, and either the injection was bad, the needle was bad, they hit a nerve. My brother could never walk again. [emotional voice] The ankle was dead. All during the war, you had to carry him. And he got all the good food, whatever the doctors could do for him, couldn't do anything. They said it's polio, it's a nerve system. He was mostly home reading, studying, could never work.[10]

My father and I and my mother, we worked, but the money was never enough, we had nothing. I remember clothing, I grew very quickly. When I was 15 years old, I was my size now, but skinny. No clothing, you know, it was very hard to buy.

Then I started playing soccer.

Ernest Culman tells of the downward economic pressure on his family, from the early days of opening a business to selling possessions for food and rent. They moved from downtown Shanghai to the outskirts, finally to Hongkou. Culman's father suffered especially from his inability to support his family. Culman's Bar Mitzvah and schooling exemplified the attempts to continue German Jewish culture in Shanghai.

In Shanghai there was a welcoming committee, and they told us that most of the refugees lived in Hongkou. Hongkou had been completely destroyed in the fighting between the Japanese and the Chinese, and many refugees had settled there and started to build it up. But the conditions were horrible. My mother objected. So we first went to a hotel, the Burlington Hotel on Bubbling Well Road.

We stayed there until this group of people found a house that they rented, the equivalent of a townhouse here. A common kitchen, my parents and my brother and I got two rooms, everybody else had one room. This house was in the French Concession on rue Ratard.

Then they started a luncheon business. The lunchroom was interesting, because there were a lot of single men living there who were not used to cooking on their own, and this was like home-style cooking for them. My father acted like the maître d', you know, talked to the people, sat them down on the table. The men used to go out early in the morning to the market, which was on Seymour Road, and pick up whatever they had available, and then the women would cook it. The big meal, European style, was at noontime.

The little lunchroom was not really profitable, because inflation was rampant. Whatever we charged for a meal, it cost us more to buy the food the next day. Basically what we got out of it was free food for ourselves, which was well worth it. And these bachelors loved it. They complained every time they raised the price, but the price had to be raised because of the inflation. Finally everybody got so sick and tired of it, they stopped the lunchroom. Then everybody was complaining that they stopped it.

The other couples moved to Hongkou, but my mother still didn't want to go to Hongkou. So my parents rented an apartment with another family even further away from the city than where we lived up until now. So we moved out to Kinear Road, way out.

Our furniture and all was in storage with a freight company in Hamburg. They were told to hold on to it until we tell them where to send it. We cabled the freight company, go ahead and send our stuff. It got on the ship, got as far as the Dutch East Indies when the war broke out and all German ships were told to enter a neutral port. Well, Holland was still neutral in the beginning, so they entered a port called Sabang, a little island off of Sumatra. And it cost us a lot of money to get it transported from there to Shanghai. It was worth it, though, because we had all our possessions in there, and by selling many possessions we could live on a day-to-day basis.

In Shanghai there were so many diseases, smallpox, cholera, typhoid, typhus. Typhus you get from bites of an insect. Typhoid you get from bad water. Those were the primary things. Through my father, who insisted that we have that done, I was inoculated every six months. When my father was looking for a job, one day he applied and almost got the job at the leprosy colony. My mother put her foot down, that just goes too far.

You had to have boiled water to clean your teeth, you couldn't take any unboiled water and put in your mouth. We couldn't eat any raw vegetables, or anything raw as far as that's concerned. Food had to be boiled or boiling water poured over it before you could eat it. Salads were almost unheard of. One couple decided to put a filter on their water fountain and said, "Then we don't have to boil it." Unfortunately they caught cholera and died. There's another couple, the man caught rabies, God knows from what. As they were taking them to a hospital, he kissed his wife good-bye. He died and a few days later, she had rabies and she died. I didn't know these people, I just know of them. You had to be so careful. You couldn't go barefoot because you would catch what they called Hong Kong foot.

At one time, there was some fish that they were selling. It wasn't herring, but it tasted like herring to most people, and you know, Jewish people generally speaking like herring. My father didn't like herring, and I didn't like herring at that time. We were the only ones who didn't get sick, everybody else got what they called liver worm. Don't ask me what that really is today, but it wasn't critical, I mean, it wasn't a fatal disease, but it was very uncomfortable.

The Chinese themselves, they had absolutely no hygiene. The fields got fertilized with human waste. You could walk through a field and you would see people defecating right on the field. When the babies died, the poor Chinese, they would wrap them up in newspaper or blanket and put the body out on the sidewalk. When I walked to school I often saw those, flies and other insects all around them. I used to go on the other side of the street.

Theft was rampant. A man would ride on the streetcar with a hat on, somebody outside would grab the hat and run away and everybody would just laugh.

In the meantime, I had been signed up to go to the Shanghai Jewish School, which was on Seymour Road, where everything was taught in English. The school was not a free school, we had to pay. Both my brother and I entered that school, where we were put in lower classes than our age, because our English was minimal.

The teacher, of course, was aware of my background. I had that half year of English, I knew enough to make myself understood. The first class, I believe, was a dictation, and she corrected every word I misspelled. I can still see in my mind this piece of paper with the red ink on practically every word. The teachers were very patient, and the other kids were very patient with me. But at nine years of age, you pick it up very quickly. In a year I was almost fluent, they put me in a higher grade, and I did very well in school. Learning came easy to me, but the teachers were good, excellent teachers.

In the Shanghai Jewish School, they served a hot lunch to everybody, but as it were mainly the people from the Middle East that were running that, it was extremely spicy, curry, and I hate spicy food to this day.

Maybe six months, maybe a year later, I joined the Cub Scouts, it was a British scouting organization. I became very much involved in that, took part in some jamborees and things like that. I also remember Baden Powell, the founder of the Scout movement, died while I was in the Scout troops and we had a big memorial service for him. These were not just refugee children, these were children from the Russian Jewish community, which had been in Shanghai since the end of World War I, and Jews from Iraq and the other places in the Mideast, who had settled in Shanghai as early as Shanghai was made an open port, we called them the Arabian Jews. Some of them became very wealthy, many of them were not. But these were the larger group of kids in that school. They were Sephardic, and the synagogue that was there was actually a Sephardic synagogue.

My father could not get a practice started. Through this major in Batavia, he got letters of introduction to two German Jewish doctors who had come to Shanghai in 1933 or '34. They were younger than my father, they had graduated medical school in Germany, but then were not allowed to practice. They were very helpful to him in that they explained a lot of these crazy diseases that we had there, but still the Chinese didn't come to him. The refugees went to the free clinics. And my father was a little bit of an idealist, he didn't believe in socialized medicine and didn't join up with this clinic. So we struggled with what to live off of.

My parents had no real income. My father had a patient here and there. Doctors had it very tough in Shanghai in the Jewish community. Number one, you had the free clinics, number two, there were more doctors per capita than average, so that each guy was cheaper than the next. One guy would charge three dollars for a visit, then the next guy would charge a dollar for a visit, and somebody charged as little as 50 cents for a visit, and it didn't make any sense. My father couldn't make a living and was deeply depressed, especially in that period where we were living on Kinear Road so far away from everybody else.

In Germany, 30 years in the same place, he assisted people in their birth, and they grew up, they continued to go to him, then he helped them with the birth of their children. I remember that he got called out frequently in the middle of the night. One time we got a letter to Shanghai from Germany, "Doctor, you might be gone but not forgotten. The other day I was walking behind two people who were talking about somebody having gotten ill and one said to the other, 'Well, if Dr. Culman were still in town, he would have come over even in the middle of the night.'" Very dedicated to his profession and just couldn't handle it once everything fell apart.

We often were worried that he would commit suicide. My memory of my father in Shanghai is seeing him seated in a chair, mouth half open, sleeping most of the day away. So terribly depressed that he could not support his family. His dream had been to send my brother and I to the finest colleges in Germany. All his dreams just collapsed one right after the other. Other people were able to cope with it, but he couldn't or he didn't, I don't know. It was just horrible, and it really affected us.

They had like a doctor's association, it was just a local thing, basically just for the guys to get together. He went to the medical meetings. Gave him a way to get away from the family for a while and be with other people of his own.

So to get some money in, my brother went to work at the age of 14. One of the doctors that my father had been introduced to knew a Swiss man who had a machine shop, but it was at the other end of Hongkou, and we were on the other side of the French Concession. Tremendous trip. He had a bike ride of over 45 minutes each morning and night, going through the whole city of Shanghai. He was like an apprentice, and they were horrible. I mean, how my father could send a 14-year-old boy into such a work situation, I don't understand and my brother doesn't understand. Some very hard feelings especially on his part that he was put through this.

My mother tried to cook German-style as much as possible with the available things there. Rice was the thing we had most of and cereal. Because there were a lot of Russian people there, a lot of Russian food got introduced into the Shanghai market. There was a cereal called *kasha*, which tasted horrible, and it's still available in grocery stores here. I wouldn't touch it with a ten foot pole. I was a very bad eater as a child, my parents must have had a horrible time with me. One thing I remember, they bought rye bread, it was the only thing available there as bread, and I had my mother take out every kernel of rye before I could eat it.

My mother baked cakes that she would sell to people. Butter was very expensive, so all we ate was margarine. All the cakes were usually done with margarine. There was one person who ordered a cake done with butter one day, they had the money and they wanted it with butter. My mother baked it with butter, it was a sheet cake, so she cut it apart to make the delivery, cut a small slice for all of us to taste what the difference would be between a cake made with butter over a cake with margarine. Of course what we also enjoyed is when a cake didn't rise fully or didn't come out right, because then she couldn't deliver it, and we had it.

On December 8th I went to school, I hadn't heard anything during the night, and I get to school and all the kids are all excited. "Didn't you hear the shooting?" What had happened was the British and American gunboats were being shot at by the Japanese. It was December 7th in the United States, and the Japanese were beginning to occupy the city. The whole school got called into the auditorium, and the principal got up and told us all that. When the lecture was over, we went back to our class for a little while before we started to go home. The Japanese were marching past the school, occupying the American Marine barracks across the street, and I personally saw the American flag being lowered and the Japanese flag being raised in its place.

I get home, and my parents had absolutely no idea what was going on. We had no radio. My parents heard from me about Pearl Harbor and the Japanese taking over the city. In the meantime, my brother had gone to work that morning, all the way to this Swiss machine shop. He came home in the midst of the occupation. He was driving back by bike through this mob of people. Eventually through other friends he found a job in a different machine factory, where he was treated more humanely.

When we moved from the French Concession out to almost the suburbs, it was still in the city limits, but very far removed from everything. They felt very isolated there. After the Japanese occupation, they finally decided that they need to live within the Jewish community and decided to find an apartment in Hongkou. In Hongkou, you had the whole Jewish community, your neighbors were refugees like yourself, and I think that was what they felt, that they should live within the Jewish community, so not to be so isolated.

We moved to Hongkou sometime in 1942 on East Seward Road. Again we shared this place with another family. The move was weird, because it wasn't trucks. We moved through town with these handcarts. Chinese were pushing the carts, we were walking along them to make sure they don't steal anything. It was a long walk with these pushcarts all through the city.

I transferred from the Shanghai Jewish School to the SJYA, normally referred to as the Kadoorie School. There all the children were refugee children, and it didn't take me long to get acclimated to those kids. It was not a far walk there, and I did very well in school.

In the Kadoorie School, things were more relaxed. Especially the last year that I was there, as kids had dropped out of school, this highest grade, whatever it was, we had 12 students in the class, six boys and six girls. And instead of a regular classroom, we sat at a long table, like a long dining room table, the boys one side, the girls on the other, the teacher at the head. And a lot of kidding and playing around went on in there with some of the teachers. We went of course through the Jewish Bible stories and then continued into Jewish history, and Jewish history in a way is like world history. So I had tremendous background of that and to this day I'm fascinated by history, love history. I was one of the best students in the school.

I remember quite a few teachers. Our homeroom teacher was Günter Gassenheimer, taught math and physics and chemistry and everything else under the sun it seems, an excellent teacher. What I learned through him without text books, at the age of 13 or 14, is what people here learn in high school or the early years of college. Algebra, trigonometry, math is what I really loved. One teacher claimed that I was the best math student, regardless of grade.

We had one teacher who was teaching us Chinese, he was a Chinese, who again was obviously not a teacher. The exams consisted that he would say a sentence in Chinese and we had to write it down in English. There was always one person in the class who knew the answer and he would yell it out in German. [laughs] Of course all of us spoke perfect German, so we all had the same answers, and this one exam, we all got 90. One person gave us a wrong answer.

We also had a refugee teacher teaching us Japanese. And one day he decided that we don't have any cultural knowledge of Germany, German culture, and he decided, instead of going into Japanese, to read us German poetry, Schiller and Goethe, and that was fascinating to me. We learned English history, English literature, Shakespeare. We put on Shakespeare plays in school, or parts of it. I got the part of Puck in *Midsummer Night's Dream*.

Epstein was our music teacher, and when I got to the Kadoorie School, the kids all told me in music classes, singing classes it was called, they said, "Those of us who can't sing, he lets go outside and we can play soccer or anything." I don't have a good voice to begin with, but when he tested me, I purposely sang bad, so out we went to play. Eventually some of the other teachers complained, we were making too much noise, so we had to stay in class. We didn't like that at all, so before the singing class we collected wastepaper baskets from several classes and stuffed the piano with it. He comes in there, we're standing quietly in the back, those of us who can't sing, and he starts hitting the keys, nothing came out, he opens up the piano, realizes what went on, gets furious and kicks us all out of the room, which is exactly what we wanted.

So discipline left a little bit to be desired with many of these teachers. The ones that were strict was the principal, Mrs. Hartwich, who also taught French, Gassenheimer, who wouldn't stand for any joking around unless he went along with it, which he often did. Gassenheimer, you couldn't get anything past him. He just kept the class interesting enough so he didn't have any discipline problems. Leo Meyer was the gym teacher. We had a lot of fun in school, under all those conditions, a lot of camaraderie, the teachers and students both.

I remember in 1942, I was Bar Mitzvahed. Everybody went to this Hebrew teacher to take their Bar Mitzvah lessons, Wesel, and he went into too much detail in all these things. He was from Breslau, and my cousin had taken classes from him in Breslau when he was still in Germany. So I talked to my teacher Gassenheimer whether he would give me my Bar Mitzvah lessons, and he said "Certainly." He had aspirations to become a rabbi anyhow. So I took Bar Mitzvah lessons from him in two months, I think, just enough to get me by. We then had to go to the rabbi for like a little exam, whether I have learned everything. Even though Gassenheimer showed me how to lay the *tefillin*, somehow or other I didn't get it right.[11] The rabbi was a little upset about that. But I was Bar Mitzvahed. It was very, very interesting.

The cantor was an opera singer. He looked something like Pavarotti, big and all, and I still remember him, little 13-year-old kid looking up at that man singing at full voice to me. The Bar Mitzvah was held in the school, and it was very festive, even though we were at the poorest point that we could be.

Didn't get many major gifts. The people who lived next door to us, they had a clothing store, and he had asked my mother some weeks earlier to loan him one of my shirts, because he's going to have a shirt made for his son or whatever. She just pulled out a shirt, gave it to him. Well, they made a very nice shirt, custom made for me. The only trouble was, my mother, when she gave him a shirt, gave him one that I had already outgrown. The sleeves came up to here when I got it, he took it back and put an extra patch in there. That was probably my biggest gift. I had coffee and cake and about a dozen or so people came over for that. But the Bar Mitzvah was nice. I don't remember a word the rabbi said, but I do remember the cantor singing.

The principal, Mrs. Hartwich, came up to my parents afterwards. She said, "We usually don't make this a habit, but we like Ernie, he's a good student, and as a Bar Mitzvah present he has free schooling from now on." I stayed in school another year. More and more of the children left school when they became 13, 14 years old to go to work, because the parents did not make enough money.

Herbert and Ilse Greening moved from initial luxury in the French Concession to Hongkou. As both Greenings tell it, the women of the family took over the practical task of ensuring that they had sufficient income. Herbert's medical practice brought them close to Chinese doctors who also spoke German, giving the Greenings unusual opportunities to observe Chinese culture.

Ilse Greening: When we arrived in Shanghai in April 1939, the first thing my uncle said, "We are all on our way to becoming millionaires." That's how good business was. His business at that time was British piece goods he imported for woolen suits and coats, and his customers were Chinese on Yates Road, where all the tailors were. A lot of very rich Chinese bought the piece goods, I know, because for a while I worked in my uncle's office. Some of these wool merchants lived in our building. Also a lot of the Russian furriers bought piece goods from them, but also tailors, very big companies.

My uncle supported us in the beginning, and we had a very luxurious home in the French Concession, which they sublet for us for the summer of 1939. It was on the twelfth floor, and they had refrigerators, and they had lots of servants. So we really knew very little about refugee life, except we had no money, because we only had four American dollars.

Herbert Greening: In Shanghai, I couldn't make a living. I opened a practice, nobody came. I didn't know anybody. I was 26 years old. Uncle's partner said to me, "There's one big trouble with you, and it will get better with every day. You'll get older." I mean, I had only hospital experience. German medical education is very different from the one in America. I didn't know a damn thing. I knew theoretical stuff, but I didn't know how to treat a cold. I got myself a handbook of tropical diseases and started to study. Medicine I learned in China, no question about it, by reading.

After six months in Frenchtown, I said, "We have to get away from here. Here I can't make a living. The Jews are in Hongkou." So we moved there, and there I had a very good practice, I must say, and collected a lot of experience.

Ilse Greening: In the fall, we decided to move to Hongkou, and we lived at the corner of Chusan Road and Ward Road. We had two rooms. Downstairs it was Herbert and I, who were newlywed. Our room was also the medical office, and we had a little electric stove to cook. My mother and my sister upstairs.

We lived very primitively. My mother was used to better things. We were young and for us it was an adventure. It did not bother us that we didn't have running hot water and no heat, and not too much to eat. We take for granted here showers and baths and those things. None of these things we had in Hongkou. That is something most people do not understand. My mother never complained, never, but for her it must have been very difficult.

People used to line up for tea in the morning with their teapot and just bought hot water, one ladle of hot water. Not only Chinese, refugees too, because they had no electric or gas stove, so it was too much trouble to start the coal fire just for tea.

Bedbugs we had too. My sister said, "I can't sleep at night, because I itch all over." One morning she couldn't sleep, and she was reading in bed, and a little buggy was running across the book. That's when we found out that it wasn't a rash, but we had bedbugs. That was a shock for my mother, [laughs] that we had bedbugs. Yeah, that was worse than most things for my mother. But I assured her that we were not the only ones, other people had bedbugs also. Whom did you call? Herbert Moss. His father had already been an exterminator, he was the second generation from Berlin. Oh, yes, we needed him more than a doctor. He was very important. I don't know whether he had any competition, but we only knew him.[12]

Herbert Greening: He was a patient.

Ilse Greening: And then, when the Americans came, I think he said he went on ships and he did a lot of work for the Americans with being an exterminator. And when he came to Indianapolis, he was very successful, so you don't have to be a college professor or a doctor to have an important job.

I got a job with the Chartered Bank of India and China, it is now called Standard Bank in England. This was a large English import-export bank on the Bund with all the other banks. My main job was to help the refugees who came to the bank, because relatives sent money for their support from all over the world. I had told them that I know English and French, but my French was not very good. Once in a while, they received French letters from other banks and I translated, I managed, but I wasn't that good. But English I knew. I was happy there.

They let me open all the mail. Many of the letters were marked "Private and Confidential." Then I had to decide which department they were going to, which was easy.

When the European war started, my boss, the Englishman, called me and he said, "You open all the mail. I would advise you to be careful with whom you associate, because it's quite possible that people are after the kind of information you get in those letters."

Herbert had quite a number of patients. Herbert comes from Upper Silesia, and the people from there sort of had a little club, or they met for coffee. He used to go there to make contacts, and he also had friends who sent him patients.

We needed a house and an office, so we moved to more luxurious quarters on Kungping Road. Downstairs, a Viennese had a jewelry shop, and we had the rest of the house, which was really fantastic. We were really lucky people. We had two rooms and a kitchen on the second floor, and then on the top floor Herbert had a small office in an attic, and a waiting room. And next to that, another couple rented a room from us.

Many times, there was not enough seating, and they were standing down the stairs, but yet the fees were very small. He also was reluctant to ask, so even though the people were waiting, we were not in very good financial position. The worst part was, since Herbert never asked for money, even when the patient offered, they eventually got a bill, but they still didn't pay it. We needed money badly to eat, so my mother had no choice. She used to collect, which must have been hell for her. She went to the patient and asked for money to pay their bill.

My mother amazes me. Absolutely amazing. Suddenly we had to do all this ourselves. But never once did I hear her complain about things. She was fantastic.

My sister worked and I worked, and we managed, just managed. We all had one bathroom, but fortunately it was modern. We had a WC, a real toilet, not like many, many people who didn't have that. We had a small electric stove, I think it had two burners and a small oven. We had a tub. Sometimes as a treat Herbert ordered a few buckets of hot water for me to have a bath.

One important branch of this Komor Committee was the kindergarten near our house on Kungping Road.

Herbert Greening: I went there every morning. There must have been 30, 40 kids. Every morning I had to look at the kids. They passed by, I look in their throat, touched them to see whether they have a temperature. I became known as a pediatrician, which I never was. They got food there. And I enjoyed it.

We kept this practice in Shanghai in the attic, and I was very, very busy. I enjoyed it. The fee was very low, it was about one-tenth of what doctors got in Shanghai, compared to Hongkou. I was a very bad money-maker. I don't understand anything about money. I enjoyed medicine, I enjoyed the challenge of medicine through all my life. Ilse was the money collector.

The majority of my patients were refugees. But I had some Chinese patients, and I had some Japanese patients. Of course, I saw a lot of stuff that I've never seen before or after. Like malaria, typhus, cholera, typhoid. Smallpox. Gastrointestinal diseases. Dysenteries. I loved it.

Twice a week I went to a leprosy clinic. In China, lepers are not isolated, they live with their families. We didn't have much medicine either at that time, actually no medicine, only the old-fashioned chaulmoogra oil. It's an injection that was used, without any effect, I'm sure. A Dutch physician was in charge of the leprosy clinic. I learned. It was a great experience.

In the leprosy clinic we did skin biopsies. Since the skin is insensitive, anesthetic, you can just pick up the skin, cut it off with the scissors and then sort of shred it and dye it and put it on the microscope and diagnose the leprosy. That was good.

When I came home from the clinic, first they said, "You can't eat at the same table we eat."

Ilse Greening: We were ignorant. We didn't know. I wasn't going to sleep in bed with him, you know, until he explained to us that it wasn't…

Herbert Greening: You have to sleep with a leper to get it. It's not very contagious. Once I showed to Ilse a leper in the streetcar.

Ilse Greening: He says, "Two persons away from you a leper is sitting." I was not too enthused [laughs] about that.

Before the Japanese occupation, we also went into the Chinese quarters. We mixed with the Chinese, we were interested in their life, we had Chinese friends. Once a Chinese friend took us into a Chinese temple, where we had vegetarian dinner.

When we first came, the Chinese invited us, and always big dinners.

Herbert Greening: And they licked the chopsticks up and gave it to you.

Ilse Greening: That was a special honor. I wasn't too keen on that, but you had be polite. Also we were friendly with a Chinese doctor who had studied in Vienna and spoke German fluently. He brought another friend of his, and they spoke very good German. Sometimes I was embarrassed, because they had very good vocabulary and willing to study hard, very. Chinese are like Jews in many respects, family lines and education and all that. We felt quite close to them.

Herbert Greening: Once you are their friend, you're their friend for life. It's quite difficult to get close to them, but once you have them, they are good, very trustworthy.

Ilse Greening: I have to say the Chinese are gamblers at heart. They gamble for everything, whatever. These gambling casinos, I don't know by whom they were run. If you called up, they would send a taxi for you. These things, of course, were out of the question, because we had no money, but we knew lots of people went. And you were wined and dined, and the casinos were housed in very fancy houses. We had a friend, she woke up one morning, her whole lane had a new owner. Her owner had gambled away the whole lane, those were Russians, though. At night when you walked through the streets anywhere in China, you could hear the people playing mah-jongg. You could hear the noise. They loved to gamble. My uncle also was a gambler. He liked to go to dog races.

We once went to an opium den. I don't think that you can find many refugees who went. It was devastating experience. It was a small room with bunkbeds, very primitive, just wooden slats, one on top of the other. And there they were, terrible-looking people, emaciated. They looked half dead and the smell permeated the room. They looked like the poorest of the poor. In this opium den, it was coolies, low-class people, because the rich smoked at home. We had a neighbor right across the street from us.

You could tell in the street who was an addict. You walked at night through the street, when you passed a house where they were smoking opium, you could smell it.

We also went to Das Kah, a big theater, very big. And we went for a performance there. Chinese theater, the people eat and the people drink and they talk and they take part in whatever, that's called Das Kah, means "Big World." I don't know, we went to lots of places, I had forgotten.

Herbert Greening: We had a good time. Sometimes an empty stomach.

We had a number of fraternity brothers in Shanghai. We met on Sunday mornings *Im Weissen Rössl*, and had a glass of beer or something to eat or something to drink. All men, not women. We met as a group in Shanghai, we met as a group in New York, you always be meeting.

Oh, one story I have to tell you. We were walking on the Bund and I said to Ilse, "This guy there is a classmate." Crazy. So I called him, yes, he was. "What are you doing here?" "Oh, I'm working with the German Consulate. I'm a photographer." And then we invited him once.

Ilse Greening: He said his job is photography, and he goes to outside of Shanghai and to the country, to the border, and he takes photos. And he was very eager to meet with us. I don't know whether this was accidental, we'll never know, but that was at the time during the European war.

So when we met this German guy, he was very eager to associate with us. Very. So I said to Herbert, "We have to try to get rid of him, because under no circumstances can I associate with him." So finally, he insists, he did come to the house once, and once Herbert went to his house. He lived very luxuriously in the French Concession with a Chinese. But finally we got it through to him that we did not want to associate with him. We couldn't. To this day I don't know whether he was just happy to meet a friend or whether this all was intentional. But later on, after the end of the war, we found out...

Herbert Greening: We read in the papers that he was a chief of the Gestapo in Shanghai, Kahner.[13]

Ilse Greening: Although the European war was already in progress, there was never any division between the nations. Social life between the English and the Americans and the Germans was still the same, as if nothing had ever happened. Apart from some of the shipping that did not come in because of the war, it was life as usual, which was remarkable. We both had bicycles, we were very well-to-do. Herbert made his house calls on the bike, and I went to work.

Until Pearl Harbor. On the day after the bombing, I went to the bank and the bank was manned by Japanese. It was quite a big bank, all the departments had Japanese officers, but the English people were still working there, and it was kind of peaceful. We were free to go and the English were free to go, we were all free to go.

After Chartered Bank it was Mitsubishi Gingko Bank. I had to learn Japanese, because we were 25 girls in that Japanese bank. The manager spoke German quite well, and some of the officers spoke English, not too well, but none of the girls spoke any foreign language. So one of the Englishmen, before he went into camp, and I went to a Japanese class. This teacher was using a fantastic modern method, and we learned very fast.

Food was scarce, and in the bank they offered a so-called lunch. I ate there out of desperation, it was terrible. But I sat with the girls, and I had to speak Japanese, there was no other way, but I must say I learned very fast. This teacher was unbelievable.

But life after the Japanese was not as usual. When the Allied got their orders to go to camp, my boss, the Englishman, insisted that I stay with the Japanese, although I didn't want to. He was very serious and he said, "There are going to be very hard times ahead in wartime. You people have no government to support you." We were stateless, and he insists that I keep the job in the bank, because I would be able to go into town. He said that the food was going to be scarce, and maybe in town I would be able to buy things that I couldn't buy in Hongkou. He was adamant that I should keep the job, which I hated to keep, but I finally gave in.

They told us that in those internment camps for the Allies, Chinese used to throw packages over the wall for them.

Herbert Greening: We sent my parents a landing permit for Shanghai.

Ilse Greening: The days of going just like that, when we went there, they were over. You needed a landing permit. Many people bought landing permit, I don't know from whom, from other refugees, I guess, but we went...

Herbert Greening: The kosher way.

Ilse Greening: ...the regular way. I took time off from my job at the bank, and I went to the government. I had to stand in line and fill out things, it took quite a long time, the legal way. But we sent them. I don't think my father-in-law would have considered, even if they got it.

Herbert Greening: We got letters from them, and afterwards we found out that in the autumn of '42 they were taken to the *KZ* [concentration camp]. And Mother let us know between the lines what was happening. I have a sister, she was a real RN at that time, and she went to a hospital on Isle of Wight. She lives now in Atlanta.

My mother's family was a very large one, my grandmother had 16 children, 11 of them lived to grow up. Left over are just a couple of cousins, two or three.

Because **Ralph Hirsch** *and his family arrived in Shanghai so late in 1940, their connection to their family doctor from Berlin was crucial in finding an apartment. Although nothing was normal in refugee life, even students like Hirsch, who had been to school in Europe, felt at home in the Kadoorie School, which had been created just for refugee children. He explains why.*

We arrived in Shanghai at a wharf that was not far from the Garden Bridge, during the daylight. There were a lot of people there to greet the ship surprisingly, including some refugees, and one of them was our friend and family doctor from Berlin. Good old Uncle Harry, as he was Harry Salomon and he had two daughters. One was about a year older, and one was maybe two or three years older than I, and I had known them in Berlin. He had arranged for a room for us at the New Asia Hotel, which is a Japanese-run hotel near the Garden Bridge.

He gave both my brother and me a quick physical to see how we were. Possibly he examined my parents, too, I don't remember that. But I remember that he examined me, because he always finished the examination the same way, by pinching my cheek very hard. I hated that!

I think it may have been through Harry Salomon that we found about two days later, perhaps he had arranged it in advance, I don't know, a small apartment, which I think was probably intended as a makeshift place to stay, on Kungping Road in Lane 305. The first apartment was spartan. It was an old building, very small. The structure itself was pretty rickety. If I remember right, the water supply was outside rather than inside. And some months later, we moved to the place around the corner, where we stayed the rest of the time in Shanghai, so about six years. That was in a recently built structure in Lane 909, East Seward Road. That was nominally an apartment, but in fact it was just one medium-sized room in which everything went on. We cooked, we slept, we studied. My mother cooked, and, you know, we sometimes helped a little, the kids.

Everybody came before we did. We were the last that we knew to arrive in Shanghai. I mean, there were a number of people on the same train with us, and there were other Jews who came to Shanghai after we did, but they didn't come from Berlin, or at least none that we knew, there may have been one or two.

There was a substantial contingent that came over Kobe, and they came sometime in 1941. They were not from Germany, I think they were Poles or Lithuanians. And altogether there was little contact with those who spoke Yiddish. Language was a big definer of the community. The first time I heard Yiddish spoken was when I came to Shanghai, because I'd never heard it spoken in Berlin. There was a yeshiva not far from us, and we'd see the yeshiva kids when we were on the way to school. Sometimes we'd say hello to them, but that was the extent of it. There was no real interchange.[14]

There certainly was contact of various kinds with some of the other groups that were longer established in Shanghai, some of the Sephardi and Ashkenazi who had been there for a longer time. We kids would meet some of them in social activities or play against them on teams and so on. After the war had ended, when we took the Cambridge School Certificate Exam in 1946, we met quite a lot of those kids, because they were also in the same schedule of preparations, and so we had contact with them, and to some extent that was then continued.

I started out in the first year playing a lot with the Chinese kids on the street, and I think as we got older, the play tended to be more among ourselves. It became more structured, you know, we got onto sports teams and so on. There was less contact, rather than more, with the Chinese.

We were members of the 13th Shanghai Scouts, the British Boy Scouts. In our 13th troop there were only Jewish kids, almost all from Germany and Austria.

Our school was the Kadoorie School on Kinchow Road. The school had been set up by a teacher named Lucie Hartwich, whom my parents, as it happens, knew in Berlin and who had been the headmistress of a school. A lot of the activity that my brother and I had, and to some extent they were different, because we were somewhat more than three years apart in age, revolved around activities that were tied to the school in some way, the astronomy club, various sports teams. The big sport was really soccer, *Fußball.* We also played table tennis and we played tennis, and although the school itself didn't have any facilities for swimming, we managed to do that through the Scouts, and that I think was the other major activity center.

After a little over a year in Shanghai, we heard the shore batteries firing at and sinking the Yangtze patrol, like thunder. That distant sound of cannonading was our notice that the war in the Pacific had broken out. We found out about Pearl Harbor, only, I think, a couple of days later. And then the Japanese marched their troops into Shanghai and started interning the Allied citizens. We had several British and American teachers in our school, who were all women, and those one morning just didn't show up. I think it may have been late December or maybe January.

The big change came in January and February of 1942, when a whole batch of teachers was recruited to replace those who had been interned, and these were Germans and Austrians and Czechs and Hungarians, all central Europeans. What I think was pretty remarkable was that, by and large, they were more qualified, had more training and so on, and in some cases were university lecturers. But they were not subject to being interned as enemy aliens by the Japanese.

And some time later that year, it may have been in the summer, the whole school moved to a new building, which was a large, U-shaped, airy structure, very open, very inviting structure. Very different from the old school, which was kind of rundown.

The school was in many ways a model of what a school could be in those days. Certainly it was better than any school that I had seen in Germany. The facilities were ample for the size of the student body, which was probably around 600. What was lacking was equipment for doing

Photo 5   Leo Meyer leading exercises at Kadoorie School

science. The musical part of the education came too short, I think. There was an old piano. It was very hard to get musical instruments to teach the children to play, so that was rather neglected, although a number of the children got that privately. But in terms of the humanities and so on, the school was very well equipped and certainly the instruction was extremely competent in almost all fields.

One of the very nice things about the physical arrangements was that we had a running track and a playing field right in the middle of that U-shaped space. So we could run out and play out in the open during breaks. The two long legs of the U had the classrooms in them and some other supporting facilities, the sick room, there was a doctor in the school full-time. The principal's office was on one end, and the assembly hall and the library and so on were on the cross section of the U. It was the school that I attended then for the next four years, and I think got a remarkably good education, quite aside from the circumstances in which that education was administered.

The Hongkou community had two German-language newspapers and an English-language paper and some others that we didn't read, but were aware that they were there. There was a Yiddish-language one, there was a Polish-language one. Every now and then, somebody managed to get a paper from Germany, or from America, from Britain, but those were always very old, so it was no longer news, it was just interesting to read.

The *Shanghai Jewish Chronicle* was actually a pretty remarkable paper. I think it came out every day. I remember it being hawked in our street. There was a news vendor with a particular chant, which always amused me, because he would chant, "Ay Croollee Gay," like that, "Ay Croollee Gay." That was supposed to mean *Jewish Chronicle,* but if you didn't know it, you would not have known it. [laughs] The paper was sort of a crusading journal. Its editor was a man named Ossi Lewin, who again and again challenged the Japanese censorship. Sort of a controversial figure in the community. He was my parents' generation. He obviously was very dedicated to the principle of a free press, and he was willing to go to jail for it, which he did a number of times. I think a lot of people, including my parents, thought he might have been better advised to be more circumspect in his challenges to the Japanese. But he kept doing it, and every so often the paper would be suspended for a day or a week, but it always came back.

You know, listening to the radio, or trying to receive a shortwave broadcast, was a pretty thrilling occupation. Nowadays, it's hard to think back on the quality of the radio in those days, particularly if you think about the inability to replace components. Trying to buy a radio tube, of course, all of those radios operated with tubes, was a major enterprise during the war. So radio was a technically very different kind of thing, but a lot of people spent much time listening to the radio. I think we were more inclined to read.

My parents had a number of friends, quite a few were people whom they had known in Berlin. Almost all of them lived in Hongkou and would visit back and forth and occasionally go out to a café and spin out a cup of coffee for a very long time. There were great many cafés, and particularly the Viennese brought with them the institution of the *Kaffeehaus*. I learned to appreciate various types of *Torte*. Some of them managed remarkably well to get ingredients to bake *Linzertorte* and *Sachertorte* and all those other good things that the Viennese have contributed to civilization. I remember that sometimes my parents went to join their friends and shared a piece of *Torte,* or something like that. Particularly as the war went on, it became harder and harder to afford those things.

But quite often, my mother would bake a cake and we'd have friends over. The men usually played *Skat* and talked about politics, and the women talked about family things. The talk about politics was usually very, very immediate, about the policies of the Japanese and what the chances are that the Americans would take new initiatives and so on. There was not much abstract discussion that I can remember. When I got older, of course, we older kids talked about such things among ourselves, but that was quite separate from what the adults talked about.

Melitta Colland was a very enterprising 22-year-old. After a difficult beginning with bedbugs and cockroaches, she was able to start a clothes-making business in the French Concession with small loans from doctor friends of the family. But it was not possible to bring her father out of Germany.

Paul, the oldest brother, arrived in Shanghai. And now comes my story about doctors. The group of nine doctors were invited, I don't remember the name of the doctor, but he was very well-to-do, he has been there for about 20 years, had a fabulous home and a lot of servants, which were very cheap in those days in China. And he invited these young, so-called "colleagues" to his house for a banquet dinner. They were served by Chinese boys with white gloves. Behind every chair was one waiter. There was a long table, the food was absolutely fabulous. At the end of the dinner, the doctor got up, and made a speech to these young doctors, and said, "My dear colleagues, it's nice to welcome you all here, but I'm sorry to tell you that there isn't really very much future in you being here. You might just as well go right into the Yangtze River, because to make a living here as a doctor is a very tough thing." That was his warm greeting to these young doctors. And all nine of them got up and said, "Thank you very much for your hospitality, but since we have come that far, we don't choose the river right away. We are going to try our best." Each one of them was able to get a job somewhere, not within Shanghai, most of them. They all went out. The psychiatrist went to Nanking. My brother went to the interior of China. I don't know what the others did.

Paul married a Viennese doctor, Stella, he'd studied medicine with her in Vienna. She was related to the Orbachs, of the department store Orbachs. And they had sent her an affidavit to come to New York. But she was in love with my brother. When my brother wrote to her that, "If you want to come to China, we will get married," she, of course, chose China.

Her parents also went to China, they were in Shanghai. The mother was always someone who would rather save a penny than spend it, you know. My brother Henry in Panama had sent a little money to her, he couldn't afford much in those days, to prepare housing for my mother and me when we arrived beginning of July of '39. And she prepared according to what she thought we refugees are entitled to. That was a room that was as wide as this, from the wall to here, and as long as that, with a little window, on the upstairs floor of one of the White Russian women who had bought several houses like this and made a lot of money by renting out these rooms. Of course, one bathroom was for the whole building. I don't know how many rooms she had in that building. And we arrived and went into that room.

My mother had a little couch to sleep on. The rest of the width was wide enough for one of these little army cots that were folding up, when the one chair that was there would be put on top of the table. I was supposed to sleep on that. And as I opened it up, it was full of bedbugs. These big flying roaches came running in and out of the window. We just sat up all night crying, because it was hot, hot. "How can we live here?" We didn't have any more money for rent, and in spite of that, next morning we asked the lady, would she give us some of the money back? She said, "No, no, absolutely not." But someone was nice enough to rent us a slightly larger room, which was clean at least. And that's how we started.

Paul was not allowed to travel from the interior. He couldn't even come to Shanghai to greet us when we arrived. So my brother had sent a man he'd befriended, an American doctor, Dr. Brooks O'Neil, I'll never forget the name, he sent this man a few days later to say hello to his mother and sister. This Dr. O'Neil was a medical doctor on the ship "Luzon." He came and said, "Now how do you plan to earn your living?" I said, "Well, so far I tried to make some artificial flowers," which I had learned in Vienna how to do, and luckily I had a little bit of the material you needed for it in my personal luggage. I started making those and carried it from store to store. I tried to sell them some of these artificial flowers for evening gowns. He said, "Yeah, but this isn't going to feed you and your mother forever." I said, "No, it surely won't." He said, "Well, what else can you do?" I said, "I finished fashion academy in Vienna, I know how to sew, I know how to fit garments, I know how to cut them. But the Chinese tailors do much better and cheaper than I can do." He said, "Well, the only way you can earn a living that way is to own your own business, and employ Chinese tailors." I said, "Yeah, but that takes money." He said, "Well, you go and inquire, how much money does it need to go into business."

I went to a renting agent. I inquired about a very nice store in the French quarter, what the rent would be. I inquired what it would cost me to put a few pieces of furniture in and one sewing machine. Didn't even think to buy fabrics ahead of time or anything like that. So I said, "Yeah, I think with about 700 dollars I could start in business." Dr. O'Neil said, "I give you 350, if you can find one more person that is willing to lend you 350 dollars." And I knew one other doctor, who was a gynecologist, his name was Lustig, Dr. Lustig. He had also known my brother already, when he was in Shanghai for a short time. I went to him, and told him the story. And he said, "Yes, I have helped a few refugees. After all, I was lucky enough to come here 20 years ago and make a lot of money. I'm willing to give you 350 dollars." That's how I started in business. I was 20, just about.

That was just maybe four weeks, five weeks after I arrived. So I rented that store. Didn't know anybody or anything. One Chinese came in and said, "Me tailor, number one tailor." I said, "Fine, you're hired." [laughs] He brought the others that I needed, as business increased. And he stayed my number one tailor for the duration.

Then a lady, highly pregnant, walked in, and said, "I am supposed to attend the festive evening at the French Club, and I am, as you can see, very far gone in my pregnancy, and I need something that I will look halfway decent in." She was the wife of the Danish Consul. I didn't have the money to go and buy the fabric, and I was ashamed to ask her for a deposit. My mother had a winter coat in her luggage with a little chinchilla collar. There was a furrier on the corner of this building where we had the store. She took the chinchilla collar off, went to the furrier, and sold him the chinchilla collar. And with that money, I bought the first piece of fabric to fill my first order. I made her a lovely gown.

Through her, I practically had all the different consulary wives, because she really helped me a great deal. Among them suddenly came in the wife of the biggest Nazi in Shanghai, Herr Glimpf.[15] His wife, who never had any children, I don't know whether it was her guilty conscience or what, but she loved me as if I had been a daughter of hers. She brought on the customers, not only from Shanghai, but she told them in Tokyo at the German Consulate about me. And I had to make garments that were taken to Tokyo by the German couriers. How I came to that, I never know. But I went in and out in her house, as I say, like a daughter, came to fittings to her house. They knew I was a refugee. He was as jovial and nice when I came to the house as anybody could be.

In six months, I was able to return the money to Dr. Lustig, who nearly fainted when I came back with a check. He said, "I have given money to a lot of grown men. I have yet to see one dollar back. And this young girl comes back with the money." To this day, it bothers me that I was never able to give it back to Dr. O'Neil, because he was on high sea, in Manila and everywhere. We never heard from him again.

In the beginning, we couldn't afford any household help. So Mother cleaned and cooked and did everything for me. Trying to help me make ends meet. She had to watch the workroom. Trying to hold things together when I was in the front of the store, waiting on clients or fitting them. The few linen sheets that she'd packed in her own luggage, she sold to buy the next meal. She was too proud to go to any Hilfsfund.[16]

My brother in Panama was really the one who kept us from having to go for soup kitchens. Thanks to Henry, who sent us a little money, we never had to do that. If you exchanged one American dollar into Chinese money, we could eat a whole week from it. And that's what we did. To give you a sense of what money meant, when I lived in the French quarter, I befriended a man who worked for Shell Oil in Shanghai. His salary was 100 American dollars a month. And he could live like a king on that. He lived in all luxury you could possibly want.

The worst part for my brother in Panama was that when the war broke out, they interned all the Germans, the refugees with the Nazis together. Until they could sort out who was an escapee.

Very shortly before Pearl Harbor, my father wrote and said, "Now is the time to get me out of here. Please try your best." And then Pearl Harbor came, I couldn't do anything.

Doris Grey's nursing skills were her and her husband's most important asset in Shanghai, more valuable than the Käthe Kollwitz drawings he was able to bring to China.

My cousin picked us up from the boat, he had a butcher store. We had somebody there, which made a lot of difference. He rented a room for us from a Russian lady, Jewish people. The first night, my cousin gave us a mosquito coil. You burn it, and the mosquitoes don't like it and they leave you alone. We put the mosquito coil on, and my husband was awake and he said, "I can't sleep." I said, "I don't feel any mosquitoes." He said, "I don't see any mosquitoes either, but there's something." And sure enough we put the light on and the bedbugs, full of them. So we told our landlady. She said, "Oh, that's Shanghai, that's nothing." We didn't have any money then to do anything about it.

Italy entered the war, and we were running after our money for a week or longer. We finally got the $400 in the smallest notes you can imagine. And we never touched it. That was our reserves.

What was very bad when we first came, all the beggars in the streets. The women had the children tied like a dog with a leash, you know. And they hit them and molested them, until they cried and begged, and then they came, you should see, *"Gnakoning, gnakoning! Mibau, mibau!"* You know, bread, bread. That was terrible. And it was so dirty in Shanghai.

We lived in the French Concession on Avenue Haig. We had one room to ourselves. The room was nice, and we were glad to be without any strange people. My cousins took us around first, you know, show us the city. We were fascinated, of course, went to the China Sea. And then very soon we made contact both of us professionally.

A few days later, the phone rang, the Jewish community, they were very rich and well-known, Jews from Baghdad, from Russia, all over, and in charge of the committee was the certain Mr. Ellis Hayim, he was very well-known, and he did a lot for the emigrants. I was asked whether I know English or not. So I said, "Listen, I speak a little English." "You have an appointment in three days."

I had that appointment, and he sent me to the Country Hospital in the English Settlement. The matron said they don't have any vacancy right now, but would I be willing to do private nursing? So I said, "Yes," not thinking that she would call me right away, because we really needed some rest, after all that wartime in Germany and all we went through. So sure enough, the same week, they called me. You might not believe it, my first private case was a young Catholic priest with gonorrhea. I nursed him for four weeks, I had to do everything for him, I had to catherize him. It was not a very pleasant case, but I made two American dollars a day, that was a lot of money then. You know, one dollar was 16 Shanghai dollars, and you could live quite nicely, you could have a good meal every day.

Willy took his Kollwitzes under his arm and some other things and offered them to stores. There was a very well-known German art store, the name was "Modern Art," and he knew of the people, because their father was well-known, they come from Dresden, non-Jews. That's how he started, buying and selling, yeah. He was in contact with America, too. And very soon he had a Kollwitz exhibition. He made a few exhibitions in Shanghai, too, at Wing On, that was a very famous department store.

Very soon we made money, and I had some more cases. After six weeks, we got an exterminator, we threw all those furnitures out, and we ordered everything that just fits in our room from a French cloister, beautiful, combined closet for dishes and for our clothes. It was done beautifully. Then a special closet for my husband's graphic, and then we ordered a beautiful set, table and two armchairs and four chairs. Then after a few months, the Country Hospital employed me, and I was there till we went to the ghetto.

After some initial economic success, **Ruth Sumner**'s *life, like that of many other refugees, was turned around by the outbreak of war in the Pacific in December 1941.*

I can give you more memories about Shanghai than I can about Germany. We came to Shanghai, and they picked us up from the ship. Even though I was very young, I was very much aware that my life had changed. There I had been in first-class luxurious Japanese ship, and then we were in a home with army cots and blankets.

We didn't stay but three or four days, because my father had money. I don't know how much he had. He probably had much more than I thought he did. He was very industrious, self-sufficient, he was always business, business, business. He always made a buck. He never sat on his behind, not earning.

My dad was in the restaurant business, he had bars and restaurants and all that kind of stuff all his life. He opened up what they called a nightclub on the roof garden. He had a couple of partners, and he had a good business going, successful. The first year or so he did real well.

We lived well. We had our own furniture, we had a nice house. There was three bedrooms, bathroom, kitchen, living room. We had servants to clean until towards the very end. *Amah,* or boy, they call them.

And then, of course, World War II broke out, and that was the end of that. It was December when the war started. The roof garden closed, and then he never opened up again. And he started another business. He had another little restaurant, and it never worked out. Then he started selling things. He was always industrious, making money.

I learned English in school, and I was bilingual for many years. Now I've forgotten German, my accent's very poor. My father, he didn't learn English until he came to the United States. He spoke with a very heavy accent. But us young people spoke English with a British accent. And we had no problem, I mean, we spoke mostly German at home, when we went somewhere we spoke English, we could use both. It wasn't until I came to the United States but what I quit using the language. I don't even think in German anymore. You know what I mean, it's there and I can still read it, my ear has to get used to it. But you don't forget, it's just not used. It's rusty.

My formal schooling ended, I think, when I was 12 or 13. The school closed down, just before that they took me out. They figured I wasn't learning enough. I was not a particularly good student. I was average, you know, the best of the worst, [laughs] that type. I had to work first. If I had to memorize something, it took me some time.

Hongkou was a little city within a city, we took our culture with us, that was German, Jewish. We had theater, we had a synagogue, there were sports. We had libraries, I mean, it wasn't public, it's somebody that brought a lot of books with them. And we read. I used to have a very big complex about my lack of education until my daughter, who went through college, said, "Momma, if you don't tell anybody, nobody will know. You're self-educated." So I quit having a phobia about it. It doesn't bother me anymore, because we were well-read and we had our culture.

On the street corner, they used to have vendors, and there was big old pots and they heated it with charcoal, they baked the sweet potatoes like that. We paid for it, we'd get sick. Peanut butter, I never had peanut butter before, that's what we used to buy, lick, eat it. The Chinese candy, all that junk, we were told not to do it, but we did it. Because we knew we would get sick, and we paid the price every season.

The only time I really got sick, I'm sure at that time is when I picked up my tuberculosis. I really got a bad cold, and it wouldn't go away, the doctor kept coming back. Then Papa took me into town to a hospital to have my chest X-rayed, and it came out clear. When I was 39, I came down with tuberculosis. I think that's incubated in me for all those years. I mean, that's just a feeling I have, because I remember how sick I was, and I was not in school three or four weeks, I was about 12.

When we were living there, you recognized the beggars. I mean, stumps wrapped in things, rotting limbs, shoving themselves across the street. And you just walked by them, you don't pay them any attention. You learn to live with that. It doesn't bother you after a while.

There was no communication with the Chinese either. I never once remember going into one of their homes. They stuck to themselves, and we stuck to ourselves. The only way you communicated is if you had a servant, to come and clean. We had a lot of Japanese, Japanese soldiers, Japanese women and children. I even learned a smidgen of Japanese at that time.

I have always been the religious one, if that's what you believe in God, a faith in God. My daddy went high holidays. I don't remember my sister, but I always went. I've always enjoyed it. I've always talked to God. God has always meant a great deal to me, yes. I've always prayed. But I didn't go to synagogue on Friday and Saturday anymore, not in Shanghai. We were the typical three-holiday Jews.

The only Russian Jews I met was later. We kept pretty much to ourselves. Wherever from Germany you were from, that didn't matter. There were mostly German Jews and Austrian Jews, that didn't make any difference. In Shanghai, we had some of the very religious Jews from Poland there, the pious in the black hats. I remember they lived right across the lane from us. We didn't associate with them at all or nor would they with us. As far as they were concerned, we weren't even Jewish.

CHAPTER 4

In the Designated Area

The remarkable thing about Jewish life in Shanghai until 1943 is that there was no persecution. The Japanese, allies of the Nazis, already held de facto control over most of Shanghai by 1939. In December 1941, when the Pacific War broke out, the Japanese officially occupied the entire city and later put citizens of the Allied nations into internment camps. Yet the central European refugees continued to live undisturbed.

Nazi emissaries constantly attempted to convince the Japanese to kill the thousands of Jews under their control. Wild schemes were proposed, such as putting all the Jews of Shanghai onto boats and then sinking them at sea. The Japanese promised to consider the issue, but procrastinated and did nothing.

They finally took action targeted at the refugees at the beginning of 1943, perhaps in response to German demands, perhaps for their own reasons. On February 18, the Japanese authorities issued a Proclamation that forced all "stateless refugees" who had arrived after 1937 to live within less than a square mile in Hongkou. The February Proclamation showed the ambivalent nature of the Japanese attitude toward the Jews so despised by their German allies: the word Jew was not mentioned in the Proclamation, and the existing Baghdadi and Russian Jewish communities in Shanghai were not affected. About 8,000 central European refugees who lived outside of this district had to move within three months.

Although the Japanese used the innocuous term "Designated Area" to refer to the place where refugees were confined, the refugees always called it the ghetto. That word had first been used to refer to the district in Venice to which Jews were confined in 1516. Since the Holocaust, the word has taken on deadly meaning, because Jews in Nazi ghettos were all destined to be murdered. Jews in Shanghai did not know that in 1943, when they adopted the word "ghetto" out of their history to describe the restrictions on their movement. Beyond confinement, there was little antisemitic content in the creation of the Designated Area. Jewish religious services were unhindered, and Japanese officials occasionally attended them, watched refugee soccer games, and visited school classes.

Most important, Jews in Hongkou were not physically brutalized. Stories about those few Jews who were harmed by the Japanese thus took on great importance. The refugee who was found drowned after arguing with some soldiers who had hit his bicycle with their truck, and the nearly fatal beating of Hermann Natowic, who was accused of spying for the Allies, are often mentioned in interviews and memoirs. The contrast with Japanese treatment of the Chinese, which during the war approached genocidal proportions, demonstrates what might have happened if the Japanese had also been infected with virulent antisemitism.

This is the context for our narrators' repeated stories about Kanoh Ghoya, one of the officials in the Japanese Bureau of Stateless Refugees. Ghoya was the gatekeeper for Jews seeking daily passes to leave the Designated Area. His outrageous and unpredictable behavior is described even by those who never met him. But Ghoya saw himself as the "King of the Jews," not as their gravedigger. Why

1. Kadoorie School (after 1941)
2. SACRA building
3. Bureau of Stateless Refugees: Ghoya's Office
4. Ohel Moishe Synagogue
5. Ward Rd. Heim
6. Ward Rd. Jail
7. Wayside Park

Map 2   Designated Area, 1943–1945

read many stories about Ghoya? Only by seeing how many people his behavior affected can we recognize his real significance.

Germs were much more dangerous to refugees in Hongkou than the Japanese. Europeans had no immunities against the deadly diseases that inhabited Chinese slums. Sickness is another common thread in Hongkou stories. Close physical contact, polluted water, inadequate clothing, and an ever poorer diet made the refugees susceptible to dysentery, scarlet fever, and tuberculosis. Death did threaten in Hongkou, but it was not a constant visitor. About ten percent of the whole community died in Shanghai, mostly in the difficult years from 1943 to 1945.[1]

Refugee stories about Hongkou focus on the most basic material conditions of daily existence. Most families lived in one room. The repeated descriptions of food and putting together meals demonstrate how much energy was consumed getting enough to eat. No European starved in Hongkou, but thousands of the refugees were kept alive by the communal kitchens, especially at the Ward Road Heim, run by the community leadership and funded by American and Baghdadi generosity. The international transfer of funds by the Joint Distribution Committee to Shanghai was a lifesaver for the refugees.

Stories about communal faucets, the need to boil water, bedbugs, and toilets show how painful these central Europeans found their confrontation with what they considered primitive Asian living conditions. Here, generational differences became obvious. Jewish children in Hongkou just adapted to what they had, as children do everywhere. Adults used to urban bourgeois life in Berlin or Vienna still expressed horror at hygienic conditions in the Shanghai slums in interviews 50 years later. But families pulled together, pooled resources, and survived.

About 2,500 Jews spent their Shanghai years in camps, the so-called Heime. *They are not well represented here. These five complexes housed mainly men who were alone, but also many families, in huge common rooms. Most of the funding was provided by the Joint. Life in the* Heime *was not unhealthy or oppressive, it was simply degrading, and most of its stories remain unreported. The former refugees who keep in touch through reunions, have written memoirs, or have given interviews tend overwhelmingly to come from the majority who could avoid the* Heime. *Of our narrators, only Gérard Kohbieter lived in a* Heim. *The opinions about the* Heim-*dwellers offered by others appear to be based on little direct connection.*

Missing almost entirely from the memories of German-speaking Jews are the 2,000 Polish and Lithuanian Jews who arrived in Shanghai in 1941. Their life journeys had been entirely different. They had escaped in the months before the German invasion of the Soviet Union in June 1941 escalated the intensity of mass murder to a level unimaginable to anyone but the Nazis' own ideological leadership. A substantial number of the Polish Jews were male yeshiva students, including the entire Mirrer Yeshiva. They spoke Yiddish and did not dress like the Berliners and the Viennese. Religious culture kept these two communities separate. To the assimilated, occasionally observant, often mixed Jewish families from the Third Reich, the Polish Jews were religious fanatics. The Germans felt intellectually superior to the Poles. To the Orthodox religious teachers who led the Polish community, the Germans had betrayed their Jewish heritage. The Poles were better Jews. As Ruth Sumner said at the end of the previous chapter, to the Polish Jews who were their neighbors in Hongkou, "We weren't even Jewish." Although the Japanese put both communities into Hongkou, they barely interacted. When they did, it was often over religious issues, where mutual distrust leaped to the surface.

The isolation of the German-speaking Jewish refugees from the other Jewish communities in Shanghai was deepened by their confinement in the Designated Area. Shipwrecked in a sea of impoverished Chinese, these Jews created an island of central European culture and waited for the war to end.

Ernest Culman *describes the meaning of the Designated Area: shrinking of living space, lowered hygiene, more reliance on free meals provided through American and Baghdadi charity. The occasional cup of coffee made from used restaurant coffee grounds indicates deprivation, but not starvation. Although Culman recognizes that the Japanese were not cruel to refugees, he tells all the stories he knows about individual acts of cruelty.*

In February of 1943, the Japanese brought out this Proclamation that everybody has to live in a Designated Area. The word ghetto was not to be used, and there were no barbed wire around it. East Seward Road was the dividing line. Trouble was, we lived on the wrong side of the street, and we had to move again. It was very hard to find a place to live. We had 90 days. The Jewish community, primarily the Russian Jewish community, because Russia was not at war with Japan at the time, purchased an old school building, known as the SACRA building.[2] Half of it was a Japanese radio station, the other half they divided up the classrooms into smaller rooms and large rooms where single men could live in dormitory style.

So we moved again into the SACRA. We had a room, oh, I don't think it was as big as this living room for the four of us. You had to pay a certain amount of money to get in there. The only way we could do it is for my father to sell his microscope, which again had an emotional effect on him. It basically told him that he couldn't do anything. He was very proud of his microscope and microscope work that he did.

Every time we moved from one place to the next, it was smaller. Initially we were in this house with our friends where we had two rooms, then we moved into that smaller place out on Kinear Road, and when we moved into Hongkou, East Seward Road, that was even smaller, and then from there to the SACRA building, which was one room. So my mother and I used to make a chart, a diagram by centimeter by centimeter to figure out what furniture can go where, and what furniture do we have to sell or give away before we could move in there. Sometimes it was within a quarter of an inch or it wouldn't have fit.

Now my mother was a good decorator. She took that single room and with some wardrobes divided it up, so she had like a kitchen area, could do the cooking, a table where we ate. My parents had a pullout couch that they slept on, my brother had a bed that came from Germany. Initially we had two of them, one for him and one for me, which folded up against the wall with a bookshelf on top and then like a curtain in front of that. When we moved in the SACRA, my bed had to be given up, and I had to get an Army cot which could be folded up and stuck in the corner when not in use. In the morning when Henry and I went to work, my father had to stay in bed, because there wasn't room for all of us. The bike was also in the room, that we used to get to work on.

Things always got less and less, and there in the SACRA we didn't have a private bathroom any more, there was a bathroom there for everybody. You could take showers, men from 6 to 9, women from 9 to 12, or whatever it was, it wasn't that long. But taking a shower once a week was okay. Often we did our washing just out of a little basin, like a sponge bath is what you would call it here.

When the ghetto was formed, there were a number of people who decided not to move into the ghetto. They were given a one-week jail sentence, which sounds fairly mild considering it was a war situation. But what nobody knew was that these jail cells were infected. People came out of the cells, within a week or two they died of cholera, typhoid, whatever diseases they had. It was horrible, I think like 12 to 20 people died from just being in jail for a week.[3]

Many areas were destroyed by bombs from before we got there. In the SACRA building where we lived, in the back there was a bombed out building, where the second floor cement hung down like this at an angle. We used to jump up and down on that thing. Thinking back on it now, we could have been hurt quite badly. At other times we dug around ruins. One time we found pieces of a mahjong set, where obviously the house got bombed and the mahjong set all over the place. As kids we played a lot there.

Then my parents decided when I was 14 that I should go to work, too. In the meantime, my brother had gone to this other factory which made lathe and drilling presses. It was owned by a Korean, and what he did, he took an American lathe apart and reproduced the pieces piece by piece. There was a small area where all the small parts were made, the screws and nuts and bolts, headed by a man by the name of Kurt Lorenz, also a refugee. And that whole department had about half a dozen refugees working there, including my brother and another boy, really, you can hardly call them men, who I'd been friends with. They got me a job in there. I was an apprentice learning how to make parts. I loved it. When the boss came in, he always wanted me to just clean up every place, but I enjoyed working there very much, I learned a lot, most of it taught to me by my brother.

We had some Chinese working with us, and we used to kid around with them. There was one guy, he and I kidded around and I used to say to him, *"Du bist so nett,"* which is the German of, "You're so very nice." But I made it sound like a cuss word. The end result was that when he got angry at me, he used to tell me how nice I am. Henry and I still get a big kick out of that these days. And I worked there until the war was over.

The factory was outside the District and we had to have a passport every time to get out of there. The issuance of the passport was administered by one man, Ghoya. The passport was valid for one month. Frequently he let you wait in line for a month before he would bring you your passport. Ghoya was quite a character. He was short and hated anybody that was tall. A tall man came in looking for a passport, he'd jump up on the table and say, "Me big potato, you short potato, out, no passport," without any reason. He considers himself the King of the Jews. Our sporting activities was basically soccer, you know, we had soccer matches. He would be out there watching the game, and before the game we had to parade in front of him, just like others would parade in front of the king.

My mother had a Singer sewing machine with the pedal, and made alterations for people. She also did knitting, like she would knit a sweater for Henry, and as we outgrew it, she would undo the sweater and redo it sleeveless, you know, and after Henry outgrew it, then it became mine. Everything was used over and over again. Socks got darned. Now if I would give socks to be darned to Anya, she'd throw them out the window. In Hongkou is where things really got bad for us, you know, that's when Henry and I brought in the money that we had.

In the meantime, my father eventually got a job with the clinics. And between him and my brother and I working, and the fact that we were getting charity, we were able to make things work. We applied for charity, they came in to inspect your place, to see if you have anything else to sell, before they would give you charity. The charity that we received was in the form of one big pot of stew divvied out to everybody. My parents used to dig out the meat pieces to give to Henry and I, and they lost a lot of weight. My father lost over 50 pounds in the years in Shanghai.

The Jewish people had their own little police force, the Japanese made them be the guards at the entrance and exits of the ghetto, called *Pao Chia*. One guy, he was somebody in the *Pao Chia*, lieutenant, captain, or whatever equivalent, he was riding with his bike one day when a Japanese army truck hit him, accidentally. He didn't get hurt, but his bike got ruined. He wanted these two soldiers to replace the bike for him. Of course they wouldn't. "Take me to your superior," and people standing around yelled at him, "Stop it, be glad you didn't get hurt. Forget it." He says, "No, I am so and so of the *Pao Chia*." Eventually they told him, get on the truck with them. He was never seen again. A week or so later his body was fished out of the Yangtze River. These are foolish things that people did.

The Jewish community had its own mediation board, I guess would be the closest thing in English. When people within the community had disagreements, they went to this mediation board and they tried to resolve things without taking it to the Japanese authorities.

There were a lot of things to do. In sports, we had soccer and track meets and things like that. Ping pong was a big game for us. I actually became pretty good at ping pong. One time in school, I was playing ping pong and in my enthusiasm broke a window, so I was very concerned about what this will do to me. My parents would have to pay for it, and this was a time when they had very little money. So I walked in to the principal, and told the principal what had happened. And she said, "Okay, don't worry about it." Went back to class and then the custodian comes running into our classroom, yelling and screaming at the top of his lung, "I know somebody in this classroom has done it. Whoever it is, I'm going to see to it that you get punished, I will take you all to the principal." And I held up my hand, "I'm the one that broke it and I already told the principal." The custodian was just flabbergasted, he didn't know what to do.

We had a board game called Shanghai Millionaire, which was identical to Monopoly. I think somebody in Shanghai built it, using the same type of board and just changing the names of the streets. The Bund was the most expensive part, then there was Nanking Road, which was the next part over. I think Bubbling Well Road was on there. And we used to play that on a rainy day for hours at a time. We'd start at ten o'clock in the morning until six, seven o'clock at night. We took this so seriously, one

Photo 6 Playing Shanghai Millionaire

kid would leave, somebody else would take over his place like an ongoing crap game, you might say. But of course not for money, it was all just for the fun of it.

My parents couldn't afford to buy one of those things, and another kid and I, we actually copied it. We took a piece of cardboard and painted everything in there and we made a game for ourselves.

On a more adult basis, there were theaters. They had operas and operettas and simpler operas. In our building was a man by the name of Gyula Singer who painted the backgrounds. He became a friend of the family, and he snuck me into the theater so I could watch it. I saw the *Fledermaus*, I saw *Carmen* there and several of the other Viennese operettas, and got my first taste of music, which I still love to listen to.

Of course, cooking was something else again. In the SACRA building, there was one kitchen, and I don't know how many people lived in there. If you were lucky, you were able to use this gas kitchen for 20 minutes, 30 minutes, whatever it is. So everybody was cooking on what we called Chinese stoves. They were little charcoal things that we now enjoy for outdoor barbecuing, but it was no joy for us there, because it was a necessity. Sometimes the charcoal was too expensive, so we bought just powdered coal dust, mixed it with water and made our own charcoal. Hands became pitch black by doing that. There was one woman who worked in a restaurant, she used to come back to this SACRA building and brought the coffee grounds back. "Who has an oven going with some hot water, they can share a cup of coffee with me." My mother missed good coffee tremendously, so she often kept the oven going for this woman to come back and she could have a cup of coffee.

As the water always had to be boiled, at every street corner practically there was a place where you could buy boiling water. We had to make sure that we saw the water bubbling before we would take it, and then it got poured into a thermos bottle. We took it home, either made tea or sometimes just drank hot water. At the factory where Henry and I were working, we just drank hot water usually with some loaves of bread with salami or something on there, frequently no spread on it, that was our lunch.

My father was so worried about everything. I mean, he wasn't really cheap in the pure sense of the word, but he didn't want us to spend money on anything that wasn't necessary. My mother had a very sweet tooth, and I inherited that sweet tooth, and my brother did, too. So sometimes when my father was out at these doctor meetings, she would send my brother or I out to buy three pieces of candy for whatever it cost at that time, and we'd enjoy each one piece of candy.

Eric Reisman talks about some psychological difficulties of being a Jewish refugee under the Japanese. But he also got a good job and had fun with friends.

We moved into the Designated Area, my father was able to get a room there. Although you could call it a ghetto, it was a forced detention area. I don't think the Japanese felt antisemitic, because I don't think they knew antisemitism. So we all moved in.

My father knew fruit, there was no citrus fruit as such, that was his speciality. He opened a vegetable stand in the market and bought vegetables from the farmers and sold them to the public, to those people that lived in there and could afford it, and that's how he made his living. After I finished the Kadoorie School, I went to work in a pharmacy, and I worked for the majority of the war years in a pharmacy. The pharmacist taught me how to package things and distribute the things. I helped fill prescriptions, I made some money, and we were able to put it all in a pot. With my brother working and I working, we were able to subsidize the living that we needed. There was never, "You made this and I made that." We all took out whatever we needed, the meager requirements that we had to have.

Each Japanese soldier was a representative of the Emperor, and whenever you saw him you bowed, you had to humble yourself. That was very degrading, of course, to all of us. I'm sure the adults were more conscious of that requirement than the young ones. We were like a young tree able to bend much easier than an old established tree, which broke if bent too deep. They were the authority, and we had to adhere to that. Subsequently their requirement was, we had to start to govern ourselves, which was an experience that I will never forget too easily. There was a lot of nasty occurrences where our own Jewish people would turn in another Jewish family, because they did certain things that they were not supposed to have done.

I know from friends that they would shun certain individuals, because they were what they called *Spitzels,* you know, they would squeal on you, and I would have nothing to do with those people. But there was others that were put in prisons within the Designated Area and had to endure punishment by the Japanese, because they were being turned in. A friend of mine was active in the money-changing business, and he would trade in black market dollars. His mother and father had a restaurant, and he was doing this on the side. He was older, he was my brother's age, and he was turned in by one of them. He was in the prison and got cholera and typhoid and what all the other diseases that were predominant under those circumstances, and he died from that.

This was a group that used to hang around together, and of course when you're young, you take a lot of things in stride, much easier than when you get older. We had fun days, I mean, not every day was a dreary day. We found ways to entertain each other and it was all clean fun. Costume parties and socials that we had in his house, Zunterstein, Alfred Zunterstein, yeah.[4] I can mention some of the names that I still remember. Rita Schlosser, Ernstl Stern, Harry Loew, he was a real good soccer player, he and I were very close. At that time, you didn't fool around with girls. You married the girl, then you could fool around. There were friendships that to this day we're friends.

While I was in China, I took up boxing, and the guy that used to train us, he turned out to be a boxing champion. I took up boxing for the simple reason that I was tired of being pushed around, I wanted to know how to box and defend myself. There was no way of using any weapon, I don't have a weapon in the house. I felt that our Jewish people under the Nazis and under the Hitler Youth were so meek. If I know that I'm going to have to die, I'll take somebody with me, and that's why I learned how to box. I never needed it, but one instance. One of the Chinese was trying to steal something from me, and I knocked his block off. [laughs]

I was in the ring for about three years. But all as an amateur. They wanted to make me semipro, and I fought a Japanese in the ring. I knew I won the fight, and they wouldn't give me the win, and so I said, the heck with that, I'm not going to fight anymore, [laughs] I can't win with them, fighting the Japanese. So I gave it up.

Kohn turned out to be a boxing champion. "Lako" we called him, *der lange* Kohn [the tall Kohn], Lako. He became a professional fighter in China. He's a furrier from profession, and he subsequently emigrated to Israel. *Der lange* Kohn, he was a good boxer.

Alfred Kohn, boxer and soccer player, explains how sports offered a semblance of normal life in Hongkou, although he is modest about his own accomplishments. He saw how much harder refugee life was for his parents' generation.

Then the ghetto came, and that was even worse. We had to give up the apartment. We go into the ghetto, and we lived in a Chinese house that belonged to a Jewish guy. In one room lived a father, mother, and a little boy, another room was a single guy, on the next floor was a family with a daughter, and three bachelors, there was another bachelor in another little room, and we had the attic. You had to walk up two flights, it was very hard on my parents.

The only tap of water was downstairs, you go two flights down. There was a pot in the corner downstairs, that was the toilet, which they picked up every morning. The roof was leaking. In the summer it was hot as Hades, in the winter it was cold.

It was tough in Shanghai, the heat and the cold and living in an attic, four adults, no privacy. If my mother wanted to wash herself, we kids had to leave the room, be downstairs. And above all, you had diarrhea all the time, no matter what you did. They said, drink the water only if it's cooked. Everybody had diarrhea. Two, three, four, five times a night people had to run down on that stinking pot downstairs, and that was for the whole house. The stink was unbelievable, and if they didn't come to pick up for a day, you know, [laughs] it was a disaster.

Nobody had heat. I met a guy here in Florida, who said to me he worked in Shanghai for the gas company. I said, "I didn't even know they had gas in Shanghai." We had one lightbulb and that's it. We had no electrical equipment, we had no radio, we had none of the essentials that you imagine today are in America normal. I was a very rich man, I had a bicycle in Shanghai, and I put my brother on the back to take him to the soccer game, you know. A rickshaw was impossible, it was expensive.

My parents suffered terribly, my brother being sick. I had it a little better. I was active in sports, and some of the sports people helped me a little bit. I got a job to work in a kitchen, and I had at least food. I was the main provider by working and bringing home food. It was wonderful. And hoping always the war should end.

Before the ghetto, I worked for a while as a radio technician in a store. The guy who eventually became what we called the King of the Jews, who ran the ghetto, Mr. Ghoya, I installed a shortwave radio in his house with an antenna on the roof. He could hear Japan, and he was the happiest man in the world, and that guy had a memory like an elephant. It was a hassle to get out of the ghetto, I'm sure you must have heard. Hundreds of people standing in the sun waiting for Mr. Ghoya outside his office, and he questioned you about all kinds of things. Whenever I came in with my father, he said, "I remember you, you put that radio into my house and I still thank you," and no question about it, I got a pass to go out.

We did work outside the ghetto also at the time, working in the fur business. Russian Jews were not affected by the ghetto. The Russian Jews, the furriers, didn't need us, they could have had it done for half the price from the Chinese furriers and any Chinese laborer, but they employed us outside the ghetto. Because my father spoke Russian, we had a good job and we worked, but you always had to compete with Chinese labor. We also got some lunch at the time from Shelter House, which was mostly for Russian Jews who were destitute, they got one meal a day. We were permitted to go there, because the Russian boss of ours was a big contributor, and he says, "I have a poor man working, he speaks Russian," and the few words of Russian that I spoke was all right. So we had at least a meal. The Russian Jews took very good care of their own and us refugees, they helped enormously.

But life in the ghetto was very tough. You know, it's no comparison to what the Jews went through in Germany or Poland or Russia, forget it. The Japanese were cruel, they were strict, and they cooperated with the Jews, they made no distinction, they were very fair, the Japanese were just.

Everybody that did anything against the Japanese, having a shortwave radio or something, or when it was supposed to be darkened at night when there was air raid, you got caught and the light was on, there was severe punishment, severe punishment. But I have to come back to the point that the Japanese really did not believe in this business that a German who was a Catholic or Protestant is different from a German or an Austrian who's a Jew, and that was our luck. Otherwise we'd be all dead.

Of course, people got killed. I saw with my own eyes, a Japanese caught two Chinamen stealing kerosene. They have the canister, five gallon of kerosene, they want to put it on the bicycle, and they saw them. So they got on the bicycle, took off, the other guy got caught, they tied up his hand, they put a block of wood on the floor, with a samurai sword they chopped off his hands. And when we had air raid, I saw how a Chinese guy wanted to take off a ring from a dead person, and a soldier came and killed him on the spot. He told him in Japanese a few garbled words, boom, dead. That was Japanese justice. These are things I saw.

Sports kept us alive. We had an organized little boxing club, one of them was champion of Germany.[5] So we boxed a little bit, we played soccer. And that was the main attraction for the youth. In the Chaoufoong Camp we had a soccer field. We had a junior league and a second division and first division, and we played soccer Saturday or Sunday. There was a big rivalry between the teams, you know, and that life was more or less normal. But everything was in a much lower grade.

And even during the ghetto time, our Jewish soccer club played against the German soccer club. It was not the nicest games we played. Some of the German non-Jews in Shanghai were very pleasant, because many of them had to leave Germany because they were Communist or something, but the German community was then controlled by the Nazis. In fact, in our boxing club we had a German, a non-Jew, he was a policeman in Shanghai during the war, he was friends with us. That is on a personal level. He was a big husky guy, very nice fellow.

There were of course Nazis there. We went to the American school to play soccer, and there were some German boys, and they called us dirty Jews. We couldn't do much about it. After the war, I worked for the Americans, and one of these kids worked for the Americans. So I went over to the officer in charge, I said, "This kid over there during the war called us 'dirty Jews.' I don't think he should work here, and if you're not going to get rid of him, we're going to get rid of him." And they fired him. Which was minor, but you know, what can you do?

Jewish crime there was, people were stealing because they were hungry. Prostitution there was. But essentially everything was done in the German way. We had theater, we had opera, not on the level that you wanted to, and we young people didn't have money to go to the opera, but we could always find a way to sneak in at the plays and watch. We had two wonderful comedians, Herbert Zernik and another guy, forgot his name, and even they ridiculed the Japanese. Some Jews always were spying for the Japanese, they told the Japanese, and then they arrested him.

Life was very hard, particular for the older generation, for my parents and other parents.

Survival in Hongkou, as described by **Lotte Schwarz***, was a slow descent into poverty.*

There was a couple from Vienna, Berger, and they had a little coffee shop. So when we couldn't do anything anymore, we went there. There was a refugee family, Margaret Mattes, her parents baked kind of a Danish, and they made *Negerküsse* [literally, nigger kisses]. It's inside marshmallow and outside chocolate, we called that *Negerküsse,* [laughs] that's what we called it in Germany. Margaret went around with a big basket and went to the different little shops and said, *"Brauchen Sie heute Negerküsse?"* [Do you need Negerküsse today?]

So we sat in Bergers' little coffee shop. First we bought the *Negerkuß* and a coffee, and we had either sugar or milk, whatever we wanted. Then we didn't have the money anymore for the *Negerkuß,* so we just had a coffee with a little milk or little sugar. And then we didn't have the money for the sugar anymore, and we only had a little black coffee. In the end we couldn't buy anything anymore. Instead coffee we had tea, that's when I learned to drink tea without sugar and anything.

Everybody was sick from our people, because the terrible food we could buy and eat didn't agree with us anymore. I was so thin. One time I was sick, we all had that terrible stomach ailment. And the doctors were all refugees, too. He looked at my stomach, he said, "I don't even need an X-ray, you are so thin, I can look through." And many times I just had enough for my husband and for my daughter, and I didn't eat anything.

We had kids, you know, couldn't feed them anymore. Next to me lived an Indian family, from Bombay or so. And they had a cow. But there was no place where they could put the cow outside. So the cow was with them in the house. My husband worked in the committee for the refugees for a while, and he got a little money there, so every time he got money, every week or every two weeks, I bought little milk next door for my daughter, you know, she was two years old maybe at that time. And that was till we could finally leave.

The Japanese were never bad to us, in all those years. Their people couldn't talk our language, we couldn't talk their language, so "Uh, uh, uh," you know. At night the Japanese watched that we didn't have any lights on. So I had a candle, we had only one little room, and I put the candle underneath the bed and fed my daughter. You know, boy, when they saw a little light, they knocked at the door and they screamed. We had to be very careful, yeah.

I brought beautiful things. I had a beautiful wedding band, which was my husband's mother's ring, with a big diamond, that was the first we sold. I had from my mother a beautiful brooch, and it had a diamond in and a pearl. We sold it all in Shanghai. As long as we had the shop and had the other little shop, you know, didn't sell. Part I remember I sold when we bought Bayer out, because his drinking was impossible. And the rest I sold piece by piece. I didn't care anymore. I never cared for jewelry, so that wasn't hard. And I remember my husband said, "Now look at all this stuff and take what you want to keep." And I said, "I don't want to keep anything, it's no use anymore." You had to get rid of everything, just to buy something to live with. There was one woman, her name was Leschnik, I never forget that, and everybody sold their stuff, and Leschniks had little store, and then the Japanese came and they bought it all. And at the end we didn't have anything. My husband didn't even have a suit anymore. We sold it all.

And then the Red Cross came with a big machine there, at noon in the middle of the street, they put up one kind of a big kettle, you know. The last year or so, it was every day. Terribly depressing to go there and go to that thing and get food. We never did. I would starve first. Everybody lived in a *Heim* get their meals in a *Heim*, because nobody there made money either anymore.

The thing was, we didn't think at all anymore. We just didn't know what was going on. You know, you were kind of numb in Shanghai. You lived from one day to another, and you hope you have something to eat for your family the next day. And that was about it. And that heat in summer, oh God, was it hot! 120 degree, 110 degree. It was terrible. And when I was thinking, I was thinking to get out and that I could still make a living for my family. But otherwise, you know, we were all together and all in the same boat, so you really didn't think very much.

Gérard Kohbieter describes living in a Heim, *not only the degradation and depression, but also the inventive efforts by petty entrepreneurs to make a little money. He offers rare insight into the administration of the* Heime. *The quality of his refugee life depended on a few dollars.*

In between magic jobs, it really got too tough. I would put the tuxedo in a pawn shop, and they took the patent leather shoes on another occasion, and the shirts. I even pawned my rings, the magic rings that link together. Then when I got a job, I had to go borrow money from somebody and get all my shit out of the pawn shop, do my job, and pay this guy back. Transactions. But most of the time you just lay there and read.

And I read a lot. There was a time when I read a book a day. Jews are readers, more often than not. There were lending libraries where you had to pay and free ones. I read my way through the Second World War, which isn't a bad, bad way to go through the Second World War, let me tell you.

There were guys going around to the non-Jewish German community and selling things. Somebody made German sausages, and they went around to German households and were gladly received, because where else could they get German sausage? I was dealing German books to them, and I was very well received. There were German bookstores that were selling books, not just the lending libraries, and I knew one of the guys, Heinemann, very dear man, very knowledgeable, a real book person. He let me take books on commission. He gave me a suitcase full of books, and I made appointments. I don't think they bought it out of pity. They were glad to get German literature. What I didn't sell, he got back. It was good for him, it was good for me. I didn't do that very long. It was a little stopgap, I think is the word that wants to get off my lips.

I spent considerable time in camps, in and out. The camp I was in, Alcock, used to be a huge factory building that had been cleaned up. There were at least two huge halls, and there were, I don't know, 80 or 100 people, but on double beds, so half the number of beds. Just one next to the other.

One guy was a head of the room, which you needed, that would sort of take care of disputes between people which would arise invariably, and just made sure that the place got swept out and that whoever was on duty actually did that and so forth. Tempers flew high, particularly when there wasn't much to eat, and once in a while something got swiped. Then there was a big ado, of course. It was run alright. It was something that I could adjust to. It was a fact of life. There was nothing you could do about it. And I was glad that you had a place. You would put your suitcase under the bed, and I think they had a place where you could store things, for people that had too much stuff. I didn't. I had sold everything, little by little, everything. I was down to one pair of pants, man, and that's when poverty really knocks on your door, when your last pair of pants, they go in the knees first, and you see the first thread there, and you say, "That's it, Charles. That's it."

You had a huge dayroom that had the stage. It had a billiard table. It had long wooden tables with benches and all around it. Then there was a courtyard, and there was a tinsmith that was building tricks for me once in a while. There was a barber, and that was about it. It was right next to the huge jail where my burglar acquaintance spent the winter.[6] There were other camps that were for families. This was mostly for singles. The families got sometimes rooms of their own, or maybe two families, and things were a little more genteel there, I think. But I only know that from visiting.

You got meal tickets. In the beginning, for each day there were three coupons. Then it was two. And then it was one. During the really bad times, there was a time when there really wasn't enough to eat, where you lived on what one would consider a fairly large roll. That was your daily ration. It was interesting to notice how people coped with that. I knew one guy, he took out a napkin, put the bread on it on a little piece of wood, and he cut it in three pieces. He made himself three meals out of it, and he very disciplined ate one piece in the morning and so on. We usually, the young ones, just ate it all up and hoped for the best and managed to scare up a bowl of soup.

The *kvetchers* were a big pain in the ass in Shanghai. Attitude is everything, you know, and there were people who were *kvetching*, man, and that were really driving you nuts. *"Ah, Mensch, hab' ich einen Kohldampf."* [Man, am I hungry.] Well, this was senseless. Everybody else was in the same boat, man. You're just simply reminding people, "Oh yeah, that's right. My stomach is empty." Whereas other people had the wit to divert, entertain themselves somehow. They read something, or they talk with each other or played billiard or something. I said, "Man, look at the alternative."

People had all kinds of enterprises in these camps. You had some Frankfurter people who were cooking something that you could buy. There was one guy that was selling cigarettes out of the open package, one at a time. Then there was one guy that was selling pastry, manufactured, I think, by refugees. And then, of course, there was a Viennese cat that was selling coffee. Some of them gave credit. I had a pretty good credit standing there. There was one guy that had brought along a little machine that sharpens razor blades. So he would sharpen razor blades for people. It cost pennies. But, you know, he had a few pennies.

And so you sat there. In summer you spent the night on the roof, because they had bedbugs. There wasn't a damn thing they could do about those bedbugs. You can't sleep with bedbugs, man, it's just impossible. And the minute it gets light, they go away. Kerosene was hard to get, it was very expensive for our standards, and some guys had little tin cans with kerosene and put the legs of the bed into these cans in the hopes that the bedbugs couldn't crawl up there, but they fall off the ceiling. I don't know how they do it, maybe they can fly. But I spent many a night on the roof, just talking with people, and then curiously the minute the sun comes up, you went to bed. That was an unpleasant part of it.

Whenever I had a little money, I rented myself a room. People would talk about it, "Hey, there's a room free. Do you know anybody who needs a room?" Or there'd be a sign in a window. It was easy to get a room. Anyway, I never had any trouble as long as I had the change in my pocket. What did a room cost? Well, if I had a couple of engagements, couple of weeks here and maybe a month somewhere else, I probably made enough money to rent a room for six months or something like that. I was in and out of that place.

I had some pretty adventurous pads, as one used to say. One in a bakery. At night I had to go through the back and they were baking bread. You'd get the smell of freshly baked bread, man, and sometimes I couldn't buy one. The meal tickets I could still get.

When I didn't have the money anymore, I'd go to the camp. It was easy. At least you had a place. Everything was free. Perhaps some people had to pay a little, if they had an income. There were people that were working and lived in a camp anyway.

There was a committee, huge office with desks and so forth, social workers who would assess the situation and what to do with people and where to put them and what's available. Can we put this family there? Do they have to separate? It was done reasonably. It must have been a lot of headaches to keep 20,000 people together, under the circumstances. I have no beefs. I mean, I have a beef that I had to go there in the first place, naturally. Let's have no mistake about that.

Otto Schnepp's ability to both earn money for his family and study at St. John's University made his life hectic, but fulfilling. He used his language competence to become unusually integrated into the social life of Chinese students. That probably made the extreme Chinese poverty in Shanghai even more conspicuous.

Where we lived in Hongkou was in a small room. We got that place from a committee that had been set up to support the refugees. I slept on a camp bed that was set up for the night and then folded up. There was a washroom somewhere. It was cold, and heating was kind of nonexistent. My mother cooked on a little hibachi stove. The life there was very, very limited for most people. There were camps where people really deteriorated, and it was very bad. These people who lived in camps, they were probably people who were the less vital, the less active elements. And so, I think, they just went by the wayside. One of my deep impressions was how harmful, how difficult things are for people.

I couldn't afford to buy anything too expensive, in spite of the fact that I worked so hard. One important thing in my personal experience, eventually I didn't have any clothes to wear. Through Switzerland money came, and then this Jewish committee had shoes, all this was sponsored by the

Joint, I got some there. And a very good friend of mine, a Russian Jew, he collected some clothes for me. Some Chinese invited me for lunch, I was very grateful. It was really desperate in that sense.

And my difficulties were also that there was blackout at night, and I was only allowed to use kerosene lamp, electricity was forbidden. Eventually I got some arrangement. The *Shanghai Jewish Chronicle* was very close to where I lived, and they had permission to use electricity and work at night. There were Chinese typesetters, and there was a refugee proofreader there at night. I was allowed to go there and study and work and so on. This proofreader had also a day job, and he fell asleep [laughs] half the time, and I learned how to do proofreading. It's strange.

I had no life really inside the District ever. I came home to sleep, and I got up in the morning and I left, and I worked on weekends also. Sunday mornings was the time I was at home, and by noon I left to do some more tutoring in the afternoons. So I had very little connection, if any, with the people inside the District. The only connection I had was with others who went to St. John's University. Very few were fortunate like I was to live outside.

I got into studying Chinese more when I went to St. John's. The official language of the University was English. But there were courses for Chinese who had not had a good Chinese education. They came on many different levels. I was able to join the lowest one that was offered. So I went for five semesters with those courses.

I was the only one who attended of any foreigner that I know. Chinese were all over the place, and Chinese language was all over the place, and the writing was everywhere, you know. And yet the refugees kept completely apart from China. It was too far to go, they had so many problems. English was bad enough, you know, to deal with, I guess.

At St. John's I was more integrated with my Chinese co-students because of that. I attended social functions, and I could get on with them. They spoke Shanghai dialect mostly, but there were some who were from North China who spoke Mandarin. But I could get on with some Shanghai dialect. I think it put me on a somewhat different footing. One of my classmates invited me to his house. His father was a principal in a school. So there was an interaction, and I understood more of what was going on. I think that made a difference.

I had to deal with Ghoya. I had a pass to stay out till nine o' clock or something because I was a student. I was allowed to go all over the city. We had these badges, *"Tong"* it says on it, which means "pass." You had to wear this badge everywhere outside. A number of times I was late returning. One day I was caught, it was just a very little late, I think, maybe I was 15 minutes late. That time I came by streetcar. There were Russian policemen there, and the Russian policeman took away my pass.

Then I had to go to that police station. I'd been scared silly of these Japanese, I must say. I had to go there to get issued a pass, and it was always a very traumatic experience. That time I was very frightened. I don't think it's specifics. You see, when you face a power, where you're completely powerless, you're completely in their hands, you know, that is something that goes very deep, and I have great trouble accepting that. I had had that in Vienna, and I felt that very, very strongly again there. At that time I was no longer a child, I was already reasonably grown up. So I really felt very upset about that, very frightened also. It was dangerous there, because some people died from being put in jail there.

They published a list of names on the notice board to come in whose pass had been taken. Ghoya made a big fuss, you know, "St. John's University, small university," I don't know, he screamed and shouted. He gave me back my pass, but he curtailed where I could go. He wouldn't let me go to the French Concession to teach, only just back and forth to the University. Well, he couldn't control where I went. There was this resistance to being so controlled. I said, "Piss on them." I went to the French Concession, and I continued tutoring, teaching. It was interesting, I actually took off that badge when I went to the French Concession. I thought if I had a badge, somebody could ask me for my pass, you see. But this way, nothing ever happened. I got away with it. It was an important thing for me to rebel, not to conform to their rules. That was the only time I got my pass taken away.

In retrospect, I was pretty dehumanized in many ways for years, because the life there was so dehumanizing. You had on the streets beggars. You had people diseased, starving in the streets, Chinese. People died in the streets. You literally step over bodies. I can't see how people would not be affected by seeing poverty and starvation and disease and death as an everyday occurrence on the streets of Shanghai. Shanghai does not get cold, it rarely gets below freezing, but I remember from somewhere a statistic that in Shanghai on a cold winter night about 100 people would die in the streets. Because it was wartime, there were many refugees from the countryside that came to Shanghai, and it was just a terrible life. Look, it was terribly dehumanizing to take a rickshaw, which was an everyday occurrence, that's a dehumanizing experience. You must say to yourself, "This man is not human." Otherwise how can you do it? And I guess one way to deal with that is to just kind of retreat and to defend yourself from that.

Herbert and Ilse Greening both had good jobs and suffered less from material deprivation. Scattered through their stories are portraits of how the lives of "people who were used to better things" were affected by scarcity and deprivation. What you brought and then sold could be crucial to the quality of life in Shanghai.

Ilse Greening: Many refugees lived in the French Concession and in the International Settlement. For them it was disastrous, because they had to give up comfortable apartments or houses and move into very primitive. We knew people, doctor friends of ours, who had to have the so-called honey pot in the middle of their living room. Many times you were sick, because a lot of people had intestinal disease, and there you were sitting in the middle of the living room, and there was no other place.

We had friends, they lived in one small room, there was only room for one narrow bed, so the wife put a board on the tub, which happened to be in that room, and then a mattress, and she slept on that. Of course those were all people who were used to better things.

We were fortunate. We were not affected since we lived in the Area already, which was accidental, we were renters in Kungping Road. The only thing was we decided to buy the house. We were able to buy almost the whole attached house. You couldn't buy the land in China, you could only buy the building. So we started to sell most of the stuff that I had received as a wedding present, china, dishes and a lot of things. For instance, we had a very beautiful precious silver coffee and tea set, which must have been very valuable. Those very expensive things were bought by Germans, not directly, through dealers. There was a German jeweler on Bubbling Well Road, I think, who bought most of the stuff.

The rationing was terrible during the war. Whatever came into the city was controlled by the Japanese, that's why really we had the shortages. Flour and sugar especially were rationed, but it was terrible, the flour was inhabited by all kinds of weevils and the sugar was very wet. But my mother managed from this rubbish stuff, she still baked cakes. [laughs]

That doesn't mean you couldn't buy it, you could buy everything if you had money. Everything you can imagine was available in Shanghai in the black market, whether it was coffee or butter or imported medicine, was always available to those people who could afford to buy it. There were lots of Chinese who were in that kind of business, and Europeans.

Herbert Greening: We lived on tea in the morning, and bread and soy milk and bacon and lard. We didn't want a child in Shanghai.

Ilse Greening: You didn't want a child. He always said, "We're going to have a child after the war," but there was no end in sight, and finally I insisted, I wanted a child while I was still young. In 1945 I became pregnant. When I was pregnant, I drank soybean milk, and I ate soybean cheese, which now everybody thinks is ideal. There was milk, but it was very expensive.

Herbert Greening: We had three hospitals. We had the refugee hospital on Ward Road, we had General Hospital at the river next to the post office, and we had the hospital in Frenchtown, Great Western Road. On Chaoufoong Road, yeah, another refugee hospital. I never set my foot in there.

The General Hospital was maintained by nuns. They were not nice. I brought a Chinese guy in with an acute appendicitis. The guy didn't have any money on him. So, "I wouldn't even consider admitting you."

Ilse Greening: The Country Hospital on Great Western Road was fancier, for the people in the International Settlement and in the French Concession. I visited somebody there once, after the war. During the war it was out of the question. But the refugee hospitals did the best they could.

Herbert Greening: You have to look at it with the eyes at that time. Maybe it was the best that could be done. Looking at it from today, the refugee hospital was a dump. The heating in the new baby department was very primitive. They had what they called electric suns, electric heating lamps. And there was a short cut in the electricity and three babies died from exposure to cold. And so I said, not for my son. And we delivered him at home with a friend of mine.

But it was war, Shanghai was an isolated city, we didn't get anything from the outside as far as medications concerned. Only what was in store in Shanghai could be sold at very high prices. We had to do with medication made in China, copies of foreign medications, which were easily available. But a hospital is only as good as the doctors are and the doctors were quite good. Except some of them.

I studied homeopathy and made myself homeopathic medicines. I injected urine, that was supposed to raise the antibody level. We injected own blood, that too was supposed to raise the antibody level. One of the refugees, she was a doctor, started to make antidiabetic medication out of corn. I don't know how it worked out. I never used it.

Ilse Greening: When I went to Mr. Ghoya, I did not have any problem. I was scared. You know, everybody was scared, and we were standing on line and you never knew what mood he was in. I guess because it was a highly reputable bank, I never had any problems.

Herbert Greening: I first got a 24-hour passport, and that was curtailed to 12 hours later on. But the 12-hour passport I always had. And I had Japanese patients.

Ilse Greening: Remember you went across Ward Road to go to visit a Japanese, but that was not within that time limit. You couldn't refuse a Japanese. You couldn't tell him, he wouldn't understand, "I cannot come to you, because my pass has expired." Oh, I was scared until he came back at night.

For many years there was a curfew at night. We had to do something for entertainment, you know. We were so confined. We played cards and mahjong. *Mensch, ärgere Dich nicht,* that we played, too. All German kids learned that.[7]

One thing we did not do much was going to synagogue. My grandparents were very religious, and I had the feeling, but we were never one to attend services too much. And Herbert even less than I.

Herbert Greening: No, although the rabbi was our patient.

Ilse Greening: Shanghai is very low, it's below sea level, and when a typhoon came, there was lots of water. One year we had to go by boat to the synagogue, the Eastern movie house on Muirhead Road. Some Chinese used to carry the parishioners on their backs, they were waiting on the other side of the road, and some people went by little boats into the synagogue. That's the only time I went, I do not recall any other time. I can't even remember what it looked like inside.

You met a lot of different people in Shanghai, you know, and because we were so closely together, you also got to know them better than casual. And we made some very good friends.

Herbert Greening: Shanghai friends stuck.

Ilse Greening: People thought they were only in Shanghai for a little while, and many of them never unpacked. Patients of Herbert invited us for coffee, and they were the type of people I knew had better dishes. She must have seen the look in my eye, and she said, "Oh, you know, don't think this is all we have. We have everything, all the good dishes and the silver, etcetera, but we didn't bother to unpack it." Another patient of Herbert's, they had two sons that were growing and growing. And they were not dressed well. These people I knew had lots of money, and I asked her once, you know, why they dress so shabbily. She didn't unpack the clothes. The boys had tailor-made suits, but she wouldn't let them wear them.

During the war, not a lot but a few women associated with Japanese. Not too many. Many times it was the need for bread. You know, it wasn't fun or anything. They needed to support their families.

Herbert Greening: One patient I had, she admitted to me that she was a prostitute for Japanese only, and she hated it, but it was a good income.

Ilse Greening: It was more surprising, because most of the women were from middle-class Jewish families where you didn't expect it.

Oh, I have another thing I have to tell you. While I was working for the Japanese in my old English bank, most of the Chinese employees were old timers like me, and especially I was friendly with two older men. We were not allowed to listen to shortwave radio, it was forbidden. We were not that brave. But every morning these two got me into a corner, and they told me everything that was happening outside. They had shortwave information, these two. I never asked how and why, and they gave me information about battles, you know, what was won and what was lost.

We were plenty scared. The Japanese were not easy to get along with.

*Even though **Doris Grey** had an important job and some financial resources, her husband could no longer earn any money. They ended up in a small room with no toilet. She is stoic about the tragic end of her pregnancy and very informative about the difficulties of providing hospital care for thousands of refugees with minimal resources.*

One day, we opened the newspaper, and it didn't say Jews, it said all people who came to the French or English Settlement have to move to Hongkou. So we went house hunting, so to speak. House, it was a hut. Downstairs was one couple living with mother, then a half floor up we were living. Again that gentleman who was the owner of "Modern Art," he was an architect, too, so he came and we made a drawing exactly how our furniture will fit in that small room. I remember we got the last Simmons couch at Wing On, which opened up into two beds. And then we had this table, and on one wall those two closets for art and there we had a big box, where we kept our clothes and our winter clothes. [laughs] When we went to bed, you know, we had to move all the furniture, the chairs went on that box, so we were able to open up the bed, but this was all right. We lived among the lowest Chinese, we didn't have a bathroom for three and a half years. We didn't know what's coming, if you would have known, you wouldn't want to live.

My husband was not allowed officially to do anything in his profession. What could he do in Hongkou? Who had money in Hongkou? But we survived, that's the main thing.

I was pregnant just when we got to the ghetto. I got to the doctor, who said, "In these days, Jewish women shouldn't have children." Maybe it was fortunate. But you know there were so many children born. When my husband passed away, I thought maybe it was meant that way, you know.

What would I have done with a 12-year old, working, not being able to take care. So everything has a purpose I believe, I don't know.

There were several *Heims,* you know. At least we lived in a room. I have to tell you, you might not hear it from other people, I never knew that Jewish people can demoralize in such a way, it's terrible, you have no idea, they didn't start to work or do anything. People sank lower and lower. It was really depressing. They got their food, the Kitchen Fund, they called it. The food was mostly noodles, sweet potatoes, and all that. But it was nourishing, you know. Bread they got, too.

Ghoya was the most dreaded person in the District. He was hitting the people and made it very difficult to get a passport. My husband got a pass twice. I never went out, all those years, I never left the District. It was very, very difficult.

So I started out in the Ward Road Hospital. It consisted of 35 beds with lice and straw.[8] We had an office administrator, I was in charge of the nursing staff. It was difficult for us to get used first to the new surroundings. You come from a first-class hospital and start with dirt and lice and straw, you know, it's quite a job to be done. But we were young, and we were willing to do it.

The doctors were all qualified doctors from Europe, you know, mostly Viennese. The internist was a Dr. Mannheim, he came from Vienna, and he immigrated to Israel. Then we had on the surgical floor, first Dr. Flater was in charge, he was from Berlin. And we also had Dr. Wiener from Breslau. After they both died, Dr. Marcuse was the surgeon. Dr. Marcuse was allowed to live out all the time in the French Concession. Dr. Neger was an assistant doctor from Vienna. And he immigrated to Israel, we were very good friends. I'm in touch with his wife, he passed away. Then we had a younger doctor, Dr. Kraus from Vienna, very, very nice, a very good doctor, and also Dr. Elias. Elias is in New York. And who else? Those were the main ones. And then we had a lady doctor, Dr. Landau, she was from Krakau. We had a pharmacist, who used to have his own pharmacy in the French Concession. Then he came to Hongkou and was in charge of our pharmacy. His name was Landau, too, but they were not related.

We started to train people. For instance, I knew a girl who was a tailor, so I knew she will be good with getting the sutures, and we trained her, and later on she was even operating nurse in New York.

We had sometimes Chinese patients, mostly private patients. People who could pay were on the private floor, very few we had. That helped too, yes. But the average didn't have to pay. Mostly refugees, and you have no idea, we counted everything. People were stealing knives, forks, spoons, everything. You see, people who were not there don't know, you had to watch, they took linen if they could. And personnel stole, too. So you had to have your eyes all open. Yeah, I had to control everything, because I was in charge of everything and I was responsible. There was an operation, I had to be there. If a baby was born, I had to be there, you know.

I did a lot of anesthesia, too. Sometimes I had to assist, because we didn't have enough doctors. We had many difficulties, of course, for instance, sometimes we were out of power. So I remember one appendectomy we did with flashlights, and we even had a bicycle in there with a big flashlight, you know. We had lice, and we had to disinfect everything, and we had maternity, a lot of children were born. And, of course, we had infectious disease, too. On account of the circumstances, we had sometimes infections of the wound after the operation, you know, so we had some medication, like certain antiseptics powder to put on.

It worked. But we lost 3,000 people out of 15,000.[9] Mostly they were very undernourished, that was the main reason, because they had no resistance to whatever sickness they had, no matter what we did. Maybe some of them didn't want to live under the circumstances. And some of them were so sick that you couldn't help them. There were complications like in any case today, too, diabetes, amputation, and gangrene, and all the everyday sickness. But the worst part was that we didn't have enough medication during the war. We just had aspirin and salve.

One of our nurses died in Shanghai, too. Her name was Brigitte Singer. She immigrated to Bangkok, and then from Bangkok to Shanghai. We were both at the Country Hospital, but I left early, she left half a year later. She worked in the operating room. She had a gall bladder operation. Before she had operation, we disinfected everything just to be sure, you know. She got *Gasbrand* after the operation, it's a bacillus. We couldn't save her. It was very tragic.

Then we had another tragedy. Six babies, newborn, died in one night. And, of course, at that time we didn't know any better, and they thought because it was not heated. We couldn't use any electricity. But we kept them with hot water bottle and blankets and everything. It was a virus, we knew it afterwards. But people were saying they died of frost cold, you know. They didn't. There's another lady I know, she lives in Berlin, now I think. And it was so terrible, I met her through a friend of mine, and then she said, "You don't remember me. I'm Mrs. Ascher, I lost my twins."[10]

We could've saved more, yeah, definitely, but I think we gave them our best. I'm sure we did. I don't think we had any cases which died due to unsufficient care or malpractice. I think we were there with a heart, we really were. You know a patient was a patient, although most of the patients didn't think so, because we didn't have enough beds, and we didn't have help and attention they should get, and we needed the beds. As soon as they got better, they had to leave. So I remember, I met a lady here, a lovely lady, and she said, "Doris, you know what you did? You sent me home." I said, "I sent you home?" She said, "Yes, I was not ready." I said, "Listen, we needed the bed for other people." She said, "Today I know it, but then I didn't know." So that was a big problem.

I remember once, I was walking with Dr. Neger from work and somebody called, "Come in, come in, come in fast!" I said, "What's the matter?" "The woman is losing her baby." So we took a kitchen knife, boiled it to make it sterile to cut the umbilical cord, she delivered her baby. But most of them came to the hospital. And they stayed a week. It's not like here. It was a happy surrounding. We usually gave them a slight anesthesia. Nobody was bothered those times with natural childbirth.

We had inspection from the Committee, you know, the people who gave money. The Committee paid us all. We didn't get much. I worked with all of them. One of them who worked very close and was in the Committee was Dr. Kunfi, I think he was originally Hungarian.[11] He lived in Vienna, he was a gynecologist. As a matter of fact, he started out with the hospital as a surgeon. The Jews from Baghdad, Ellis Hayim, they were the most influential people, and some Russian Jews, too. They were always very understanding. They knew we did our best anyway. They praised us already after we started, after a short time, even with the few things we had, that we changed the whole thing, cleaning up, and so on. The personnel didn't like us very much in the beginning when the two of us, Brigitte and myself, were there, because they were not used to do things the way it should be. They were laypeople, didn't know any better.

Then we needed more beds, we had more patients. We bought another house, the hospital consisted of house one and house two later on. We couldn't do enough for the people. We started out with 35 beds. After the war we were supported by the American Joint, and by the time I left, it was a real hospital with 175 beds, with all the medication, trained people, everything you need in a good hospital. But during the war years, we didn't have anything.

I got my food in the hospital, and I brought it home, so that my husband could eat, too. So we didn't have to go to the Kitchen Fund, yeah. We didn't want to depend on them if we didn't have to. We didn't want to take somebody else's away. You know, we could manage that. My husband was sick once, but of course he was my husband, so he was on the private floor, he was in a room with several others, so he didn't mind. We didn't have to pay.

In the ghetto, one day he came home and he said, "I saw a picture in that little store." You know there were stores, they bought and sold things, all kinds. "And I'm sure there is something original underneath." I think he bought it for 12 dollars, and sure enough there was a Goya underneath that was just painted over. He knew what to do with it. He knew art.

In Shanghai, he lectured in art. But you know he was so modest. One night, he gave a lecture and had an exhibition in one of the school. A cousin of ours lived in the same hut we lived, and we were very close. And he said to me, "Do you know what? Willy is giving a lecture tonight. He is making an exhibition." So we didn't say anything to him. We surprised him. We were sitting there in the classroom, you know, and he came in, he looked at me and smiled. [laughs]

We had always had a big social life during the war. We had wonderful friends, and circumstances kept us even closer together. With all the troubles and all the worries, we had regular concerts in the ghetto, we had a theater, we had opera, we had our synagogue, we had everything. Not to eat and not to dress, but we kept up our spirits, you know, like the Jewish humor, but it was very, very hard, it really was, I tell you.

It was terrible in Shanghai, the Yeckes and the Austrians.[12] I never knew it before, I never experienced it before. They were like enemies at times. I don't know why, I mean, I personally had no experience. Some of the people, they envied each other, because one was a little better off than the next one.

Lisbeth Loewenberg tells of the various reactions she saw among the central European refugees, from her husband's nighttime terrors, to the despair of those in the Heime, to the determination of some to make the best of their time in Shanghai. She and her husband, Bruno, ran a lending library that supplied books to people like Gérard Kohbieter and Ruth Sumner.

Then came the Proclamation. We weren't married then yet, and I moved with my mother into what was called a special club for people who were in one way or another connected with Czechoslovakia. Because my father was born in Czechoslovakia, that's why my mother and I could move in there. You know, any place that had regular toilets and showers was a luxury. Because in those lanes, all those places had no toilets, but pots that you put out in the evening.

Bruno moved somewhere else, and he opened a lending library on Ward Road. Not right opposite the jail, but three blocks further up. It was an old mandarin house. There was a narrow entrance that you went in, and then there was the first courtyard, and then there was the second entrance for the second courtyard. There was a big room on this side and a big room on this side. And there was a huge hallway, and that's where the library was. He brought the books from Seymour Road. He made a partition at the end of it and he lived behind that. There were lots of other rooms, and a second and a third floor on top. Every room was another family.

Then Bruno and I got married. I had to get a special permission to change my name from Mr. Ghoya. Epstein was my maiden name, from Epstein to Loewenberg, on account of marriage. That's funny, isn't it, when you stop to think of it?

We got married in a civil ceremony, and the way civil ceremonies in Shanghai at this time were, a lawyer marries you, and it has to be in an open place, in a restaurant with the doors open, so that it's a public event. There is nothing to hide, the whole world can be your witness. So that's how we got married, on Chusan Road, in one of the restaurants. Chusan Road is where the life of the District was. The food was good. We had a beautiful Chinese marriage certificate with all kinds of birds, flowers, and everything is a symbol for something, for health, good luck, money.

When we first got married, he screamed in the night, and it was always when he was dreaming of the concentration camp. And actually had this paranoia all the time till we got to the United States. He couldn't believe that a policeman comes and asks you, "How are you?" That you don't have to be afraid of the policeman. But the United States cured him of all that.

We rented the one room on the right side of the courtyard. It was large, there were also showers and toilets in back. We had even running water, a sink in the room. Though we did not have any refrigerators, we were very lucky, we had an icebox. Nobody had a refrigerator.

Then we opened branches of the library in some other places, and everything was going well, I mean, businesswise and everything. You see, there was only so much of all supplies left in Shanghai. Shanghai was completely closed off during the war. No new supplies came in, and people had very little money. There was very little entertainment, and what could people do? People did read everything that they could get their fingers on.

Our standard of living was, for the time during the war, a little higher than the average. I mean, there were many people who worked on the black market, and they made much more money. We weren't rich at all, but we were better off than most.

The library was a place where one could get together, and there were lectures on art, architecture, literature. I remember there was one guy who had worked for the Bauhaus, so he knew about things like that, and some other artists were there, they talked about art. There were some people who had been journalists in Prague, the editors of the *Praguer Tagblatt,* and they talked history and politics, so that young people could get some idea of those things. The schools, of course, were the bare minimum.

Bruno had to go out of the District to buy books. He could buy better books in the International Settlement and the French Concession, because there was really no supply inside, so he always had to get a passport to get out of the District. Many people brought books with them from Germany, strangely enough. And he bought books from those people who had brought their libraries. English books he bought from Chinese booksellers in the city. The Chinese reprinted and pirated books, so you could get all the recent books in the pirated editions. They didn't last very long, but they were good enough.

Every time he had to go to Ghoya, because that passport had to be renewed every month, he was in a complete state of nervous collapse. Ghoya never did anything to him, because he was short. Ghoya made tall men kneel in front of him and things like that. Women never had any problem.

Bruno was a more conscious Jew than any Jew, and more fervent Jew than any Jew I have ever known. But he wasn't religious in the sense of going to the synagogue. He told me that even as a boy on Yom Kippur, he went into the woods and not into the synagogue, so we had no connection with the synagogue in that sense. We were not religious at all. My mother fasted on Yom Kippur and went to Kol Nidrei.

All the time during the war, there were always rumors going around. "It can't last, this is only temporary." You know many people never really started out on anything. Some people got into the camps, that were meant only as a place where people could stay till they got out on their own. But these people saw it, well, this is only temporary, the war will be over any day, and they never even tried to do anything. And they stayed and stayed, but it was only a small minority. The majority went out and did something, whatever they could do, I mean, tailors, grocery stores, electricians, bicycles, whatever.

When we had to move into the Designated Area, which was a bombed out, burnt out place, you wouldn't believe in how short a time this turned into a thriving little self-contained community. Because the majority of people did have guts and enterprise and did something about it, remodeled the houses and opened little shops and restaurants and bars.

You have no idea of what was going on, the poverty and the beggars and people dying in the street in winter. There was absolutely no social consciousness, no social conscience, in the old regime. Nobody took care of anything or anybody. The beggars in the streets, the children, there were no orphanages, nothing for anybody. The only institution that I saw that did anything was in the entrance of our lane in Weihaiwei Road in the International Settlement, the Salvation Army had a soup kitchen there. You should have seen the lines of people standing there every day at noon to get one bowl of thin rice soup. Ever since that, I have had a soft spot in my heart for the Salvation Army. You know, in the *Threepenny Opera*, they tried to show the beggars, how they make them up. Those are elegant gents in comparison to what Chinese beggars looked like at the time, with open sores and open wounds. And nobody did anything.

In that house there was a narrow entrance that you went in, and then there was the first courtyard. At the narrow entrance, a band of young Chinese beggars were living. Children, orphans, which nobody took care of. They lived in that house entrance. All the other people started to kick them. One winter my husband gave them an old overcoat that they could use as a blanket. From that day on, they were like his slaves. He used them when he had to transfer books from one place to another and gave them something, a little money, and they did everything for him, because he had given them that overcoat.

You know, somebody in the house where we lived was the proud possessor of a record player. We had records, and we bought records, and he bought records. Once a week we had a musical evening, and people came and listened to records. We served coffee and cake. Now that was the epitome of luxury. To come together an evening with coffee and cake and listen to classical recorded music. You can be very happy just doing that. You don't have to buy opera tickets for 50 dollars. That's what it taught me. It taught me that if you have things, it's very good, but you always have to know that you can also do without.

Ruth Sumner *describes the social gulf that developed between those who could afford their own room and those with no income, who lived in the* Heime. *She is candid about the traditional sexual customs of teenage refugees.*

When they put us in the ghetto, all sources of income stopped. Everybody had to move into Hongkou, we happened to be in there, so we didn't have to move. My father rented all the rooms out, including the bathroom. We had eight people living in one house with one bathroom. My aunt and her son, Gerry Schaie, and his wife, they lived downstairs in our living room, and they were a family. My cousin spoke English before he came to Shanghai, he spoke several languages. He worked for the Municipal Police, then later on he was the detective, he was off the street. He worked for the police department to the very end.

My bedroom was next to the other bedroom, we just had kept two rooms. We had all those people. I remember I cleaned, Papa cleaned. He sold kerosene, and then he sold things like on a flea market we had on the street. He was always making money. But at that time, to make a living, we rented all those rooms out. And things got worse as the years got worse.

My dad was a loner, he was not social. He was a very unusual man, very temperamental, he had a violent temper. He never could hold friends. He used to say people like him only for his money and what they can get out of him. I never knew my family and my relatives because of that, because he was the rich one. Money, money, money, money, money was very important in his life.

My dad always had money. But that was his money. In my diary I'm complaining, he made me pay my own doctor bills. I was about 16. Because we used to eat junk from the road stands and then get diarrhea, dysentery.

Tante Erna, she was a good cook, I wanted her to cook some kind of pudding for my birthday. To buy a can of cream was a major purchase, any kind of canned goods was hard to come by. So I bought it from my dad, I mean, he wouldn't donate it, I had to buy it. Then I got sick and couldn't eat it, I probably had diarrhea, because I ate some of the junk. And he ate it all, and he didn't give me my money back.

At four o' clock, there's coffee time, this is European, I don't know if you're familiar with that. You have a cup of coffee, a piece of cake, because you eat a late supper, a sandwich for supper, and the big noon meal. Downstairs they used to go out and buy those little mocha cups, little cups of coffee and cake, and brought it in. They didn't have the money to buy extra for me, so they kind of sneaked it, and I knew they were doing it, and I felt left out. But I was also mature enough at the age of 16 or whenever to realize that they couldn't do anything else. There wasn't enough to share with me, and they didn't want to share, I didn't belong.

I did not have a family. There was no loving relationship. My friends were my family. I lived at home, and I obeyed the rules of the home, but I made my own living.

I was very independent as a teenager. I stood on my own two feet from the time I was 14. As a matter of fact, my father tried to talk me into doing something with him, and I wouldn't do it. He wanted me to make baby clothes, they sold real well, and at that time I didn't want the responsibility. At one time I worked for Kitty's Paradise, they sold children's clothing, as sort of assistant.

But I'm artistic, and my dream in those days was to become a fashion designer. And I did, I learned, I took classes. I've got a talent for clothing, merchandising. I made my living teaching fashion designing and selling my designs, when I was 16, 17 in Shanghai. Yes. Because there was nothing available. And I was pretty good at it.

Go out, in the mornings I sold my designs. Tailor shops. That's what I had my pass for. Yes siree, you had to stand in line, and it was sometimes for two, three days to get that little badge. And I then taught at the SJYA school, the new one they built. Mrs. Hartwich was the principal. She hired me then in the afternoon to teach kids a couple of years younger than I was fashion designing. I got a free meal out of that.

In the evening we used the buildings, the clubrooms, for fun. We had one of the boys play the piano and we danced all night. I mean, it was very simple, we made our own parties. We had fun as kids. Then when we grew out of it and we got a little older, the younger generation took over. I wish my grandchildren would have that innocent fun that we had when we were growing up.

I remember, God, my aunt and my dad, they would read to each other. My room was right off their bedroom after we rented the house out. They knew I was in the other room listening in. They came to a spicy story and they quit. [laughs] They figured that was no good for my ears. [laughs]

A hunchback little man and his young wife had opened up a library.[13] He must have loved books and brought a lot of books with him, and then he bought some more books, and he started a lending library, only you paid, that's how he made his money. Everybody went and checked out books. And I remember Eva and I going down there and going through the stacks of books he had in there and trying to find that book, [laughs] that we thought had such a spicy story. I mean, that was our excitement. You know, we were very naive.

Eva, I met her in school, and Inge, from the very beginning we were friends, and we stayed friends, and we're still friends.[14] Eva's father had a little export and import business. He had a little office. And they had a nice place. There were one, two, three families living in that one house. They shared the kitchen, each one had one or two rooms. That was quite common.

Inge's parents had a little grocery store. I mean, you bought a quarter pound or two slices of something and it's very precious. We had parties in their closed grocery store. It was a little teeny, dinky thing, but they had a little counter. It wasn't a big space, was about the size of this living room, not even my dining room. That was a good place to dance. Yes, we had parties. We had fun. We had costume parties, we wrote plays, we listened to music, we fell in love and out of love, typical teenage stuff. We were kids. But we always had a good time. My memories are not bad. They're good. They're very positive.

We kept busy pretty much. I'd go to my girlfriend's house, and I crawled into the bed at night, if it was cold, and we'd sit there talking. If I didn't go to my girlfriend's house, she was at my house. I mean, what did we do for fun? Our entertainment was walking for miles. She'd pick me up, and we'd walk around town as far as we could. Then they had all kinds of sports. And we had the club, and we danced and we kept busy. Instead of TV, I was in bed with a book. Every night we read.

In that little ghetto in Hongkou, my friends were all Jewish. Most of my friends did not live in the *Heime*. People lived all those years in those places. There were some that had children my age. We did not associate much with them. It just so happened that's the friends I made. The majority of the friends that I had, had little houses. I came from an upper-middle class, and I got to Shanghai, and we still went around with the same kind of people. That's why I guess we did not associate with the kids in the *Heime*. Does that make sense to you?

But there were thousands that depended on American money. I worried about it, about the people that were absolutely destitute. It was important to me, but that did not keep me from having a good time. Because I was young and carefree and not burdened down. I'm sure that the generation ahead of me that had children to worry about, they probably were more concerned. I was having fun. I haven't any regrets.

In our group, none of the girls were sexually active. We were 17, 18. I mean, it isn't like today, there was no sex involved with none of us. I can guarantee you that. That was just something you didn't do. It wasn't as free a society. Why didn't we do it? Because we were raised with a standard of morality, a girl just does not go all the way unless she is completely committed. And this is very interesting in my diary, that boy I had, he wouldn't commit himself, and I wouldn't go any further because he wouldn't commit himself, so we were at a standstill, that was a very healthy one.

The good girls played around a little bit. They kissed and touched a little bit, but that was it. I mean, we had no opportunities, there was no parked cars or nothing. We had parties in the boys' houses, but it was always a group situation. And the only time you were alone with a boy when he walked you home, and you stood in the hallway of your house or at the door frame, that's the only privacy we had. Because it was always groups, and that's a good protection. Boys would try to persuade girls, but girls wouldn't get involved, they'd say "No." And that's the way it was. Boys had respect for us.

In my days it was the bad girls went all the way. There was always a few, but they were well marked. They were known as loose livers. You didn't associate with kids that were, that was unusual, you know. There were some girls, I know the names, but I'm not going to say.

My father and my aunt didn't talk to me about that. We talked about it, usually young people that are not sexually active do nothing but talk. When they're doing it, they don't need to talk about it anymore. So we talked a lot.

When my daughter was growing up, it was still the majority of the girls were decent. She's in her forties now. Now it's the other way around, the girl that keeps pure, they're marked in the other direction, they call them a prude. You know, the decent ones are in the minority. I mean, in this day and time, you find junior high school kids being sexually active. Because this is the accepted way of living now. But the majority of my friends, it's just what was expected of us, and that's what we did. I wish society would go back to this, because it's much healthier. For women it's a lot of problems. You wouldn't have all these babies and abortions, etc. And I liked it.

We were very starved for some of the proteins. But it never bothered me, because everybody else was in the same boat. The main meal was eaten at noon. We used to laugh, because everybody knew what they had for lunch. For supper you had a slice of bread and some tea. Cooking on those little old flower pot things, those charcoal burners. We bought hot water. We never had any milk. Soya bean yogurt stuff was what we ate. I remember eating lard, you know, baking grease, fried out on bread. It's delicious. It was nourishing. In my diary, I'm putting down how prices went up, you know, exchange rates and how important to know all of that. I wouldn't have remembered, had I not had it in my diary.

And then during the last years, we went to the *Heime* for free food. My aunt always compensated, she added to it. We were never completely dependent on it. That's one of the ways I made my money. I went and got our food and some other people's food and my cousin's food and his wife's food, and I got so much. I remember going with pots all the way, carrying it back, to bring it home, yes.

We were on our own independently. Paid our own bills. We never depended, except for that one noon meal, on any other handouts. And that we did only towards the end, you know. But you could barely survive on that one meal a day.

Times were hard, yes, but we survived. I'm sure had I been the adult I'm now, I would have worried about certain situations or things. But at that time I was having a good time, caring about boyfriends, and doing the things that young people enjoy doing.

Melitta Colland and her mother put together funds she had earned before 1943, remittances from her brother in Panama, and, after she was married, her husband's earnings as a physician. That enabled her to purchase occasional luxuries, such as canned peaches, when she was pregnant.

After Pearl Harbor, Paul and Stella had to move to Hongkou. We had to move almost immediately. Mother and I were able to save a little money in that business. I remember that Mother and I went looking, and we saw that little Chinese house that looked kind of halfway decent, in an area that was fairly clean. We decided to buy that little house. We still could afford a houseboy, who was cleaning in the house and who was cooking for us a little bit. And that was it. [laughs] We made it liveable for Western living.

We couldn't work there. We lived on what we had. In other words, we used up our reserve. And Henry in Panama, in the meantime, did very well for himself. And he pretty regularly sent us money, which was very helpful. He sent me packages from Panama, or rather, they came from New York. He ordered them through a friend who came to New York, to send nylon stockings from Woolworths, which I sold for a lot of money. In those days nylon stockings in Shanghai were very, very highly regarded, because nobody had them yet. So I made a little money on that.

I continued a little bit afterwards to earn money. Mrs. Glimpf and a few other ladies. One lady was a French lady who was married to a Chinese. She was a very, very private lady. But then one day something must have happened at her home, because she came in for a fitting. And she said, "Melitta, just make sure of one thing. Don't ever marry a Chinese." I said, "Why not? You have two lovely children, they're beautiful children, and I thought that you're happily married." She said, "A Chinese will always be a Chinese. He met me in Paris. He was a perfect gentleman. He studied medicine there. He was just like any gentleman I would have known in Paris. But as soon as they come to their own country, they might even have the spittoon right next to their dining table." [laughs] That's how she expressed how unhappy she was.

What would a day be like? We would get dressed, we would go walking, promenading. [laughs] What could we do? I didn't have much money for going shopping for food. Grocery shopping primarily and meeting friends somewhere for a cup of coffee, and talking, and really not too much. It wasn't very exciting, [laughs] the life. We went a lot to the movies. We went a lot to philharmonic concerts. The Shanghai Philharmonic was a very good orchestra. A little guy by the name of Pacci was the conductor, an Italian.

And there we lived until I met my husband. He still had his position as a doctor for the Swedish legation. He studied in Berlin. And in '33 he was thrown out of his job at the clinic because he was a Jew. Went to Rome, made a state board for the Roman license. From '33, I think, to '39 he lived in Sardinia and worked there until he had to leave again in '39, and went to China.

We befriended a couple of sisters, which were perhaps in my age group, who introduced me to a very nice Hungarian refugee who wanted very much to marry me. And I knew a young man from Finland who also wanted to marry me. I had told my husband about it when I met him. I said, "I don't know. There are two perfectly fine, nice guys, who want to marry me, but I don't know which one to choose really, or if any of them." He asked me to arrange for dinners. He wanted to meet them, each one of them. And after he had met them, he came and told me, "I have your solution for you." We were married 1944.

He was allowed to see his patients, but he went on bicycle and then had to be back at a certain hour, I think it was 8 o' clock in the evening or something like that. If there was any need for him to come at night, then he had to call a colleague who was within the area where they lived, because he could not go out. It was no fun. [laughs]

We didn't [laughs] have too much luxury. I remember when I was pregnant, much later, and I was so, so longing for peaches, canned peaches, and they cost an arm and a leg. [laughs] I bought them. Felt very guilty about it, spending that money, but I wanted them so badly. [laughs]

Ralph Hirsch's family managed to get by without taking the free meals served at the Heime. *That put them in the upper ranks of the refugee community. Still they did not have enough to eat.*

My father tried to find work in his field of economic consultant, tax advice, and so on, but there wasn't much market for that. He got a job with the Joint Distribution Committee administering one of the relief programs. He also did some other work on the side, whatever he could pick up, sort of accounting things and various financial advisory work. And he supplemented that in a way that, I think, was foreign to his nature, but very many people were forced to do it, just by going out in the street and selling some of the more valuable things that we had brought along from Germany.

My mother, who had worked at home since probably shortly before I was born, went back to her profession that she had trained for, as a hat designer and milliner. She opened a small shop where she, in an overly optimistic mood, made elegant hats for the ladies of Hongkou. But the ladies of Hongkou didn't have any money to buy elegant hats. A few did, you know, sometimes for special occasions. But it was not a business that had a future, and that became more and more clear as time went on, particularly when the Designated Area was set up in very early 1943 and living conditions became more and more miserable. So nobody really thought of wearing fine hats or dressing up generally, except for very, very few special occasions.

But my mother then retreaded and learned to make candy. She gathered from all of her friends their best recipes for candies, pralines, and so on, and tested those out, and in the same premises she opened up a candy shop. Where the hats didn't sell, the candy sold very well. But the problem was, it was very hard to get decent ingredients. I remember that was great fun for us kids to be in the candy shop and to help out with the making of the candy, except that, of course, we had to be watched because we would snack on the ingredients from time to time. It was made clear to us that that was not acceptable.

In that way they managed to get enough so that they never had to take any of the charitable food. Although food was scarce, we never actually starved. We got pretty thin. I remember it was an occasion when we managed to get half an ounce of butter, that was a big deal. Most of the time it was rather spartan fare that we subsisted on. At the school, we got one meal a day, usually some sort of gruel, I grew to hate the stuff, but it was better than nothing. And so we kind of muddled our way through.

We tried to follow the progress of the war as best we could, with what was seeped through the Japanese censorship. There was a rumor every two hours, a new rumor. The rumors were called *Bonkes*.[15] There were new *Bonkes* every day about what was happening in Europe and what the Americans were doing, what the Japanese were up to, what the latest plans were to further restrict the refugees in Hongkou, whether the Germans would succeed in setting up a concentration camp in Shanghai, which they had tried to do. And probably the telling and retelling of *Bonkes* was the major indoor sport in Shanghai.

CHAPTER 5

The End of the War

By 1944, the tides of war had shifted in Europe and Asia. The Nazi armies were in full retreat on both eastern and western fronts. So were the Japanese forces in the Pacific: by the end of 1944, the Americans had reached the Philippines and were bombing Japanese positions in southern China.

The long-awaited end of the war in Europe in May 1945 brought little relief to refugee families in Asia. More important was Soviet newsreel footage from newly liberated Auschwitz. Newspapers all over the world now printed incredible stories of gas chambers and crematoria, piles of dead bodies, and the murder of millions. Shanghai Jews had no idea that those relatives who had said good-bye at train stations were nearly all dead. Auschwitz had been invented to kill them.

The Pacific War still dragged on, but the occasional appearance of American planes over Shanghai was greeted with cheers. The Japanese were falling back toward their islands. By summer 1945, air raids over Shanghai were more frequent, bringing both danger and hopes of an end to war.

Every refugee wants to talk about July 17, 1945, when American planes accidentally dropped bombs on refugee houses run by the Russian Jewish relief organization in the Designated Area. The death of about 30 refugees was a unique tragedy during the years of Shanghai exile. Jewish doctors came to the aid of the refugees and the hundreds of wounded Chinese. Like the insistent focus on Ghoya as the symbol of repressive Japanese domination, stories about the bombing show where the balance of life and death lay for Shanghai Jews. Multiple deaths were uncommon, so that moment sticks in refugee memory and must be told.

American planes dropped atomic bombs on Hiroshima on August 6 and on Nagasaki on August 9. A rumor that the war was over brought refugees into the Hongkou streets to celebrate, but the Japanese quickly dispersed them. They surrendered officially on August 15 and silently disappeared from Hongkou. The ghetto barriers were gone, and suddenly there was more food.

The end of the war brought immense relief, but this joy was mixed with pain. The refugees could look forward to a better life. But World War II and the Nazis had devastated Jewish families all over the world. Family suddenly meant something much smaller and more scattered. It was not uncommon to have relatives on three continents, so distant that communication was completely disrupted. The refugee families were now only remnants, saved by their decision to cross the world to Shanghai. For many, the final threads that connected them to Europe had been cut. They had survived, but were now alone.

Ernest Culman's home was hit by American bombs in July 1945. Fear of death from the skies spread through the whole community. The Kadoorie School now added a new role as barracks and bomb shelter.

After the war in Europe was over, the United States concentrated more on Japan and the Far East. We had never heard of Okinawa or Iwo Jima before, but these Koreans we worked with showed us on a map where it was, and we realized how close to Shanghai American troops are coming. After Okinawa fell, that's when the planes started to fly over Shanghai. I remember the first time seeing these gigantic planes, they were probably B-29s or something like that, flying in formation over the city, so high up that the Japanese anti-aircraft couldn't touch them. Probably they were taking photographs, whatever. And then we often heard bombs falling in the outskirts, never paid any attention to it until it hit us.

In July of 1945, I was home with a cold, virus or what, you know, nothing serious, didn't go to work. The air raids went off, but we never paid attention to the air raids, because usually the American bombers bombed the city outside, the naval facilities, the airport. We didn't have any cellars either, because Shanghai is basically at sea level, and you can't dig a cellar in there. All of a sudden a terrible noise, I look up and I see the ceiling falling down on me. Our house got hit, where there were several hundred refugees living in. And I was actually in my brother's bed with that bookshelf on top.

I put my head down and my hands over my head, tucked in my feet, and the bookshelf fell on top of me, with one leg above my head, and all the ceiling stuff fell on top of me. But I was really not hurt. My parents were just outside the door to that room. That part held because it had a archway, and at first my mother couldn't open the door because of the air pressure. Finally she was able to open the door and yell for me. They tell

Photo 7   SACRA building after July 17, 1945, bombing

me I didn't answer right away and they thought I was dead. But I was obviously alive, and we were safe. There was about 13, 14 people killed in that building that day, and many more all around us.

My father was called immediately to help people. My mother and I went out to the back, sort of a backyard, I guess you would call it, and I still had a temperature from whatever illness I had.

My brother was at work. At work we frequently went up on the rooftop when the American planes were bombing, watching them. And he saw that, in the direction of where we lived, fires were going. So he decided to come home, and the closer he came to home, the more devastated things were. He asked people, "What about the SACRA?" People told him, "Oh, everybody's dead in the SACRA, it got hit." Not until he was a block and a half away did he meet someone who knew that we were alive. So he suffered more coming home than we who stayed there and knew we were alive when it happened.

The building actually didn't collapse in its totality. There were certain areas where the bombs fell in, but they were not such big bombs that they would destroy everything. The decision was made to bring all of those who were homeless into the school. My mother again didn't want to go. So the first night we stayed in this bombed out building. You could see the skies through the ceiling. During the night somebody yelled, there's a fire breaking out over here, over there, so the next morning my father says,

"We're going to the school." Took our mattresses on our backs and went to the school. Well, we were about 20, 30 people in a room, man, woman, child, one mattress right next to the other. We dressed and undressed under the covers. We had no showers there really, we went once a week to a *Heim*, they had showers that we could use.

I remember at the school after the bombardment, they would bring in these wagons with big kettles of stew. It was not too tasty, but it kept us going. Neither my brother nor I wanted to go back to work, scared as everything. I mean, the war in Europe was over, and now it was hitting us in the Far East.

We were living in the school. And a thunderstorm came up suddenly. I had looked out and seen the black clouds. A thunderbolt struck, and I heard it and I dived under the bed. Of course, everybody started laughing, including me, but the fear was so great. When the dive-bombers bombed, it sounded like they were always overhead. No matter where in the city they were actually bombing, you heard that sound, and when you heard the bomb dropping, you looked up to see if it hit your house or not. It seemed like they came over every day. And I was so scared. As a matter of fact, other than that July 17th, the ghetto area was not hit again. But the fear stuck with us. It was only a month before the war was over.

When we heard about the atomic bomb, of course, nobody knew what it really is, it didn't affect us. But on the night of the 10th of August, which happened to be my mother's birthday, the principal came in, turned the lights on, which was unheard of because of blackout, and told everybody she had just heard through Kadoorie that the war is over. And everybody just became jubilant. Somebody started playing the piano, my father started leading a conga line through the school building.

The next morning the Japanese still showed their authority, they arrested some of the people who had torn down the signs of the ghetto, you know, do not go past there. But then an American plane dropped leaflets which said that surrender will be on the 14th of August and the Allies will be coming in a couple weeks after that.

We were so elated, we all just were so grateful that it was finally over. We were still afraid what would happen when the Japanese move out before the Allies move in, I mean, anarchy would exist. But as it turned out, it was done very well. The American troops sent a liaison in, then the Chinese troops came with them, and on September 3rd or 4th the whole Seventh Fleet steamed into Shanghai harbor, about 700 ships, British, American, other Allies. And then the sailors went wild in the city. I was walking along the street and some sailor comes up to me, "Hey buddy, you got a sister?"

Ralph Hirsch's family also feared the worst when the bombs hit.

There were a number of very big events that are still clear in my memory, that sort of broke the everyday rhythm. I think the biggest one was the air raid in July. It was very common for the planes to come over. Although we often heard gunfire or bombs being dropped in the distance, it became so routine that people mostly didn't even take shelter anymore. But on this occasion, the bombs were dropped on the heavily populated area, in fact, Tongshan Road was hit by several fairly large bombs. A number of houses were destroyed, others were heavily damaged. Several dozen of the refugees were killed and many Chinese. We knew a number of those who were killed, and in particular the mother of one of my classmates was killed.

Normally, all of us would've been on our way home from school at about that time. This particular day, I got caught up in something, I don't remember what exactly, maybe one of the club activities at school, although it was not part of the regular education program. All of a sudden, we heard the planes as we did every other day, then came great bursts of clouds and concussion, and we saw the smoke rising just a block or two away. So we dove under the desks and stayed there for a few minutes. There were one or two teachers still in the school that came around and checked to see whether anyone was hurt. To my recollection, there were only a few window panes broken in the school, but nobody was hurt. But the area along which my brother and I normally would have walked was devastated. It was Tongshan Road, that was the normal route that we took, and my mother, of course, didn't know where we were. She knew only that I hadn't arrived at the normal hour, and so she raced up Tongshan Road looking at all the bodies to see if she could find me. We met, I think, somewhere out near the school gate. Yeah.

Herbert and Ilse Greening tell about living under bombardment, desperate for news of the wider war, and about helping their Chinese neighbors.

Ilse Greening: In the summer the bombing started. During the bombing, I commuted by bicycle to the bank for a while. One day I was out with my bicycle, and there was an alarm. These Japanese trucks were racing up and down, and I didn't want to be killed by a Japanese truck. I moved from the street to the sidewalk. And one of the soldiers said I was not allowed to. I acted against the law, and they said that I had to get to the police station. I met a friend, and he said to me in German, "Have you tried to bribe the guy?" I said, "No," being a good German, did not occur to me. So this friend offered the policeman money on our way to the police station, but the policeman said it was too late, because we were already in view of the police station.

It was very dangerous in the police station, because the cells were lice-infected, and people died from typhus after they had been in those cells. I was terribly afraid. And this friend who had seen me going to the police station alerted Herbert and also some of the European policemen who were in charge, and they managed to get me out. But it was very scary. Later on I walked and I took the bus.

We were told in the Japanese bank that if there was an air alarm, we would have to go into the safe down below. The idea of maybe dying in a safe like that without any air, without any escape, that really did not appeal to me. So in the middle of summer when there was heavy bombing, I walked home from the Bund to Hongkou. By the time I got home, I was absolutely hysterical, and I never went back.

When they had the real big bomb in July, there were quite a number of casualties. We were on Kungping Road, and the main bombing was about two blocks up. Herbert opened a first aid station in our lane, and I helped, and quite a number of other women helped. We had prepared by rolling bandages, and we also had had a first aid class for this eventuality, so we were prepared for that. There were hardly any Europeans, most of our patients were Chinese, shrapnel wounds. That was much appreciated, a lot.

Herbert Greening: After the bombing, yeah, we set it up in our courtyard. I removed shrapnel without anesthesia and bandaged them up and sent them to the central station. And the central station was Dr. Didner.[1]

Ilse Greening: Word must have gotten around because they kept on coming, the Chinese. And they were very grateful, very appreciative. Until the Japanese indoctrinated them, the Chinese were very friendly, and we had a nice life with them. Unfortunately they were poisoned by the Japanese, who were against all foreigners.

Herbert Greening: We only had the Japanese radio station, German radio station, and a Russian radio station. Only the Russian radio station told us the truth, they gave us the battles, who lost, who won, and that was the reason that I started to learn Russian. I wanted to listen to the Russian radio station. Some other guys and I had Russian lessons. I was very good in memorizing the alphabet, I could write Russian script, and we learned some of the vocabulary, but I didn't have it for long.

Ilse Greening: Oh yes, we had a radio. So I said, "Why do you always have to put on this station?" And he says, "I have to know when the war is going to be over." That's why he was listening to the Russian, which you couldn't understand anyway. So I said, "When the war is over, people are going to shout it in the streets, we won't have to listen to any radio," and that's what happened. We were walking along the street, and a man we knew, he was standing in front of his apartment or shop, and he called us in, and he said, "The war is going to be over very soon." He told us about the bomb. We didn't know that, he told us about Hiroshima.

*For **Doris Grey**, and nearly everybody else, the tragedy of the bombing and the celebrations at the end of the war a month later are the most significant memories.*

One day, we were sitting outside and having lunch and all of a sudden, at first we didn't know what it was, they bombed just our District. People in the street, they were torn completely, couldn't find them, by the bombs. They brought the people in, 37 people among our refugees died. And I was worried, what happened to my husband. All of a sudden, he came with a bundle, you know, and he had all our papers. Our lane was completely down. Everything was gone.

They brought people, some of them were dead right away. But most of them we couldn't save, because they were hurt so badly. And some of them were paralyzed from the waist down, you know. They brought some Chinese victims, too.

After the bombing, you went in the streets with the mess like that. You couldn't stand the smell, it took them days to take care of all the dead bodies, it was terrible.

One night, my husband's cousins came home and said, "What? You are all sleeping? The war is over." So my husband said, "If that is true, I never make any special celebration, but this year I will celebrate my first day." And sure enough, as soon as the war was over, we went out of the ghetto and bought Chinese rice wine. My husband surprised us all. He engaged an accordion player, a Viennese, we had a big party. We put two rooms together. One of the inhabitants of our house was a tailor, so they had a long table, you know, where he did the patterns, cut the material, so we put the top of the table over two stands and the lady who was in charge of the kitchen of the hospital, she fixed special sandwiches. Of course I paid for that. Then my husband made a nice drink, *ein Bolle mit dem Reiswein mit Erdbeeren* [a bowl with rice wine and strawberries]. As soon as we had not even one glass, we were all drunk and in seventh heaven. He even ordered a photographer to take pictures, and you could see that ruined lane after the bombing. But we lived, that was the main thing, and young we were, too.

Then, afterwards, of course, we went back to the city to visit with friends. People moved back to the city. It was nice, because then we had everything. We got the CARE parcels, and we got parcels from our relatives. But we knew that we will leave soon. We knew that.

Otto Schnepp describes the isolation of European Jews in Shanghai, waiting for events over which they had no control.

We didn't really know what was going on in the Pacific. We did know what was going on in Europe, because there was a Russian radio station that broadcast throughout the war in Shanghai. The Japanese did not interfere with that. There were some people who in the dark of night listened to BBC. It was risky and dangerous, forbidden to do that. So we didn't really know if this was going to go on forever or what. When the planes appeared, and we could see how the Japanese could not reach those planes either by anti-aircraft or by their planes, it was a very reassuring symbol, in spite of the fact that then one felt danger. I was at an age that I felt that I was in no danger whatsoever.

When finally Americans came to bomb us, that's the way I put it at least, I felt a great elation to be bombed. [laughs] Because we felt so isolated there, you see. The tremendous feeling of isolation in the world is a very deep thing, it was feeling you're out of touch, nobody knows. All around you sort of an alien culture, alien things going on. And then being dominated that way, so powerless. All of a sudden there was this connection to the outside world.

Then one day these bombs fell in that District. People became hysterical there. It was a big building that was full of refugees that was particularly hit. I went that night, it was one of the interesting experiences of my life, I went to that place which had been bombed. And, of course, many Chinese were killed there. I saw heaps of bodies there. I myself, you know, have not been in a battlefield, I sought that exposure there. I wanted to see what was happening.

First the rumor of an atomic bomb spread, and then the rumor spread that the war was over. People of the Jewish community, with a lot of stored up anger, came out and chased away the Japanese from the police station, took over the police stations, and then the Japanese came back. I did not participate in that. But then came the time when it was actually over. For me it was like a tremendous liberation, opening. We spent the whole night just celebrating basically. And then, of course, the major effect was that one was free. One great disappointment, just an aside, was to see Chiang Kai-shek's army come in. [laughs] They were just as torn and just as poorly dressed as the soldiers of the puppet government of Wang Ching-wei. So I was free.

Ruth Sumner The night we heard that the war was over, we were up all night. That's the first time in my life I was ever up all night. The war was over, it was my birthday, it was in August.

Eric Reisman was puzzled by what was missing: the Japanese took no revenge on the refugees for their final defeat. Their policy of treating Jews in Shanghai with respect never changed.

When the war ended and we were liberated by the American troops, that was a puzzle to me, suddenly the guy who was the administrator, Ghoya, he vanished, I never knew where he went. I understand some Jewish people got him cornered and gave him a beating, but he just disappeared. And the Japanese vanished, there were no Japanese around, you couldn't see them anymore. Where they went, I don't know. But they sort of cleared the area, and the gates were opened, the barbed wire disappeared.

For **Lisbeth Loewenberg** *the end of the war meant light replacing darkness and the sudden absence of deprivation.*

There was complete blackout. You could use electric light only in certain hours, because the city was practically out of coal and you need coal for electricity. So you could turn the electric light on only, I forgot what hours, from seven to nine or something. There were little oil lamps that we used. That's normal, all cities in the world, if there's war and there could be bombing attacks, had blackouts.

One night, all of a sudden, it was like a rumor spread. The war is over. In the same moment, the reaction was, in the whole city, in the whole street where we lived, in the whole Ward Road, everybody turned on the lights and took down the blackout and opened the windows. The lights went on. It was like a symbolic show of freedom from the complete darkness of blackout.

Then the next day, it turned out the war was over two days later, but the Japanese tried to punish everybody. They said the stateless refugees had performed just so wonderful during the bombing attack. Which they had, because they opened first aid stands in the street and they helped the Chinese, the Japanese, whoever was injured and everything. That was organized by the refugees. But now, because we all turned on the lights, now we will be punished. That wiped out all the things that we did during the bombing attacks. But that lasted only one day, it was the next day the war was really over and we could turn on the lights, and American soldiers and sailors came in.

It was the Japanese out and the American in, just as one day the English were out and the Japanese were in. All of a sudden was a great economic boom. That was the great influx of business and everything. Like we could afford to buy coffee and sugar.

Gérard Kohbieter When the war was over, you had the town full of Yanks. Wherever you went, there were Yanks. They came from Okinawa. They had spent terrible, terrible months there, trying to push the Japanese off that island and had accumulated pay. They had no way to spend money there, man. They were busy loading the machine guns or whatever. Some of these guys come from small towns where they're not used to having money. They're simple souls, and the money burned a hole in their pocket, so they were spending it really freely, all over the place. Every bar was making money.

War's end brought new life for **Melitta Colland***.*

When Shanghai was bombarded, I happened to visit Paul and Stella where they lived. I was pregnant and hungry always. And the siren went

Photo 8   *A Shanghai family: Melitta Colland, mother Sarah Sommerfreund, and daughter Asherah*

on for an air raid alarm. I went under the dining room table. Stella always laughed, she says, "Soon as the off siren went, Melitta went right back to eating."

Well, it was almost hard for us to believe that the war is over. It's something that takes time to sink in. But of course then everybody was jumping with joy.

By that time I was married. My husband earned a good salary, and Asherah was born. I had to take care of her. In fact we did rent a nice apartment, back in the French quarters. And we had an *amah,* a maid, who took care of her. You never hear their names, other than *"amah."*

Right after the war, I did not have the business anymore, but Frau Glimpf saw me occasionally, and I would still make some things for her myself and bring them to her. She came with a double strand of pearls and said, "Melitta, I want you to have these. They won't let me take too much out, and rather than give them to anybody else, I want you to have them." Those are the pearls that Asherah are wearing.

CHAPTER 6

After the War

The end of the war brought to Shanghai a new occupying force. Beginning in September 1945, thousands of U.S. troops arrived, changing the atmosphere and the economy. In high spirits after their long march to victory, the American military brought Army rations and CARE packages, candy and jobs, and a way of life that seemed to promise freedom and equality. Their spending revived refugee businesses. The U.S. military hired about 1,500 refugees in a wide variety of jobs at high pay.

Soon, more direct relief arrived. The United Nations Relief and Rehabilitation Administration brought immense quantities of basic foodstuffs and clothing. The Joint invested money to improve the Heime *and opened a Jewish Community Center at the Kadoorie School. Sports competitions, Boy Scout troops, and theater and musical productions were revived and expanded.*

But the inflation that had developed at the end of the war worsened from 1945 through 1947 and then skyrocketed in 1948 and 1949. Even more worrisome was the civil war between the Communist Red Army and Chiang Kai-shek's Nationalist government, which broke out once the Japanese were defeated.

Not all refugees believed the Nationalist propaganda stories that the advancing Communists would kill Europeans. But the old Shanghai that had given them refuge was gone. In 1943, the international enclaves had been officially turned back to the Chinese. The former Western elite had fled or spent the war in Japanese internment camps. The privileged colonial lifestyle of the Europeans who had dominated Shanghai was no longer possible. Across the globe, colonial power was under attack.

Any white person in Shanghai could sense the change in the Chinese who surrounded them, as politeness and reserve were frequently replaced by an unfamiliar hostility. The former Chinese elite had to contend with much less subservient workers and peasants, who were encouraged by the advance of the Communist forces. Both Nationalists and Communists desired to regain China for the Chinese.

Life was better, but the refugees, like hundreds of thousands of other Europeans across the globe, were displaced persons. They did not belong in China. While refugee children enjoyed the expanded opportunities for entertainment, their parents thought about the uncertain future.

New American friends brought **Herbert and Ilse Greening** *pajamas, canned peaches, and penicillin.*

Herbert Greening: After the war was over, they thought, it's going to be terrible. The Japanese would be in top position, the American and the Allies wouldn't be here yet, and we would expose to everything they wanted to do with us. We were scared. Nothing of that type happened. It was very quiet.

Ilse Greening: You know, to be left with the Japanese, maybe they were furious about the ending of the war. We were really scared. We were so excited when the Americans came.

Herbert Greening: And thirsty for knowledge about what happened.

Ilse Greening: The soldiers came off the boat, and we were standing there, and one of them said, "I would like to buy a camera, where would I go?" We said, "Well, you know, they take advantage of the Americans here. Why don't we go along with you and try to find an honest dealer?" So, he said, "You people have a German accent, where are you from?" So I said, "Where are you from?" Well, he was from New York. His parents came from Schlüchtern, a town near Frankfurt. I said, "My grandmother came from Schlüchtern also." He knew my family over there. A strange coincidence. And we became friends, we helped him with his camera, but he also took us on board the hospital ship, which was for Herbert most interesting, because we didn't have any penicillin.

Herbert Greening: When the Americans came, there was a hospital ship for American troops, "St. Olaf." He gave me the first bottle of penicillin and sulfadiazine tablets. We had only sulfa products in Shanghai. We didn't have any injectable antibiotics, or antibacterials, and that was the first penicillin I saw.

Ilse Greening: All these friends, they were hungry for family, and we invited them to our place, but food was a problem. I said, "What would you like to eat most?" He wanted potato salad. Potatoes were very scarce, we hardly ever had potatoes. We had sweet potatoes, but not regular potatoes. So we finally got potatoes, but mayonnaise or things like that were out of the question, so my mother made mayonnaise from flour? I don't remember. Anyway, my mother made potato salad, and the other one wanted dill potatoes, I don't know whether we had dill. My mother managed to feed them. I don't know how, but she did.

Herbert Greening: She was a great lady. The best years of my life. She lived with us for 22 years, and I was always right.

Ilse Greening: [laughs] They loved it in our house, because for the first time they had home cooking. But they did bring stuff, you know. He gave us butter, apples, that was very exciting. When I was pregnant, he gave me flannel pajamas, which were in the supplies, which were marvelous for me over the winter. Yeah, they loved to be in our house.

Herbert Greening: I get a call from a bar in Frenchtown. My cousin Helga was a bar girl there. She said, "I have two guys here, and they don't want to drink. One of them are sick." American soldiers from a boat in the harbor. I said, "Well, let them come to my office." I had an office on Hong Kong Road, that's off the Bund. These two guys, and one has a urinary obstruction, secondary to gonorrhea, he couldn't pee. So there's only one thing to do, stick a catheter in and empty the bladder, which I did there, and I gave him sulfa as an injection.

They were soldiers, and they were not allowed to say that they got gonorrhea, because they had to go first for condoms before they went ashore, and they didn't go, so they had sex without condoms. They were very grateful, they paid well, and I had to go out with them. They took me to one of those dance halls, and they gave me ten dance tickets, and I should dance. And they ordered for me a coke and rum, that was *the* drink at that time, coke and rum. But then I said, "I have to go home," so they took a rickshaw for me and drove me Hong Kong Road.

Ilse Greening: Our son was born in December, 1945. So then I stayed home and helped in the office. Answered the phone and things like that. Herbert started working at the British Red Cross, but he will tell about that. And we had money. Not much, but we had quite a nice life, until the Communists came closer and closer.

Herbert Greening: After the end of the war, a friend of mine, a German diplomat for the British Army, came to me and asked me would I want a job with the British Consulate. I got a job taking medical care of one of the internment camps before they were repatriated. And that was not only a nice job, but a nice salary. I even got a uniform. There I stayed until we left Shanghai.

Ilse Greening: All the camps, just like Ash Camp where Herbert worked, they were open, but people had to find a new life. So while they were waiting for shipping or evacuating or whatever, the camps were open. But my people from the bank, the manager and all the other employees, it was hard enough to get things, but we collected cigarettes and stuff, and we sent them for Christmas, etcetera, little things. We didn't have much. For the Jewish holidays, remember, I cooked food, we took a sampan across to bring holiday food.

After the war we took trips down the Huangpu River towards the ocean, I don't know, half an hour? Somebody had a little café there, a Chinese, especially when our son was little, to give him a little treat. And we could walk around. That was a big treat, because for so long we were so confined.

Also before the war, Herbert had a patient outside the city, refugees who had a pig farm. And we used to go out. Then after the war, when the first American ships came in, this man used to buy their waste to feed the pigs. But with the waste, he also got large tins of fruit, like peaches. Once they opened these big containers, they were not allowed to keep them on the boat, and so with the waste, he brought all these tins, and since there was no refrigeration, he distributed among the friends and we really were in heaven.

Lisbeth Loewenberg was impressed by something else that Americans brought: democratic disdain for colonial customs.

There was this horrible thing that these horrible GIs did. You know what they did? They rented rickshaws and told the rickshaw coolie to sit down, and they pulled the rickshaw. And the old former English people, "What are they doing? They are undermining the whole colonial effort." You know, the English used whips when the rickshaw coolies didn't run fast enough. The Chinese might have the idea that maybe they are not extremely inferior to the white foreign devils, if the American GIs did that. Well, they were all young guys, and they thought it was the greatest thing in the world. In other words, they upset everything, the old colonial traditions. And then many people got jobs with the American PXs and so on.

Otto Schnepp experienced the dangerously changed attitudes of Chinese toward foreigners.

After the war there was great animosity on the part of Chinese towards foreigners, deep-seated animosity. That was there, I think, all the time. During the war, there was the Japanese to oppose, so they were the enemies, if you like. But then once they disappeared, there was more animosity towards foreigners.

Once I was stopped by a mob in Shanghai. What happened often was that Chinese women would push a child in front of a foreigner or a bicycle or whatever it was, and then accuse them of hurting their child. That would bring a mob. And I was in such a situation, and the fact that I could speak Chinese made a lot of difference. I was surrounded by a mob of Chinese, who were all very, very hostile. That woman wanted money, I'm sure. But what the mob wanted is difficult to know. Express anger, beat me up, I don't know what. It was useful for me at that point to be able to speak Chinese and to defend myself. I remember that scene very clearly. It was probably pretty scary.

I, together with some others, moved out to St. John's University. I taught, and eventually I taught at the Shanghai Jewish School, for a year or two, until I left. So all that made an enormous difference to me, to what I could afford. I worked at the school part-time, earned money, and it was worth a lot more, and I could buy clothes. Eventually I graduated from the University in 1947.

Photo 9 Otto Schnepp at graduation, 1947, in front of St. John's University dormitory

*For many refugees, like **Eric Reisman**, skilled jobs with the American armed forces catapulted them out of ghetto poverty.*

Everybody pursued their vocation and tried to make a living. I worked in Kiangwan for the U.S. Army in aviation. I was schooled by the U.S. Army, got a 747 rating, which was an aircraft mechanic's rating. The initial flights into Shanghai, the experimental FAA flights, landed in Kiangwan, and I got to know the people from the Northwest Airlines to the point where, when they got their regular flights going, they hired me as a mechanic. I made a decent living, especially since in China life was a lot cheaper than in the United States. With the salary I made, I was able to move into the French Concession and live on Avenue Joffre in a very, very nice area. During the time that I was working in the pharmacy, I got to know quite a few of the Russian Jewish people and associated with them, and I lived there in the French Concession.

Ernest Culman tells of young people's entertainments, centered at the Kadoorie School.

During the war we didn't do much Scouting. Then towards the end of the war, we formed a new Scout troop in Hongkou. We met at night and we didn't do it officially. There was a curfew, you had to be home by a certain time, and frequently we just did it by minutes, I mean, I was scared when you ran home, trying to be home before the curfew started. When the war was over, we became official Scout troop again, went out to some camping sites and things like that.

After the war, we formed a little club called the Tikvah Club, and we met in school, that's where we had our club meetings. That became a fairly close-knit group, late teens basically at that time.

We did it on our own. The school let us have the room. We weren't supposed to have any alcohol in there, but what they didn't know didn't hurt us. We used to bring in vodka and Coke and mix it, put a big sign on the vodka bottle, "water," and you know, we didn't get rowdy. They had some of these little theater shows going on in this school, and they often came in to us to borrow a chair, this or that for their show, for that we were able to get in free to the little cabarets that they made up.

*As **Lotte Schwarz** tells it, life in Shanghai did not improve for everyone.*

War was over in '45, we worked all as waitresses in different restaurants. There was nothing for us to do. I didn't work much at that, because then my daughter was there, and my husband was there. There were some men, they sold materials for making suits, wool and that stuff. And he did

Photo 10 Postwar costume party at Jewish Community Center. Top row, from left to right: Hank Topfer, Horst Schlochauer, Rita Schlosser, Robert Langer, Harry Loew, Inge Berman, Manfred Lichtenstein; middle row: Helga Michaelis, unidentified, Eric Reisman, Eva Mannheim, Alfred Zunterstein (Eva and Alfred married in 1947); kneeling: George Fischer

that for a little while. But then he was so sick, he had two heart attacks, and he couldn't even walk around anymore. He was kind of big man, and he lost all his weight. It was good to lose weight, but not in a way like that, you know. He couldn't do much anymore.

The Americans brought love and marriage to **Ruth Sumner***. But the end of the war also brought the disastrous news of the Holocaust to the Shanghai refugees. When U.S. Army headquarters moved to Nanking in May 1946, her well-paid work in Shanghai, and that of nearly 1,500 other refugees, ended.*

The U.S. Army hired people. I was a sign painter. The man that did all the advertising knew my father from when he had the restaurants, did all the art work for him, and he knew me. So he sat me down and I filled in the "No Smoking" signs, it was a stencil. I was artistic, so that wasn't very much. I made 40 American dollars a month. and that was enormous.

That's were I met Forrest, my husband. He was the sergeant in charge, a young man, how handsome he was. I met him, and I fell in love. They put us on the night shift then. He was in charge, so I didn't work. [laughs]

I signed in, and he and I used to go talk or go somewhere. And we got to know each other.

We met the last of October. His company was shipping back to United States. I guess it was in two or three weeks, he asked me to marry him. In order for him to marry me, he had to reenlist. When I knew Forrest's company was shipping back, I had made up my mind that he was leaving and that I was pick up my life no matter what, you know, never gonna let it bother me. But I didn't have to do that.

We worked the night shift then. I woke my dad up in the middle of the night, said, "I've got myself engaged and I'm going to get married. And I don't care what you say, that's exactly what I am going to do." [laughs] He said, "We'll talk about it tomorrow." And then the next morning, he asked me, "What about this marriage, is it legal? Or are you getting yourself into something illegal?" I said, "Well, he's going to go to see the chaplain, and we'll go find out what it will take for us to get married."

We got married December 23, 1945, in the chaplain's office. Had a reception, and we rented a little apartment. We were still working together.

I was eighteen and a half years old. He's a Christian, we had different backgrounds, nationalities, different religions. I'd had no idea what social background he had. I mean, he lived in Tampa, he could have lived in the slums, you know what I mean. I didn't think that far. I did not know where he came from, who his family was, and I married him and went with him. That's not a chance I would like my daughter to take, as an adult, but it didn't faze me.

He couldn't even communicate with my father. My daddy couldn't speak English, I had to interpret. When we first got married, my husband learned to say, *"Eins, zwei, drei,"* playing cards, because they played cards.

At that time some of the girls were running around, they got engaged to American servicemen, and you know how that goes. He went back with big promises, and that was the end of it, never heard from him since. And of course, my friends didn't tell me that, but they probably thought that, "Well, Ruth is one of them." All of my friends thought that marriage wouldn't last. They didn't say a thing, but when we went to the Concord, a lot of my friends that had been divorced said, "I'd never thought your marriage would last that many years." I'm over 45 years married now.

Right by the waterfront, they had one street that was full of bordellos. I remember, I think we were married, I wanted to go see what that was like. And one night we walked down there, [laughs] just curious little me, you know. Those girls, almost like you see in the movies, you know.

When I left the house, I was just glad my father wasn't living with me. I always honored him, according to what the Bible says, you honor your father and mother, and that's what I did. He was not a bad man. I'm sure he loved me, he didn't know how to show it. But the distance was very welcome. I am sure he didn't have it easy, I'm sure he was in love when he was a child, I'm sorry to say, these things happen. But I was very sure that I made up my mind, even very young, that history would not repeat itself. I feel sorry for anybody that has to live like I did. But I survived, I'm a survivor. I was going to marry the opposite kind of man, which I did, quiet, peaceful, loving, not a yeller and a screamer and a temperamental person. My husband's very quiet.

Then the Army went from Shanghai to Nanking. They shipped all the American servicemen over to Nanking, and I was left behind. Some of the guys that had worked as civilian employees for the Army went with them. I closed my little apartment up, went home to my dad, and then I followed him. My father took me on a train from Shanghai to Nanking. We had a first-class compartment. We got on the train, it was typical, crowded and no place to go. And I was sitting there crying, I didn't know what to do.

I started working as a file clerk, the adjutant general's office. I worked with personnel files keeping them in order. We lived in a hotel room. I was the first Army dependent that even existed [laughs] at that time. And we had a good time. We were making money, saving it, and paid for our first house.

My girlfriend Eva worked for the lab at the Jewish hospital, she was lab technician. And then Pit committed suicide, that was Eva's boyfriend.[1] She was devastated. This young man, a nice looking 22-year-old, took his life. He had survived and gotten out of Germany, and his whole family was left behind, he was living with an uncle. And when World War II was over, he found out. One day they brought him to the hospital, he had taken the bowl of Bayer aspirin and they couldn't save him. We never thought he would, he never said a word. They found that note, that he had just lost all hope and faith in God and humanity. But that has something to do with the personality and the faith of a person and has nothing to do with the situation. I mean, suicidal people commit suicide in the United States. I mean, don't you have friends that have everything and yet they're miserable? Well, we weren't miserable, or I wasn't miserable, and neither were my friends. After Pit died, we got Eva a job in Nanking for the Army.

Every month almost, we had a weekend, we'd take the Army transport, you know those big old things, looking at each other. I didn't realize probably at that time I was pregnant. I must have just gotten pregnant, I got sick on that thing, the bumpy road. There was nothing for me, [laughs] I vomited in Forrest's hat, I never forgot that, and there was all officers [laughs], and he was the only enlisted man, and I must have embarrassed him. [laughs]

We going back and forth from Shanghai to Nanking, about a 30-minute flight, you know. We'd get a TJ and Y, I think that is what they called it, weekends off. Stayed a day or two in Shanghai to see my family and my friends. We had all the advantages, he had a car, we had a weapons carrier for his disposal, you name it, we had it, because he was the supply sergeant. And everybody treated him very nice.

The war was over, you started fresh. Little by little, a lot of the people from Shanghai came to the United States, somebody sponsored them. The Jewish relief fund or whatever, Jews always look after each other, you know, that's one thing you can give them credit for. And I had to wait to go, I had married, you know.

CHAPTER 7

Auf Wiedersehen, Shanghai! But Where Do We Go?

Shanghai had always been a last resort for the refugees. Central European fami-lies, who had come to Shanghai because they had no alternative, now had to decide again where they wanted to go.

Nearly all refugee families wanted to leave Shanghai as soon as possible. Very few had been able to create a life they wanted to continue in China. Remaining in postcolonial China after the war meant learning and adopting Chinese cul-ture; only a handful of European Jews accepted that challenge. Chiang Kai-shek's Nationalist government expressed hostile attitudes toward the Jewish refugee community, and Mao's Communists were an unknown threat. Shanghai Jews wanted to return to Western countries. They did not hate Shanghai, but they did not want to live there.

Three long journeys competed in the minds of the refugees. America remained the most popular destination. Many had tried to get into the United States before the war, and now even more had relatives there. The liberating presence of the U.S. Army in Shanghai, bringing food, jobs, and entertainment to the former ghetto dwellers, made America even more attractive as a new home. The younger generation had learned English in school and were drawn to the excitingly free culture exhibited by young American soldiers.

The possibility of a Jewish state in Palestine attracted those refugees who were more committed to their Jewishness and to Zionism, along with significant numbers from the Baghdadi and Russian communities. Conditions for immi-grants in Palestine were physically hard, but the prospect of living among Jews was attractive to many who had been pushed around the world by antisemitism.

Many young Jews in Shanghai had joined Betar, a nationalist organization that encouraged migration to Palestine and the fight for an independent Jewish state.

A minority of refugees among the older generation decided instead to go back to Germany or Austria. Those who had invested all of their lives in being German or Austrian felt ill-equipped to go elsewhere. Highly trained men dedicated to their work recognized that moving to America would mean beginning again at the bottom, with an accent. Those in mixed marriages might have relatives waiting to welcome them. The older generation could remember Europe before the Nazis, when antisemitism seemed to be disappearing. Although most children learned English quickly in Shanghai, the number of adults who had learned a new language in exile fell dramatically with age. The very different experiences of parents and children in Shanghai often led to generational disputes over where to go.

Right after the war, however, Shanghai Jews could go nowhere. Just as the world had reacted slowly and hesitantly to the need for refuge before and during the war, little changed after the war. The Western democracies maintained those restrictive immigration policies that had forced Jews to scatter all over the world. The national quotas that had made it so difficult for European Jews to enter the United States remained in force, which was particularly hard on those considered by American authorities to be of Austrian or Polish nationality. No matter where families eventually decided to go, there were powerful forces arrayed against them. In 1945 and 1946, it was nearly impossible to leave Shanghai.

The plight of millions of displaced persons in Europe made Jews in Shanghai worry that they would be forgotten. On November 1, 1945, some of the more politically active refugees founded the Association of Democratic Germans to have a voice in their future. The Austrian Community of Shanghai was founded on February 1, 1946. That month, the Joint created the Migration Bureau.

Information about the Holocaust and the devastated state of postwar Europe that trickled into Shanghai in press reports and in personal communications affected decisions about where to go. Jews gradually learned more about what had happened to their own families in Europe. They realized they could never really go home, for their former central European home had been culturally destroyed by the Nazis and then physically destroyed by war. Many who had once dreamed of Heimat now turned away from Germany and things German.

In August 1945, almost 15,000 refugees were counted by Western relief workers. For six months, only a handful were able to leave, mostly from the Polish community of rabbis and yeshiva students. In March 1946, the Joint's emigration program finally succeeded in arranging for 36 refugees to leave for Australia. The "General Meigs," carrying the first group to the United States, arrived in San Francisco on July 19. During 1946, most of the few hundred who were allowed to land in San Francisco were Polish or Lithuanian refugees.[1]

In January 1947, the Joint was able to bring over 500 refugees to the United States, and another 800 left in the first "repatriations" to Austria. The struggle to convince the victorious Allies to allow refugees from Germany to return home finally was rewarded in May 1947, when the Allies agreed to allow entry to Berlin. On August 22, 732 German Jews arrived in Munich after sailing on the "Marine Lynx" to Naples. Most proceeded to the Soviet sector of devastated Berlin.[2] By September 1947, about 1,000 refugees from Shanghai arrived in the United States every month, and thousands more had returned to Europe.

Gradually, the Western democracies recognized the needs of the Shanghai refugees. Every boatload of departing refugees represented an international struggle for visas, transport, and financial support. By the end of 1948, nearly 10,000 refugees had left Shanghai, with thousands still seeking a way out. About 1,700 went to Germany and Austria, 7,000 to the United States, and 1,000 to Australia, but a mere 150 went to England, and only 25 to Canada. A few hundred were able to enter Latin America, especially Bolivia and Chile. Only 80 had managed to get to Palestine, because the British still severely restricted immigration. As in Australia, the arrival in the United States of refugees after the war upset those who did not like Jews. Despite heavy antisemitic overtones in the debate, Congress passed and President Truman signed in June 1948 the Displaced Persons Act, which allowed 200,000 European refugees to immigrate outside of the normal quotas.

As the British effort to keep control of its mandate in Palestine faltered, prospects for travel to the Middle East improved. Although the nation of Israel was officially declared in May 1948, fighting between Jews and Arabs continued into 1949. Eventually, in late December 1948 and January 1949, the "Wooster Victory" and the "Castel Bianca" brought nearly 2,000 Russian and Baghdadi Jews and some central European refugees on a six-week journey around the Cape of Good Hope to Naples, where they changed ships for the final leg to Haifa. Another group of 450 Shanghai Jews crossed to San Francisco in February, boarded a sealed train for a six-day trip to New York, sailed on the "General Stewart" to Italy, and then finally to Israel.

The civil war in China heightened the desperation of those trying to get out. The Nationalists spread fear that the Red Army would kill all Europeans. The Communists entered Shanghai triumphantly in May 1949, at which time several thousand central Europeans were still there. The new government welcomed the contribution of skilled Europeans who were willing to stay, but in the long run was no more hospitable to these remnants of colonialism than the Nationalists had been.

At the moment of departure, the silence of our narrators about preparations is revealing of the state to which they had been reduced. Little preparation was needed. There was hardly anything to pack or get rid of. Unlike other refugee communities in North and South America, the Shanghai Jews had nothing left but their lives.

For many Jews, the journey out of Shanghai was emotionally and physically difficult. Families like Otto Schnepp's were separated again, ending up on different continents. Before they finally arrived in the United States, Melitta Colland went to Panama and the Greenings to Australia. Eric Reisman's negotiations with U.S. immigration officials four years after the end of the war might be comical had his future not been at stake.

One of the last large groups to leave Shanghai typified the immense difficulties for displaced persons in the postwar world. The "General Gordon" was to take 106 refugees without U.S. visas across the Pacific. The Communist Chinese government would not allow the ship to anchor onshore. So in May 1950, the refugees had to take a train to Tientsin, then board barges in heavy seas to get out to the ship. When they arrived in the United States, they were put on a sealed train and transported across the country to Ellis Island in New York harbor. In June, another boat took them to Bremerhaven, and they entered DP camps, where they stayed for one more year. Finally they were given visas to the United States in 1951.

At this point, the narrators no longer tell the broad story of the 15,000 who escaped the Third Reich for the unlikely goal of Shanghai, but instead represent the history of the slight majority who came to the United States.

Gradually, the few hundred remaining Jews died of illness or old age, or managed to leave. By the time that the Cultural Revolution began to wipe out all traces of foreign influence in 1966, the Jewish communities of Shanghai were just a memory.

Alfred Kohn's family was only able to come to the United States in stages.

When the war was over, I started working for the American Army. Where I was working there was the American Consulate, and I befriended one consular guy. I think I was one of the first in the ghetto to go up to the American Consulate and talk to them, and knew that within three, four months they would start issuing visas for people that are eligible. Our relatives in America sent us an affidavit. We were one of the first to leave. My brother and I went first to Philadelphia in September 1947, to our relatives, and about a year later my parents came.

Only by getting ready to leave in a matter of days was **Ernest Culman's** *family allowed to travel to the United States together.*

The war was over, and the papers were full of articles of what had happened in Germany. Of course we had had no idea. And all we wanted to do was get out of Shanghai. So we contacted relatives wherever we could find them. Many of my father's relatives unfortunately had remained in Germany, and they were dead. But my mother's two sisters, one had ended up in Panama, one had ended up in Palestine, and her brother had ended up in Baltimore. My father had a sister who ended up in Montreal. We contacted them all, and the idea was whoever comes through first, that's where we're going.

Well, the United States came through first, and on Christmas Eve, 1946, we got our visa to come to the United States. That was a real high. We were scheduled to go on a ship leaving in February, the army transports, and we figured, well, we've got roughly two months to get everything taken care of. Then my father gets a phone call to come to this office where they handled the transports, this was January the 5th, and was told the ship in February still has American GIs on there. "We can't allow any women on board. You and your sons can go, but your wife would have to stay behind." And he said, "Well, no way, I mean we stuck together through all this, we're not going to separate now. What was our choices?" "Well, there's a ship in March where you could be scheduled to go." He says, "Is there nothing else?" And they said, "Well, there's a ship leaving on the 9th of January, four days from now, where we still have some room." And he says, "I'll take it." "Yeah, but you have to have your big luggage on in two days." "Never mind, we'll take it." I got a call at work, my boss was out, I left him a little note, "I'm going to America, good-bye." [laughs] And four days later we were aboard the ship.

My father, as a doctor, always had a telephone, which was rather rare in Shanghai. In fact, in the SACRA building it was part of our business. We let people for x number of dollars make a phone call, for half that amount they can receive phone calls with it. Call comes in, I would run through the building trying to find whoever it was. But the telephone was a very valuable asset, and downstairs from where we lived at that time there was a Chinese merchant who wanted to buy the telephone from us. There was also a refugee who wanted the phone, but he didn't come up with as much money as the Chinese. So my brother went with this guy to the telephone company, bribe the proper officials to move the phone from our apartment downstairs. We were already on board the ship, all of a sudden over the loudspeaker, "Dr. Culman, you're wanted on the pier." He goes down on the pier, there's this other refugee, he is going to give my father more money. He says, "No way, I'm already on American territory, I'm not going to renege on the deal I made with this other guy at this point."

I have absolutely no idea anymore how much, it was a substantial sum in American dollars.

But we got on board the ship, and it's a regular troop ship, you know, with bunks one on top of the other. Henry was on the bottom, my father in the middle, I on the top, and my mother was in the women's section on the other side. During the day of course we were all together. It took us 13 days to get to San Francisco. When we arrived there, it was four or five o' clock in the morning, but none of us could sleep. We ran up on deck, and eventually we could see the sun rising behind the Golden Gate, and really it looked golden to us, and steamed into San Francisco.

Some friends from Germany were there to greet us, from our little town in Liegnitz. The Jewish community, the Joint, I think, saw to it that we had a hotel room. It looked to us like a very fancy hotel. And one of the first things Henry and I did, we went into the bathroom, opened the faucet, and drank the water right out of the faucet. It tasted delicious, because seven, eight years we always had to have everything boiled. And then these friends in San Francisco tried to talk us into staying there. Why go east? Everybody from the east is coming west. My mother wouldn't hear from anything they said. "I'm going to my brother, he's in Baltimore, we're separated long enough, too much has happened."

When we came to the United States, we all made it a point trying to assimilate as much as possible, including eating with the fork in the right hand. On the train from San Francisco to Baltimore, my father said to us, "You know, you all got to go to work when we get to Baltimore, so consider these three, four days like a vacation. Order whatever you like from the dining car." So we all ordered fried chicken, and trying to eat fried chicken with knife and fork in a dining car is almost an impossibility. So the head waiter comes up to us and says, "Here in this country you can take chicken into your hands." We all did it and enjoyed it that much more.

Lo and behold, we get to Baltimore, we settle down, a few weeks later, my uncle and aunt tell my parents that they have a chance to move to the west coast. My mother was furious. By this time, Henry and I both had a job and my father was just about ready to have a job, already made friends, we really settled into Baltimore very fast. So they went to San Francisco, he couldn't find work there, a month or two later they came back.

Doris Grey left in the same month as the Culmans, perhaps on the same ship.

The war ended in '45 in August, and we left in January '47. They started to call up people with an affidavit in late '46, and we were among them. We went with the troop transporter "Marine Lynx." Was I sick! It was terrible. We had big, big rooms. The men in one room. But the food was good, for us like heaven. And you know what was so nice? People came on the boat before we left and the Americans fed everybody. Americans were very nice to the children, too.

Ruth Sumner and her husband could travel with the Army on a different route to San Francisco.

Then I got pregnant, that changed the situation a little bit. And his year was up, so we came back to the United States, we came on an Army transport. I was an Army dependent, so he was in with the soldiers. We went from Shanghai over to Philippines. I saw Battan, Corregidor. Forrest had been there during the war, so that was very interesting to him. He saw all the ships still in the harbor, belly up, sticking out. From Manila, we came over to San Francisco, it must have been February '47.

My sister and her husband picked us up in San Francisco. My sister was pregnant, both of us were pregnant. Mary was born in March, and Jackie was born in July. The baby boom had started. I stayed there about three weeks, and Forrest got his discharge.

We took the train to Florida, and his dad met us at the Union Station down here. I'll tell you something that might amuse you. My husband was born and raised in Tampa, typical middle-class Americans, hardworking. He's the oldest of five children. Then four years of World War II, then he comes into Shanghai, war's over. He writes home, "I found me a girl. I'm going to get married. I'm going to stay here another year so we can get married." My mother-in-law says, "I got a letter. I thought, my God, I'm going to have me a Chinese daughter. I am going to have to ask the Lord to help me to love a Chinese." He forgot to tell her who I was. [laughs] She told me, she cried. She was so glad when she saw me and who I was. Little old me, big, and I was not Chinese. [laughs]

Ralph Hirsch's family, like many refugees, was able to enter the United States because a relative was already living here.

My family left relatively early, in May of '47, which had to do with the fact that we were on the German quota for immigration to the United States, which was very large, and also with the fact that my father, I guess, was determined not to be caught making too late a move once again. So he got very busy quite early and managed to get us passage. We were probably among the first 20 percent or so to get out.

It was always clear to us that Shanghai was only a transient home for us. The only question was how short that transition would be. By the time the American immigration policy had changed after the war, to make it possible to take the Jews on the German quota, it became clear that the conditions for us were pretty good, because that was the second largest of all the immigration quotas after the British. We had relatives in America, and my father, by now, knew the ropes. We got out fairly quickly, and the United States was the only destination seriously considered.

Gérard Kohbieter also needed the crucial affidavit from a relative in America, assuring the U.S. Government that he would not become a public burden.

I wanted to get out of Shanghai in the worst way. A friend of mine was with Chiang Kai-shek's army. He spoke fluent Chinese, and he wrote me from the interior, "The Communists are winning the war." He wrote me that early in the game. The Communists, one of the first things they did was to close all the nightclubs, because they felt that it was counter-productive, or that there is no need in a poor country for that kind of conspicuous consumption. And I figured, well, I'll be dead, because that's all I knew then. I'd learned a lot, but nothing that you could turn into cash. So I tried to get out and didn't quite know, repatriation was out. I applied for Australia on an outrageously racist application form. They even wanted to know the color of your eyes and the color of your hair and that kind of nonsense. Then a friend of the family found out that I was in Shanghai and asked me, "Would you like to come to the States?" He was ready to give the affidavits, everything was cleared. We came to the States.

Melitta Colland and her family went to Panama rather than wait for permission to enter the United States.

Everybody was trying, again like they did in Vienna, preparing oneself to leave. Since we didn't want to start all over again in China, and since everybody more or less felt that there is something coming that we don't want to be caught in, namely the revolution in China. At that time I was married to her father, who would never have gone to Israel. But he did want to come to the United States. In those days I was still the little housewife, who did what her husband wanted. This has changed a lot. [laughs]

We tried to apply for immigration to United States and we knew, we were told in fact, that it would take at least three years to get the papers. Number one, because the American Consul was terribly antisemitic. He did everything to keep us out. Not only us, I mean the whole bunch of immigrants who wanted to come to America. He kept old people out who had their sons and daughters long here, practically since 1939 or even earlier, and who never survived getting out of there. They died before they ever could get to see their children.[3]

My brother sent papers to come to Panama. We took a Norwegian freighter from Shanghai to Panama. We left in '47!

Otto Schnepp benefited from special permission to enter the United States as a student.

My parents then left in '47 and went to Kenya, to Nairobi, to join my sister. It was a crown colony at that time, where my father could not practice medicine. But my father and mother went to Dar es Salaam, to Tanganyika, and lived there, where he could practice. Then I graduated in June.

People who were born in Germany could come to the U.S. at that time in huge numbers. The Austrian quota was very small and oversubscribed with refugees. I did get eventually a student's visa to come here, which was very difficult to get, because I had to show that I disposed of lots of money, which was difficult to get together. I disposed of some money, but not as much as they wanted, so I got some guarantee.

I was there for a half a year after that, from June till January. I came from Shanghai on a student's visa to the United States, to Berkeley to do graduate studies, and I was at that point already very decided on going to Israel. So my orientations were more Zionist.

Lisbeth Loewenberg and her husband, Bruno, had to leave her mother behind in Shanghai. They had a rough passage and experienced another culture shock on arrival in San Francisco.

Then the economy went down, and people started to leave in droves. Since more people left and left, there was, of course, always fewer readers in the library, so sooner or later we had to leave, too. Since Bruno was born in Germany and had a very good quota, we registered with the American Consulate, and our quota number came up pretty fast.

1948. It was very late. Already rumors came that the Communists might be coming. "They will not come, yes, they will come, yes, they won't come." It wasn't much later that the Communists really came to Shanghai, where everybody said that they would never make it. They would never be able to cross the Huangpu. You know, when you live in a closed community like that, rumors are what keeps people alive, what keeps the community buzzing. They will never come in, they will come in, the war is over, the war is not over, it can't last longer, it can. I mean, it goes constantly and constantly.

So, anyhow, we had no problem getting to the United States. We had eaten breakfast apparently before we left Shanghai, and we left some food on the table or something. My mother said, within a second from the street like hundreds of people were coming in. They sat down, they ate what food was there and took everything out of the room, whatever I'd left in the closet and not taken with me, for one reason or another. It was all within one minute stripped.

My mother didn't come to the United States, because of the Viennese quota. I got in on the German quota from my husband. But the Austrian quota was extremely bad at that time. She left a couple months afterwards and went to England, and then she came to the United States. After I was a citizen, then there was no problem anymore.

Just as beautiful as the trip to Shanghai, just as horrible was the trip from Shanghai to San Francisco. I have to tell you about that. We made two mistakes. We had enough money to pay our own fare. Okay. And you could take $500 with you and that's just exactly how much money we had, $500 and money to pay for the fare from San Francisco. Of course, the only fare we could afford to pay was third class. Which means that like 100 women sleep in one dormitory, and 100 men sleep in a dormitory. And you don't get meals served three times a day, but you stand in line in messes and pick up cafeteria stuff. I had never eaten cafeteria-style in my life. I had never seen a cafeteria. I couldn't stand the food. It was the most horrible, cheapest type of American food, same brown gravy over everything. The only dessert was Jello. I couldn't eat Jello for years after the trip.

Not only that, it was an extremely rough trip. I was seasick all the time. I slept in this upper berth with 100 women. I was so sick, I couldn't eat any of the stuff. There was a huge toilet, you know, like 20 toilets, one next to the other, and with only swinging doors. I had never been in an open toilet like that in my life. I couldn't go to the bathroom, because there was no real privacy. I was sick anyway. Bruno didn't get seasick, it doesn't matter to him. He came to me at my bed, I was lying there in my bed. "You have to come up on board. You've never seen anything like it. The water is up here and the ship is down here." Leave me alone, I was up and down and up and down. No, it was really pretty bad.

We should have not taken any money with us, and should have gone second class. It would have been better, that's where we made a mistake.

We came to San Francisco. When we landed, a committee again greets you there. Here come the immigrants. And they looked at us, they said, "Oh, you have money, take a cab." They didn't do anything for us ever. That's why I said, we should have come second class in style, instead of

coolie class. And come here without money. We would have been far better off. But anyhow we survived very well.

The committee rented a hotel room for us in a small downtown hotel.
But we had to pay for ourselves. They wouldn't pay it, because after
all, we were rich, we had money. It was Sunday, and it's downtown San
Francisco, and I looked out of the window and there was nobody in the
streets. I thought there must be martial law. Something is wrong, where
are the people? I was afraid, because there was nobody there. That was
funny. It shocked me just as much as the masses of people shocked me.

*Lotte Schwarz sailed with the "General Meigs," which criss-crossed the Pacific
in 1947 and 1948 carrying refugees from Shanghai.*

The United States government gave us collective affidavits. They told
us when our ship would leave and we would go. So by then we had everything packed, everything was standing ready, we just had to go. Big trucks
came, passed by our main street where we lived on Wayside, all full with
suitcases and stuff. And we said, "Boy, another ship is going. I hope ours
is coming soon, too." Every two weeks a ship came and left.

We left Shanghai in 1948. We all came with troop transporters, we
came with the "General Meigs."

*Herbert and Ilse Greening could not get into the United States because he
had been born in a part of Germany that became Polish after the war. They tried
Australia, where Jewish refugees had difficulties becoming integrated.*

Ilse Greening: There were two friends of Herbert's who worked in
the British Army in the interior, they were officers in the British Army.
After the war they came and they lived at the British Consulate.

Herbert Greening: One was a Viennese, his father was an x-ray spe-
cialist in Vienna.

Ilse Greening: He had a Chinese wife. She was a gynecologist, she
had birth control clinics, which was very rare in those days. She studied
in Vienna, too, and she spoke German fluently. She was a highly educated
person, and through her we met some very interesting people, educated
people. She was pro-Communist, and she told us from the very beginning that she thought that the future of China is with Communism, they
needed it badly because the poor people were really unbelievably poor,
and under pressure. She was convinced that Communists had to come to
China to free the poor people.

Herbert Greening: We were afraid of the Communists, we didn't
know what they would bring, we felt that we had to get out of there.

Ilse Greening: The Communists made it quite clear they could do without the foreigners. The poorer people were indoctrinated, they became antiforeign, too. Oh yes, it must have been systematic antiforeign propaganda, because we could feel it.

Herbert was born in Germany, but it became Poland, and he was a Polish quota, and we had very little chance to come to the United States. My mother and my sister, who were German quota, went ahead, but we didn't have any chance. This friend in Australia offered to send us a landing permit, so we decided we had to leave the country, because the Communists were getting closer and closer, and we finally left for Australia.

Herbert Greening: Twenty-second January of 1949.

Ilse Greening: He had told Herbert that he wouldn't have any trouble to get his medical license. But it didn't turn out that way, because the Australians had all these returning servicemen who had priority at the universities, and they had priorities with housing, which was natural. They were very antiforeign. Not only antiforeign, but anti-Catholics and anti-everybody. The British they hated. So it was much more difficult than we expected in Australia.

At first we went to Brisbane, where this friend lived, but Herbert was told right away that they wouldn't accept any bloody foreigners. I found a job, I worked in the city mission, but we only stayed in Brisbane for six weeks.

Herbert Greening: We went to Brisbane, where they didn't let me in medical school at all. I tried Melbourne, they said I have to go five more years, 10 semesters. And then in Sydney they said they give me the *Physikum*, I have to do three more clinical years. After three more clinical years, there would be a lottery. There would be 12 students every year admitted to practice. And we were 36 foreign students.

Ilse Greening: We finally settled in Sydney, where the possibilities were better, and Herbert was accepted at the university. They did not recognize his German diploma. I had a small child and couldn't possibly go to work anywhere. So I learned from a friend how to string pearls, and we had quite a nice business, beads, they were not real pearls, they were imported from Czechoslovakia. [laughs] They were very fashionable, and they needed workers. I worked at home, because I had the child, and at night when Herbert came back from the university, he even helped with the beads, and we made a living.

That's when I decided to leave. I didn't take to the people at all. They were unfriendly, and my whole family was in the States, and I was really very unhappy. When I was doing my pearls and they were playing a sad song, I cried, which I never, ever did and have never done after.

We already had wasted ten years in Shanghai, I didn't want to wait around there another maybe two years. So behind his back, I went to the American Consulate, and I said, "Please reactivate our emigration, we want to leave here." And it came and I finally had to tell him that I didn't want to spend my life in Australia, I wanted to come to the States. In August of 1950.

And we lived happily ever after.

Eric Reisman's little family came to the US in three parts. His brother and parents left Shanghai in 1947. His odyssey through the immigration bureaucracy in 1949 is evidence of the difficulties that many refugees experienced before they could finally settle down again.

My brother was gone already, he married in Shanghai and he went to Bolivia. My parents came to this country. My parents did not want to go back to Europe. By that time we had family in the United States, and my mother and father pursued it to immigrate to the United States. I was still under 21 and tried to come to the United States under their quota. Lo and behold, as luck would have it, I turned 21 before the visa was issued. My birthday was the twenty-sixth of April, but they got the visa issued on the thirtieth, so I missed it by a couple of days. The Consul said, "Eric, you got to go under your own quota." They went to the United States, and I was in the Austrian quota. The Austrian quota was not a very good quota. So I had to reapply.

I stayed on in China waiting for the quota to get my affidavit. And as it turned out, I did not get the affidavit when the Communists came, but working for Northwest Airline, I left with the last group of people in 1949. We landed in San Francisco.

I came to the United States with the intents of going back to Vienna and waiting for my visa to come through. I went to the portier at the hotel I stayed in San Francisco, I said, "What do I do, I want to get to New York?" And he said, "Well, do you want to fly?" I says, "Well, I work for Northwest Airlines, but I have enough vacation time that I can take a train, and I'd like to take a leisurely train to New York." He says, "I think I can get you on the Vista-Dome train, it's the first maiden run." People were waiting for months and months to get on that train, and he got me on the train, and I was with all kinds of dignitaries. [laughs] Stopped at every whistle stop there was, with bands meeting us, [laughs] and I came across. Usually you had to change in Chicago, but that train went straight through to New York. My mother and father, I saw them after two and a half years for the first time again. They met the train, there was a band there. [laughs]

I went to the immigration authorities in Manhattan, and I told them that my parents are here, and I am on my way to Vienna, but I would like to stay with my parents longer. They gave me a visa to stay, but it was a visitor's visa, and they gave me I think six months or so.

I met a lawyer in New York, if you killed me I couldn't remember his name, but anyhow he said, "Eric, you don't want to go back to Vienna. We will try and get you a visa while you are waiting here." And so he pursued that, although I had already my deportation papers. I went to the immigration authorities in New York, and they extended my transit visa, allowing me to stay here, until they wouldn't extend it anymore and they were ready to deport me, when the lawyer came through with my visa. It cost me about $800. So I was always legal here, I never was illegal or never broke the law in any way or form.

Then I got married, and the application for my visa was granted. I had to go to Montreal and come back through Rouses Point into the United States, and that was more or less our honeymoon. [laughs] So I came into the United States.

CHAPTER 8

Another New Life

Once more, refugee families had to adapt to a difficult and unfamiliar situation. They began to make new lives, always related to previous lives for the parental generation, entirely new for the younger generation. These efforts tell us much about their personalities and desires, as well as the lasting effects of their years as refugees.

Our narrators tell of the human meaning of being a refugee in America, about going to school, finding work, becoming integrated again. Problems were inevitable. Some people welcomed the refugees, others did not. The ideas and behavior that had previously kept them out had been politically defeated, but not eliminated.

There were no perfect havens for Jews who had been chased around the world by irrational hatreds. But the United States was the freest society the former refugees had ever experienced. Antisemitism was a fact of American postwar life. The long-standing restrictions on what clubs Jews could join, universities they could attend, and social groups they could enter lingered for decades after 1945. Yet these were not mentioned in our interviews. Instead, these narrators focus on their success in creating new and prosperous lives, for which their gratitude toward America and Americans is great. Discrimination in the United States may have been barely noticeable to those who had survived the Nazis. The Shanghai Jews had finally achieved security, although it often took a long time to find a permanent home.

In the creation of their new American lives, the central European refugees gave up their German Jewish culture. Scattered across the vast North American continent, the pressure and desire to assimilate meant letting go of the culture that had sustained them thus far. Their hard lives in Shanghai helped them find success in prosperous postwar America. The Shanghai Jews were no longer a community, but merely another group of Americans with an unusual history.

The stories in this chapter present the bare outlines of 50 years of postwar life, the passing of the older generation and the maturing of the younger one, the development of new political and social systems, the whole history of the Cold War. The nature of the original interviews tended to limit the discussion of the postwar period. There remains much more to know.

Lisbeth Loewenberg *could not imagine permanence after a decade of worrying about what tomorrow might bring.*

We looked around. Of course, we had no jobs. After one week I decided I'll go and look for a job. I looked in the paper and walked around and found a job the first day, fantastic job as a typist and a file clerk. That's how I started my career in the United States. And Bruno finally did open a bookstore. He did have bookstores always. It didn't take him too long, either.

This will amuse you. My first job that I found after one week when I walked around, that was with *Collier's* magazine. This place took subscriptions, they had salesmen go running around and selling subscriptions to *Collier's* and *Good Housekeeping* and *Cosmopolitan,* and so on, and I processed these orders. People took subscriptions for one year. I said, "But how do people know that after one year they will still be at that address?" I couldn't believe in permanence anymore. I was completely shocked that some people took two-year subscriptions. It floored me. But you don't know where you are going to be tomorrow, was my reaction. And life has actually always seemed to me not permanent. It's all just transitory.

Gérard Kohbieter *was still a young man of 25 when he arrived in New York. It took several more decades before he settled in Berlin with his wife, Renate.*

Went to New York, the Big Apple, and had a marvelous year's stay. It was everything I hoped for. In Shanghai I had once tried to make a deal with God. I was willing to settle for one good year, man, with everything. One year of enough food and enough schnapps and a groovy chick and a groovy place to live. One year. So in 1947, I was sitting in New York on the veranda of the Museum of Modern Art, upstairs in the clubroom, I had immediately joined the club there, and thought, "My God, you made it." I was delighted. Saw every film that they have in their archives over the years. Quickly found my way into Greenwich Village, did some magic, did some jobs. And, of course, New York is just full of fascinating people. Once you are connected, once you are plugged in, there's no end to it.

Went to college, too, but in New York it was more like going to the theater. You know, the New School for Social Research, you could buy tickets for single lectures. You could test out the courses to see, "Do I want this prof?" which is a reasonable way of running a university. And so I took all kinds of courses, but never for credit. It was foolish, but I just took them.

In New York I used to run into people. On Broadway and 103rd Street, I had a place, it was my first furnished room in New York, and there was the cafeteria. Maybe it was further down, 86th Street or so. They were all sitting there, man, just like they were sitting around at the Alcock Home in Shanghai waiting for the war to end. They were sitting in the cafeteria waiting for heaven, waiting for Godot and looking pretty much the same, only they had a few more lines in their faces, but they still moved, the body language was still there, and you know, "Hey man," and you were glad to be out of there. Talking the same bullshit, man. It's an interesting crowd anyway, cafeteria crowds.

San Francisco really did it to me. I spent a few months there when I arrived from Shanghai. Always dreaming of San Francisco. One guy in a bar said to me, "Man, you've been talking about San Francisco for years. Why don't you just go there?" Then it happened, and I went to San Francisco and changed my life again. I was home. That rare, rare thing happened to me that I found roots again, a second time. I was at home there. Yeah. I spent 28 years in San Francisco.

Then '66, Germany and Europe. Ibiza. Spent six months in Ibiza, I was going to open a discotheque there. Took a thousand records with me. I thought maybe settle in Ibiza, which would have been insanity, because that was a madhouse then. It was a poor man's Mallorca. Nothing happened, of course, and I was just sitting around there with the rest of the guys in the cafés, man. A good time was had by all. Was it a waste of time? I don't think so. A great source of consolation has always been the saying, "When a writer looks out the window, he is working." That one really hit home.

Then I came to Germany in '78, or something like that, and met Renate, and I talked her into coming to the States. But she wasn't too happy with that. Well, we went back. She had a leave of absence, just in case, so she gladly got back into her job. Then we got the house in Portugal, because I wanted someplace I can go in a hurry in case the shit hits the fan. And it looked a few times like it would. During the Cold War there were pretty hairy situations.

I came back in '78, and then back to the States, and then back to Berlin, and then every year I would fly to California and live my California life, on and off a few years. Yeah, we've been in this place for three years. Portugal five years.

Otto Schnepp had a deeper connection to Chinese society and culture than most refugees.

I got a doctorate in '51 at Berkeley, stayed there an additional year of postdoctoral work, then went to Israel, got a job in Israel, and was for 13 years at the Technion, the Israel Institute of Technology in Haifa. And then something personal happened there, and I got fed up and came to the United States because I was invited to come and to be a professor at USC, and so I came here in '65. And I have been here since. My personal life has undergone lots of changes, but I've lived here ever since then.

I was the Science Advisor of the U.S. Embassy in China in 1980 to '82, which was certainly a very interesting life experience, and since then I have pursued some studies of science and technology in China. I've written a book together with some people on U.S.-China technology transfer. So I've been there at that time for two years and since then sort of every other year.

Herbert and Ilse Greening resumed their working lives in New York and eventually retired to Florida.

Herbert Greening: Ilse got the visa for America, and we went to America. Here I had to pass first a language exam, and then a license exam for New York. So I took a cram course, a refresher course.

The first test I flunked in anatomy. Anatomy was my speciality, I mean, I was just overconfident. And the second time three months later I passed it. In the meantime, I had a job as a house doctor in a small hospital in New York.

Ilse Greening: Everything was much simpler here. I worked for the same bank, for the Chartered Bank on Wall Street.

When we lived in New York, a Jewish classmate came to visit from South America, I think Sao Paolo, so he said, "Guess whom I met in the street in Sao Paolo? I met Kahner. Wasn't that a coincidence?" So Herbert said, "Did he tell you that he met me in Shanghai?" Not a word. You know, it would have been natural for him to say, "Here you were my classmate, guess whom I met in Shanghai?" No, not a word. And only the other day we were talking, I wonder what ever happened to him. He probably lives in South America somewhere. But did he want to meet us? Was it intentional?

Herbert Greening: One of the older practitioners had watched my work and came to me whether I want to join him, first as an employee, associate, and after a year he would give me partnership. So I jumped into that. I had Ilse, I had a baby, I had mother-in-law, and Ilse was pregnant, so I needed a job. And in a year he really pumped me and worked me very, very hard. I didn't have a day free during the whole week. I had an evening free on Tuesday night. And if there was a delivery, I had to do that, or else you didn't do any deliveries. After a year and a half, I became a partner with 15 percent, 20 percent, 25 percent, going up to 50 percent. After seven years, the practice became so big that we had to take a third guy. After another 10 years, the old guy retired and I became the boss.

We started to come to Florida in '82 for a couple of months. When we went back, I went back to work. And I did it until I got a stroke in '94.

Melitta Colland and her family came to the United States through Panama.

My brother was overly generous. He rented a beautiful apartment for us, furnished it completely. There was even a question whether we should stay in Panama or not. Because in Panama my husband could have practiced medicine immediately, without having to go through another state board. And here he needed another state board, which he had done twice by the way.

My brother was already a very highly regarded businessman who befriended a lot of the consular people. He was a very close friend of the American and British Consul. And through them we were able to get the visas to the United States in six months. I had the German quota rather than the Austrian quota, because I was married to a German-born man. We were lucky.

We thought that in order to make it easier on myself, my husband and I would come into New York first and leave the child and my mother in Panama. Mother and child could have easily stayed there very comfortably, as long as it was necessary. And we were going to do that. So we did not think of getting a visa for the child. We just got it for ourselves and thought that later on we will come back and pick her up.

Well, it so happened that my brother made a good-bye dinner for us, just a few days before we were to leave. And the American Consul came to dinner. At one point the maid brings Asherah in on her arm, and she had a head of blond curls, the most adorable baby you ever want to see. And he says, "Whose child is that?" I say, "It's my daughter." "I don't remember giving a visa for the child." I said, "No, we did not intend to take her with us right away. She will stay here with Mother, and come at a later date." He said, "Oh no. Don't do that. She's born in China. Don't do that. It may take you 10 or 12 years to get her into the United States. You come tomorrow morning to my office, and I'll give you a visa for the child, and you take her with you. I don't care if you send her back, but you take her with you into the country." And that was lucky. [laughs]

Mother stayed for a few years, and then she also wanted to come here, and we applied for her papers. She went to Canada first to be with my other brother for a while. And then I really needed Mother badly, because I divorced, and worked, and I depended on strangers taking care of Asherah, which I didn't like very much. So Mother came and was a tremendous help, because I had to travel a great deal in my work. And my mother always loved that little one, more than she should have. She practically devoted her old age to her. She totally had given up her own life. She never went to a party. She never made friends. Mother loved to play bridge in Europe, she never touched a card in this country, because she always was busy.

Alfred Kohn did very well in the fur business his family had pursued in Shanghai. His stories about old friends reveal the worldwide scattering of the remnants of central European Jewry. Like the Greenings, he worked in New York and retired to Florida.

After we came to America I started work in the fur business. My first job I made 18 dollars a week. I worked as a shipping clerk until I got into the fur union. I started my first job as a furrier with 75 dollars. Within one year I made a 145 dollars in 1948, and I worked on three jobs. Before work,

Photo 11 An American champion: Maccabi boxing club in New York City; Alfred Kohn, standing eighth from the right, won the NY Golden Gloves championship at 175 pounds in 1948

at work, after work. I made a lot of money. I went into my own business, I had another partnership eventually, I was the working partner for a big company called Michael Forrest. We employed over 80 union people. And I retired there seven years ago from that company.

I got married, my wife is also from Germany, came here in '47, have two children, son is married. My daughter's not married, she's a wonderful girl, she's very bright, works for a computer company troubleshooting software, has a very good job.

My brother came to America, and the relatives in Philadelphia made an operation, put an artificial joint in here because this was dead, and he walks. He went to school, graduated, started working in America also in the fur business, and I worked in the fur business. He became an engineer. First he worked private engineering company, then he worked for the Triboro Bridge and Tunnel Authority, and when he retired last year, he was the top engineer there. He's married, has two children like we have, boy and a girl. His son is married, his daughter is not.

I have a friend that I went to school with in Germany. In 1939, I went to Shanghai, he stayed in Germany. His parents got killed in Auschwitz. He was in Auschwitz and survived. I have a very good memory for faces. After the war, I'm standing on 8th Avenue on the subway station, 42nd Street, and I see a man who looks familiar, and I walk over to him, "Are you from Germany?" He said, "Yes." Now he had wavy blond hair, looked typical Aryan. I said, "You're from Berlin?" "Yes." I said, "Is your name Heinz Bick?" He said, "Yes." He showed me a picture of his wife. I said, "I know your wife, she went to the class in Shanghai with my brother." We're still friends today.

I went skiing once up in the Catskills, we had a house up there. And I see a guy in the ski line with an accent, and he looked very familiar. I went over to him, "Are you from Germany?" He says, "Yeah." "Are you from Berlin?" "Yeah." "Is your name Unger?" He said, "Yes." I said, "I went to school with you." He said, "No, you went to school with my younger brother."

That's my life in one short thing. I'm very active in my synagogue. We go to Israel frequently, almost every year at least once. America has been good to me. I like this country. Sometimes I figure maybe I made a mistake to come to America, I should have gone to Israel. I went to Israel after I left the army, in 1955 I was first time in Israel. It was tough at the time to be in Israel. My parents, my brother were here, so I came back. But we're very Israel-oriented, my wife and I, and we have relatives in Israel, you know, and we're committed to Jewish continuity.

*Doris Grey's brother lived in London, her nephew in Israel. She and her husband
lived in New York and thought about Paris.*

While we were still in Shanghai, my brother-in-law in New York
wrote to us that they will send us affidavit, but we have to obligate ourselves never ever to ask them for any help. No children, they didn't have
any children. I'll never forget, we arrived here, and they lived at that
time, it was very swanky, 12 East 87th Street, between Madison and Fifth
Avenue.

I started out as assistant head nurse on the ward in joint disease in
New York. At that time my name was Cohn. For me, the work at the ward
was nothing, everything was done right away. My head nurse said, "You
are done already?" I said, "This is nothing. What do you think, what kind
of work I'm used to? Sometimes 48 hours and longer, you know." A day
was at least 12, 16 hours or so, eight hours work was nothing.

I had to take extra courses here. But they were then also very nice. I
couldn't bring the proofs that I worked in gynecology and in the delivery
room, in order to take my state boards. So I worked for a half a year to make
up for it in all these different departments at Fordham University Hospital,
New York. I was then head nurse already in joint disease, they gave me
leave of absence, and I took the classes there. I worked there, and they even
paid me. I think I got $150 a month, which was nice, you know. When I
finished, before I left, the director of nurses called me, they would send me
on to college, you know, to take my degree, and would I stay with them?
That's very nice, but I couldn't do it to joint disease, they gave me half a
year leave of absence in order to take my state boards and everything. And
then my late husband said, "No more studying, you had enough now." I
took some more classes, and I became a supervisor at the hospital.

My brother with his wife finally settled in London, they always wanted
to live in London because there the best culture and the best theater, music,
and so on and so forth. His son decided to study in Israel. He had his bachelor degree from the University in Jerusalem, where he was accepted right
away. He lives in Israel, he married a Sabra. He is real Israeli.

Willy didn't want to stay in America. He always said to me, "Would
you go with me to live in France?" He always wanted to live in Paris. He
thought we would live there, and he would travel to America, bring art,
you know, and sell it. It didn't work out, unfortunately.

We just started to live, we had a little art gallery, and then one day my
husband came home from Europe, you know, he went over to buy art,
and he wrote already, he lost a few pounds. Nobody could find out what
he had until we got to Dr. Preuss. They said right away, "Six months."

My husband had cancer of the stomach. They operated on him, and in the beginning, he gained a little weight. We were always full of hope, you know. So I said, "Maybe we are lucky." He was operated in August, and the ninth of February, he passed away.

Before he died, he wrote two wonderful farewell letters to me. He said how happy we were, and he can never thank me enough, that I never let him feel that I was the one who was earning the money in the times where he was not allowed to work in his profession. It hurt him, but I was never conscious of it. I should not be alone and I could not be alone. I only should keep him in good memory, and I should get married, if I find someone. That was his farewell letter.

For many teenagers, such as **Ernest Culman**, *poverty in Shanghai meant interrupting schooling. Like the strain on the physical health of the older generation, being a refugee for 10 years had lifelong effects.*

We came to Baltimore, arrived on a Wednesday. The following Monday I walked into Ritz Camera Center and told them I did repair work and they hired me. Stayed with them for 10 years. I did all the repairs for them.

My brother was sent out to Bethlehem Steel, in the machine shop there. Again, at the other end of town from where we were living in Baltimore. Didn't have a car as yet, so took streetcars, took about an hour and half to get there, an hour and a half to come back, shift work, sometimes all night, and he hated it. Finally my parents agreed that as soon as my father has a job, he could quit there and find something else. Well, it turned out that my father did get a job about three months later, and Henry found a position with a paper company selling paper products, and stayed with that company for over 40 years before he retired. Did very well, was very happy there. But initially, again, they just demanded of us to take care of them.

We wanted to get the high school equivalent certificate, so we sent all our school books, school report cards, and what have you to the Department of Education in Washington, figuring that we would get credit for some of the things that we had learned. They ignored everything but our ages. I was 14 when I left school, so I had to take a test to be able to go to high school. I passed that, and I went to high school at night, Baltimore City College, both Henry and I. So what should we take? Well, we knew we had to take some English, and we took American history, which was very interesting, chemistry. As a language we took German, and we took tests which we passed. Not necessarily with a hundred, but in the nineties. And then we heard of the Maryland high school equivalent tests, so we took those. Both Henry and I did get our high school equivalent certificates.

But other than that, our education lacks. Whatever education I have had over and beyond that is from my own reading and so on. I've never had any formal college education. I attended some college courses, more for the fun of it than for anything else. So I feel that I lost a lot. I mean, obviously if the Nazis wouldn't have taken over in Germany, being the son of an upper middle-class physician, I would have gone to college, and I would have been a professional. If we would have come to the States directly in the early '30s, instead of when we did, actually the same thing would have been true. Coming here from Shanghai, my parents were so concerned about making a living that they saw to it that we immediately went to work. We supported our parents.

My father had, with the help of the Jewish community, been able to get a job in a sanatorium for colored people. Maryland being a southern state was still segregated at the time. So he had a position and was making money. I have some pictures in here actually of him at the hospital, and a lot of little children were in there, and they loved him. The little kids just loved him. We were, so to speak, out of the poorhouse by this time. But I continued to go to work, and so did my brother.

My father started to learn more and more English, he read English books. Now granted, he didn't think in English, basically translated everything from one to the other, you know. Some of the English words he knew from reading them, but he didn't have the proper pronunciation in his mind. I remember the two of us reading the trilogy about Lincoln, and he was very interested in it, we talked a bit about that. And he even considered taking some of these exams to be a full-fledged doctor again.

He had a goiter which developed when he was still a young man, this is during WWI, and he said, "I could have had it operated on," but he knew of somebody who had a goiter operation and became a vegetable, and he felt it was just a beauty spot, so he had that goiter. In some of the pictures I think you could see the very thick neck. But what happened was the goiter was not only external, it was also internal, and it put a tremendous pressure on his heart. He had had a heart attack in Germany. He was visiting patients and, at that time doctors still made house calls, and I often accompanied him, sometimes by car, sometimes by bike. I had just learned how to ride a bike, and we were going someplace, I was riding in front of him. All of a sudden I'm talking, I don't get any answer. I look around and I see him off the bike, standing there panting. He said he's not feeling well. A friend of ours that lived not far away, we went there, then we got a cab to go home. He had had a very severe heart attack, he was sick for a long time. But recovered, this was in 1938, I think. And then in Shanghai he had another small heart attack, it wasn't as severe.

When we came to the United States and he was working at the hospital, some of the doctor friends that he had met here suggested he have it operated on, now with modern medicine, and get rid of that goiter. It puts too much pressure on your heart. But they also were concerned about his heart, whether it could withstand an operation. So the idea was that he would go into Johns Hopkins Hospital for a week or two, you know, good bed rest, and they would check and make sure that his heart is in good shape, and then operate.

We went to visit him one Sunday, and while we were there, the doctor comes in, "Your heart seems to be fine, we've scheduled the operation for tomorrow." Next thing I remember is that he said he had to go to the bathroom, and it took him a long time, and all of a sudden we hear the loudspeakers, you know, "Dr. So-and-so, Dr. So-and-so, Dr. So-and-so." And my mother says, "Something happened to your father." And sure enough, he had had another heart attack. They wheeled him back in a wheelchair into the room, kicked us out of the room, and he died right there. What caused that final heart attack is anybody's guess. The fear of the operation finally came to him, one thought. But he was only 64 years old. And to me completely unexpected.

My father died less than two years after we got here. I was only 18 years old, I felt a tremendous loss. As I mentioned to Anya this morning, I mean, it felt like part of me died at that time.

After that, all the responsibility fell on my brother and I. My mother just demanded that we take care of her. My mother said to us, not once but many a time, "The day before he died he said to me, 'You don't have anything to worry about, your two sons will take care of you, if something happens to me.'" My mother worked very hard in Shanghai to keep the family together with the lunchroom, the sewing, the baking of cakes. She helped out. And then she must have felt like, okay, now it's my turn, you guys go to work and I take it easy. She was only 52 years old when we came to the United States, but she never got a job. She lived off of my brother and I. And I resent that, in retrospect. I don't think I was fully aware of it at the time.

In 1951 I got drafted, the Korean War was going on. After basic training, being stationed at Fort Monmouth in the camera repair school, where I became an instructor for a while, I was then sent over to Austria, Salzburg, which considering the war was going on in Korea, was very nice. But I was expected to send money home each month. As a private I think I made 80 or 90 dollars a month, and half of that was sent home. Again in retrospect, I resent that. I mean, most kids who are in the Army get money from home. Here I had to send it the other way. It eliminated me to have some of the fun that you have in the service.

After I came home from the service in 1953, my brother had gotten married the previous year and I moved back in with my mother. There was a GI Bill available for me, I did not take advantage of it. By this time I was just looking forward to making money again. I'd been working for Ritz Camera Center, they kept the job open for me. They only had about four or five stores at the time, now they have several hundred. But they found other places to do the repair work for them, and they took me back as a salesman. Eventually I became a manager of one of their stores in Washington. And then we had some disagreements, I thought that I should make more money than they thought, and I found another job with a company in Silver Spring, Industrial Photo. I was with them for 28 years as a general manager, vice president. And like these things happen, the boss and I had our disagreements, strictly on business level because to this day we're still friends, and I left there and went with a company called Pen Camera. Pen was just starting their government industrial business at the time, and I took over as manager of the government industrial sales department.

When my mother died, I felt relief, because finally I don't have to take care of her anymore. I could concentrate on my own life. I mean, it wasn't only the financial part. She never learned English. She learned enough to go to the grocery store. Go to the movies, she expected me to translate word-for-word what was going on. And you could always tell where we are sitting, because all the way around us people had moved, it was empty. I took her to see "Gone With the Wind," and during the movie interpreting or at least translating the gist of it, I didn't get much out of the movie, she did. [laughs] She became very, very self-centered and made us feel like we owe her.

A certain way, I feel like I was cheated. I was amazed how well some of the people that I went to school with or belonged to that club with did with their lives. Werner Blumenthal is an example. When his parents came here from Shanghai, he was able to go to college and have a profession that ended him up in the highest area of government and the highest area of industry. Hans Eberstark, who was in my class, who was a genius, he entertained himself by going to the library and learning the dictionary by heart. He ended up in Switzerland working for the United Nations as an interpreter, he spoke several languages.[1] Others became lawyers, and so, in other words, they had their full schooling once they came to the States.

When I reached 65 years of age I decided to retire. I enjoyed retirement, but six months later Pen Camera called me, would I be willing to work part-time in one of their retail stores. After a little bit of thought, I decided to take it, so that's what I do now, two days a week I work in the retail store behind the counter and love it, because there's no pressure on it. I'm doing something I've done all my life and it's easy on me.

This constant responsibility for my mother continued on and on, and it hurts to this day. By the way, Anya and I, this is our second marriage for both of us. My first marriage also suffered from this. There were many things that were wrong in the marriage, but one of the things was that when we became engaged, I told her that each pay day I send x number of dollars to my mother. Over the years she resented it. After a while, some of the claims to Germany, my mother got some pension, and things got a little easier.

Just about, oh, three, four years ago I was playing with the idea of going back to college and getting a college degree, and as I love math, I decided I'll take a math course first. And the college math course that I took was like going over the things that I learned when I was 13 years old, by this guy Gassenheimer. I was just amazed that it all came back to me fairly rapidly. I feel cheated in a way that I did not utilize this in my life. Part of it I cheated myself, I can't blame it all on my parents.

Ruth Sumner's family represents many themes of refugee stories: assimilation into American life, geographic separation from some relatives and reunion with others, and the continuity and recreation of family.

I came to Tampa to live, and I've been here living ever since. They took me into the Sumner family, and I became one of them, that's been my family since. This is why I enjoyed my husband's family so much and felt so secure when I come to live in Tampa, because that was a family of loving people.

My daughter was born a month after I got here, we got here in February. Mary was born in March, she was a little early, because of all the traveling I did. I think that I cheated a little bit too, I was not supposed to travel that late pregnant. And then my son was born, and that's the family I wanted, I believe.

My father coming to the United States, I don't know that much about it. He came because my sister sent the papers for him. He came the same year I came, in '47. He lived with my sister for a little while, and they didn't get along. It's very hard to get along with my father, and my sister had forgotten that. And so they had a fight, and they split up, and he found some lady and he married her.

He started out as a dishwasher. He was a very industrious man, a very hardworking person. They had a duplex house in Los Angeles, and houses in Los Angeles are not inexpensive. So my father knew how to handle money, always had money, he was never poor. He went over to Germany to get some of his possessions. See, it's part of Poland now, Beuthen. And I guess he got some refunds from the German government or something. I don't know how much money he got out, what was left. And then he died in '64, I think. His wife inherited most of it now.

The difference between me and some of my schoolmates of those days was I came to the United States as a wife, a pregnant wife, and within a month I had a child. My life after we came to the United States was different. My husband had to make it, you know, he was a typical GI, who had to go back to school, got him a job, we built our first house. This is our second house, and we're still living in it. We raised our two children, they're college educated. The other young people my age came to the United States single, went back to school. I did not need that, I was a housewife. So I never pursued going back to school.

Eva and her mother, her father had died, and her brother had died, so it was just the two women. Somebody sponsored her, and she came to the United States, to Fresno, I think. And she was real sick coming over. I think she had typhoid or something. She came a couple of years after I did. Her training was good enough for her to pass all the tests in the United States when she got here. She was a medical technician. Then she married, and they were very successful.

Eva is still going to junior college taking courses, just for the fun of it, you know. The people that came out of Shanghai in my generation became very successful, they picked up their education, which I never did, because my lifestyle was different. They all married Jews. I'm the only one that I'm not married a Jew. Because it so happened at that point of the game, religion wasn't that important to me. So it worked out anyway.

The difference in religions didn't bother me, because I figured, it's the same God. And I had always had that same deep-rooted religious, I'm the one who goes to church. My husband doesn't even really. I was going to bring my children up without religion, because I have no contacts with Jewish people. And then when my children got into their teens, I felt like they needed to have more of God than what they had. And I had met some friends up here with the Methodist church, I had Girl Scout troops. So somebody invited me one day and I went. I figured it's God's house, no matter what. It didn't bother me. And then later on I became a Christian, but I'm still a Jew.

It's amazing, with hindsight, what you've been raised you put into your children. I raised my children the same way that I was raised, that sex is an adult privilege. I told my daughter, when she was planning to get married in senior year in college, "Okay. You plan to get married, don't expect any more out of us. You're sexually active and that means you are an adult and you take responsibility of adulthood." And I feel that way. That's the cutting line, whether 14 or 25. That innocence is gone, that depending on Daddy is gone. That makes them adults, no matter what age. That's the way I believe, and that's the way I was raised. And I've raised my children that way.

Of course when I came back to the United States, I got reacquainted with my sister. I talk about Shanghai and the hard time. She tells me a different story. She came into an American household at 14. They put her back in school. She ended up on the living room couch for years. So she didn't have a bed of roses either, as a refugee girl, you know, being taken into a quote "strange" family.

There was a few letters went back and forth through Switzerland. I've got that in my diary that we've received a letter that she was planning to marry. And then we did not hear from her at all for years. Don't forget, while we lived in Shanghai, the Japanese was winning the war, until the last. We did not know.

She moved from Los Angeles to Wichita, Kansas, he was a professor at the University there. And now he's retired, and they living in Port Richey. We had been separated for that many years, because when you have young children and starting life, you don't have much money to visit. Now that they've retired, I have got a sister again. And like I said, she let me in on many things that I had forgotten from Germany. I had blocked the fact of my mother's death and the funeral completely out of my mind. I had always said that I did not go to her funeral, and my sister said, "I beg to differ with you. You were there. You were sitting right next to me." I says, "Well, if that's what you say, so it must be so." [laughs] I guess it has something to do with the personality.

We both married loving, gentle men, because of my father being such a stinker. It's amazing how much alike we are, even though we've been separated for many years. Coming out of the same household, one being raised in Shanghai, one being raised in the United States, and both of us thinking we've had it hard. My brother-in-law calls me "Little Eva," that's my sister's name, because we are so much alike, we have so many things in common. My daughter said we need to write a book about that. "Momma, one of these days I'd like to write the book Two Sisters." My sister says, "Ruth, we're survivors."

My girlfriend Eva and I, we see each other, we keep up with one another. Not close, but we keep up. They are prosperous, own their own business. She invited me to San Francisco, and I went to her daughter's wedding. There I'm driving my own car, and she's driving her own car in the fancy wedding for her daughter. And we'd laugh, "Did you ever think we'd do that?" [laughs] Inge's coming in May to come to see me, we keep up, you know. She lives in Oakland.

It's those two close girlfriends I have. The boy I used to date for years, he lives in Iowa. And we've kept up a little bit, not too much, because it's a little bit awkward. I've made a new life, I've made new friends.

Eric Reisman's work in postwar Germany as a military consultant demonstrated his professional success. But he had not forgotten the causes of his former refugee life.

While I was still basically quote unquote "illegal" in the United States, but legal to the point that the authorities knew I was here, I started going to school to the Academy of Aeronautics. We got married, I graduated, and I was legal in the United States. I went to work for Sikorsky Aircraft, I was a flight instructor.

Then I got drafted. I was at Fort Sill for the Army, ground instructor and subsequently flight instructor. And as soon as I came out of the service, I went back to work for Sikorsky, and I worked for Sikorsky all this time. Until I retired.

I was service analyst, but then I worked myself into the service engineering part of it, you worked with the customer outside. It was the one position that I was looking for, I was working for the company, and yet I was by myself. I didn't have to work with the vice president looking down at me, every move I made. What I felt I should do to the customer or with the customer, it was left to me.

From 1960 to 1964, I was advisor to the German Luftwaffe. I was in Koblenz discussing theories of operation with the ministers of defense, with the highest German government officials, who were nothing other than Nazis before, because where would they get the know-how at that time, be in that kind of position without being prior German military under the other regime. They knew I was Jewish, I never hid it, I never advertised it. If somebody asked me, I was, "Yes, it's a Jewish holiday, I'm not working today." But I was accepted by all of them, and I was respected by all of them. I liked my work, and I did it to the best ability that I could, and they accepted me. I had never had one word, antisemitic remark, never once, in four years working with the German ministries and the German Army and Air Force, never once.

When I started working for the company, I held a position of importance at the time, being assigned to the U.S. Army Depot in Mannheim, Germany. It was an overhaul depot, and they needed to have a consultant there from Sikorsky, so I was sent there. And my sister-in-law came to visit us, and we went to Frankfurt Rhein-Main airport to meet her. Being that she was a young girl, I wanted to help her carry her valises, and so I said in German to one of the customs officials standing there, "My sister-in-law is coming, I would like to help her carry the bag." I showed him my ID card, at that time I was a GS-15, which was very, very high GS rating. "Oh," he says, "You can't go past the door." So I stood right there, and I waited, and in comes a German lady and they speak together, "Oh yeah, yeah, go in." Now she goes in. So I said, this is ridiculous, if they can go in, I can go in. So I walked right in, and he put his hand on me and he told me I can't go in. I swung around and I flattened that guy, he was laying right there on the floor.

So that's basically my life story. I've been happily married, we're married now for 46 years, and we have two children. Our son lives here, graduated from Babson College, and our daughter graduated from Clark University and made her masters degree in physical therapy at U Penn and lives in New Jersey, married, has two children. My son has one child and is happily married. Our son-in-law is very, very nice fellow, Jewish fellow. My daughter-in-law is not, she's Christian, but she's a lovely, lovely lady, and they're very happily married.

Lotte Schwarz worked in Germany, worked in Shanghai, and worked in California. Life was never easy, but she is a survivor.

When we came here, we had two suitcases. We were three people and had two suitcases. We were two months on Eddy Street in San Francisco. Because my husband had two heart attacks before we left, and he got two injections in here, and they were infected, and he had to be treated right away. They gave us every week, not much, but certain money. They paid our room, and we could live with what we had there, but you could cook in there and everything.

There was a little coffee shop over at the restaurant, breakfast my husband went over and bought a thing of coffee and bought some fresh rolls. That's what we missed the most from Germany, those little warm rolls for breakfast, you know. And then we went around and saw San Francisco. We took the cable car and went to Fisherman's Wharf and everything.

We stayed two months till he got better, at least better so he could travel, you know. And then they ask you if you have relatives anywhere in the United States, because they want to send you where your relatives live. Every Jewish community was asked to take so-and-so many refugees according to how many people they have. But the only one we had was my brother in Kansas City, and I didn't want to go there. In the first place, it wasn't a good climate for my husband. He had to be where it was an even climate, and not too hot and so. And my brother married a women he met in the camp in Shanghai. She was much older than he was. And nobody could get along with her. She was good with my brother, and she was a good wife to him. But I wouldn't want to live with her.

Then we came here to Long Beach. They told my husband right away he could not work anymore, and I knew that. But he worked a little bit. The Jewish community center here in Long Beach had a little stand, now it's a little bigger, for when people come in for coffee or something, was new at that time. And my husband had that for a few weeks. But he wasn't supposed to do anything or work anymore, so he came home.

And I worked and I worked and I worked. All I thought was I have to find a job right away, because I had a daughter and I wanted to educate her and I had a sick husband and I didn't want any welfare. Never took a penny from anybody. When I came here, I worked in Judy Crib Sheet Company in Long Beach. We made the first fitted crib sheet for baby crib, like you have for the big beds, with those fitted corners.

My son was born here in Torrance. Yeah, I didn't want another child, but it happened. And my husband died two months before my son was born. He died in July, of a heart attack, and George was born in September. My boss sent me my paycheck every week. But I felt so bad that I get the money without working, you know. After three weeks, I went back to work.

I was in charge of the factory in Long Beach. I worked there 20 years. Then everybody else made those sheets, too. We hardly had any business anymore. So we closed the place. And that was just when my son started city college here, my daughter already was teaching.

From Judy Crib, I had to hire people. When the business was slow we had to let them go, and then when the business started again, then I had to call up and want new people. That lady at the employment office knew me for when we needed people. And so after Judy Crib closed down I called her, I knew her name, and I said, "You know, now I need a job." She said, "Come on down, we'll find something."

So I went down to her, it was at Long Beach, in that county building. And she said, "You know, we could find a job for you. You could work for Los Angeles County, but you have to make a test. I'll give you some things you can read, you make the test." It was Friday morning. And I said, "I make the test now, I need a job." The test was Friday afternoon. "The test," she said, "takes 45 minutes." I'm no good at math, I didn't do too good in math. All those young high school kids, I was the first one to finish the test. And two hours later I had my job for the County. I went right on up and got a job, and I worked till I had to retire with 65. I have a beautiful diploma from the Board of Supervisors, and all kinds of things. I liked the job. Everybody was nice. I made a good salary.

So my kids went to college. And my daughter's a teacher in a Los Angeles school. She's good girl, beautiful, tall girl, 5'8". And she has two daughters, 20 and 19. And George has two boys.

My brother in Israel, he's an old man now. When Heinz came to Israel in 1934 there was nothing. They had to build up everything. Every tree in Herzliyya my brother built. He knew everything. He was a really good farmer and agriculture expert, and he's still there. He's 80 years now, he's the oldest one, and he's still doing okay. Herzliyya is just beautiful. He has a lovely house. He has one son. He was born in Israel, and he lives in a kibbutz with a family for a long time. Yeah, I was there and saw all that. His wife died, my brother's wife, they were married so long, and now he's alone. He said, "During the day it's fine, I'm busy with everything, but at nights it's terrible."

My brother Berthold died of lung cancer here. It had nothing to do with Shanghai, he smoked like crazy. I visited him in Kansas City some years ago, and he smoked so and he coughed. He was a big guy. I said, "You shouldn't smoke so much." He said, "Look at me how I look, I can smoke, it doesn't do anything to me." But he developed lung cancer. And he smoked. About five years ago he died.

When my daughter got married, she was 23, she is 10 older than George. Dan, her husband, was in medical school at that time, and I thought now things really getting easier, it goes up. That day at her wedding, George got kind of sick, and Dan said right away, "Diabetic." George developed diabetic, and we had to go through that, you know. He was in school on a baseball team and everything, he was a big guy, and I had to go to school and tell him, he can't. I'm a diabetic, but very much under control, I have no problems, I take an insulin shot every morning. I always worry about my son.

And I have to say, we got some kind of money from Germany, I get a nice pension every month. That's what gets me going so nicely. And of course, I have a good Social Security, because I worked 29 years. And I was never one week without a paycheck, never.

I had a very lovely house in Long Beach, which I sold. I was afraid to live there, when both kids were out. Then I had an apartment downtown in Long Beach, a large, very nice apartment. But the neighborhood in Long Beach gets so bad. It was on 4th and Gaviota, close to Bixby Park, and I thought it was a practical, a convenient neighborhood. I didn't even need the car, I could take the bus all over. But it got really bad. And that's when I moved to Leisure World. So then I bought that thing here, in that old age home, and I'm glad I'm living in here now, and that's it.

And besides, Jack, my friend, moved in first. He was a widower from Winnipeg, from Canada. And he said, "When you move in, I'll walk with you. Every day, whatever you want to do, I'll do."

Jack was a real good guy, and a handsome man. He was just as old as I was, had a wonderful family. He had three daughters. He was a furrier, you know, it seems in Canada everybody is a furrier, [laughs] because it's so cold there in winter. But he had retired, and his wife had died, and he had a few operations before, so his daughter said, instead of flying to Winnipeg every few months, "You are going to come here and you'll live here." So I met him in our Jewish community center right after he came here. And we were together for seven years. He took that apartment further down a little bit. And then I took mine.

Jack got sick after a few years, and first he got real heavy. What happened was, it was water. His kidneys didn't function, and the water stayed in his body, you know. His son-in-law called me, he's a doctor, one day, and he said, "Lotte, kidneys you can't repair, there's nothing you can do." And besides, I didn't know he had only one kidney, you can live fine with one kidney when it's healthy, but that wasn't healthy either. His veins collapsed, there was nothing they could do. We walked a few more weeks, a few more months maybe. And then he died. Now it's too late for anything like that. So you think it's getting better, but things can still happen, you know. And you still have to live through that.

CHAPTER 9

My Life as a Refugee

Fifty years later, what remained of the years in Shanghai? For decades, most Shanghai Jews focused their energies on the present and future. Their exile experiences paled in comparison to the stories of concentration camp survivors. They gathered occasionally to talk about Shanghai among themselves, especially in New York and San Francisco, where most of them settled. Their first official reunion was organized in 1985 at the Concord Hotel in New York, and there have been periodic gatherings since then. Their story has gradually edged into public consciousness through memoirs and films.

Our narrators are ordinary people who lived through extraordinary times. They survived Nazi dictatorship, colonial Shanghai, and Japanese occupation. They settled in the United States and devoted decades to succeeding in the freest society they had known. After being stateless during the war, they once again became citizens of a sovereign nation. But they have become more than that: they are citizens of the world whose reflections describe and transcend the violent history of the twentieth century.

People do not automatically become wise through difficult or life-threatening experiences. World travel does not always make one worldly. Yet these narrators express themselves with wisdom, with compassion, and with principles won through their experiences. They spent their formative years in the first half of the twentieth century, but they still have much to tell us in the early twenty-first century, about tolerance and the consequences of hate, about wealth in money and in spirit, and about overcoming adversity. They have had a lifetime to think about their years in Shanghai. What have they learned? What can they tell us about life?

In our interviews, I did not ask these questions directly. After they had talked at length about their lives on several continents, the narrators spontaneously offered these varied reflections on their experiences and emotions, which suggested the title of this chapter.

Doris Grey

Those were the best years of our life, so to speak. And don't forget, I started so many times in life, first when I got married. Then we went to Shanghai. Then we came to New York. In New York I had to take my state boards and start all over again, and that is the only satisfaction I have, that I believed that I helped my husband to become again what he used to be, to work in his profession, and get where he wanted to. Unfortunately, he didn't enjoy it for a long time. It was very, very hard, and it was very depressing at times. But, on the other hand, it was gratifying to help people and to do the best you could with the least means to do it.

I am an optimist, and my mother taught me that already. No matter how bad things are, always take the best part of it. If I wouldn't have inherited it from my mother, I wouldn't have survived. Professionally, I had a chance nobody had. Because I had to do everything, so that was an experience more than a lifetime.

Nowadays, I wouldn't like to work in a hospital anymore. Because they sit at the desk and write and write and write. The nursing care is not so important. Helps do the nursing care. You see, we really did nursing care, and if I tell you, nursing care, it was nursing care. Here, they do your bed, and then nothing, no p.m. care, nothing, nothing. It changed completely, and so does everything in regard to medicine.

What I think of the Chinese, I can only say the best of them. Their mentality, in the beginning, it was hard to digest it. For them, we were *gnakoning,* a foreigner. On the other hand, you get used to it, and at the end, you'd know that they were very helpful. We lived among the lowest class of the Chinese, but they helped us. They showed us how to make coal out of dirt and water, how to use the Japanese oven. After the war, we reciprocated. So when our parcels came from America, from our relatives, when the CARE parcels came, we will call them to the front of our house, we always gave them something. We were glad we could do it. On the other hand, you know, Chinese people laugh or cry, there is no medium. If one of their people is dead, they engage special people just to lament and to cry.

There was a lady from Brooklyn with an accent much worse than mine. She couldn't understand that I wasn't able to speak Yiddish. After a short time, she became very friendly with me, and she knew she was taken care of. One day, that lady called me and she said, "Tell me, why did you come to Shanghai, to New York?" So I said, "Did you ever hear of a certain Mr. Adolf Hitler?" You know what her answer was? "Was it really that bad?" That shows you what you don't go through yourself, you can't imagine. Even the American Jew cannot imagine, and I'm sure that woman came from Poland or somewhere that she must have experienced something, you know.

So, like everything else, it had its bad times and its good times. And if you were an optimist, you tried to forget the bad times. I remember, for instance, when I came to South Africa, I hadn't seen my brother for sixteen and a half years then. We started talking, and he said, "Tell me, how was it when you came to the border and you had to go back?" I had forgotten about it already, somehow.

But the spirit we kept, and I think that's what kept us alive. You know we tried not to demoralize, because we saw what could happen. We are thankful for that, that it didn't happen to us.

Lotte Schwarz

You think, when you come out from Shanghai, you start a new life, now this is it, it goes up again. You wouldn't think that something could happen. You can't say nothing happened in my life.

Nazis are all over, you find them all over, here too. Here are the skinheads, you know. When I walk down the pier, where I usually go every day, I see a few of those skinheads, and it scares me. Because all they are are Nazis.

It was a bad time, but you don't know what you can do, you know. When you have to do it, this is it, and you do it. You just go on living. I don't think I could do that now, to live a difficult time. I don't think so. When you get older, you get weaker, you know.

Nobody ever liked the Jews, huh? Never. Two thousand years ago it started, and longer. I wonder why. There were afraid we are too smart. So they didn't like us.

Otto Schnepp

I became a Zionist out of conviction. I read what had happened in Europe. It was very traumatic for me to face what had happened there. The traumatic part was that I escaped by no act of my own, you know. I was powerless, as it were, a youngster there. So that identification was very strong. That was an important thing for pushing me in this direction of becoming a Zionist and wanting to go to Israel. It seemed like that was worth a good try. And I wanted to do that. I understand now that I did an enormous amount for myself in going to Israel.

It's clear to me that I just stopped being a refugee in Israel. It's a very deep experience, I felt that I was at home there, I had a right to be there and all that. I put aside my refugee status or that part of my personality. I was no longer frightened, because in Israel very primitive things happened to me. I remember very clearly that the first time I came to Israel, they still had military parades on Independence Day. I went to see that. It was something of great importance to me, you know. The idea of being defenseless was so much with me. And then when I was in the reserves, I was doing something with the artillery. They had guns there, firing guns, boom boom, felt damn good. Very primitive things, but very important, if you've lived through this feeling, you know, of being so completely overwhelmed and no defense.

Herbert and Ilse Greening

Herbert Greening: Shanghai was an experience for us. We were young, it was a wonderful adventure. We look back to Shanghai, we liked it. We would have never experienced all that we did experience in China. We went back in '88 to show the kids.

Ilse Greening: We took everything with a lot of humor, but we've been talking about it, it must be because we were young, and it was more an adventure than anything else.

Our children liked it a lot, too. We decided to go with the children, and also last summer we went to Germany, to show our children where we come from, because once we are gone, they have to know. And especially in Shanghai where a lot changed. Not the ghetto, though.

Herbert Greening: And now they want to go back to Silesia, to the town where I was born, which was called then Königshütte, which is now called Chorzów, and they want to go to Breslau, which is now called Wrocław, where I went to med school, and they want to go to Berlin.

I still feel very German, I can't help it. German education, German culture, German literature, German art, it sits there, we can't help it. [laughs]

Ilse Greening: I have to say that my parents traveled. They went to Italy and Switzerland and Holland, I mean, they did travel, but still our life would have been limited to a certain area. We would have settled in Hannover...

Herbert Greening: Or another small town in Germany. I would have been the *Pillenbeutelwiesendoktor,* country doctor.

Ilse Greening: And I'm happy we went to Australia, we went to Hong Kong and Singapore, and we know all those places. There are a lot of people all over the world we know. I'm grateful for that. And we're still traveling. Of course, with the changing times now we would have traveled also, but our outlook and meeting so many interesting people, oh yes, we grew a lot, a lot.

Ernest Culman

The Japanese were not really that cruel to us. Compared to Germany, I mean, it was nothing. And when people say to me I have to consider myself a survivor, I have difficulty with that. Because I see a survivor as somebody who survived a German concentration camp. Things weren't that bad. But they were bad enough.

I had a hard time with feelings. To some degree to this day, expressing my feelings is difficult for me, because I pushed my feelings aside to survive. You know, you form friendships in Germany, in Shanghai, in Baltimore, wherever, and then people move away, so you don't hold on to friends that long. I still have a hard time making close friends with people. Lots of acquaintances, but a really close friendship is very difficult for me. And I think that it goes back to that time, when my feelings were suppressed by me, because that is the way I felt I could survive.

We didn't have to live like we did in Shanghai, if my father would have been more willing to go to work for the clinic right away. What he did to my brother, making him work in that machine shop, is inexcusable. For years I felt guilty about these feelings. That's my whole life.

Eric Reisman

I guess all my life I was always, I wouldn't say I assimilated, because I have never denied my being Jewish, but I have never advertised the fact of being Jewish either. To this day I don't walk around with a Jewish star around me. I just don't feel that I want to advertise it, yet every Friday night I go to services. I believe in being Jewish. I have mezuzahs hanging on all the doors, but I don't have to advertise it.

I call myself Holocaust survivor, although I was fortunate never having been in concentration camp, or my mother and father. But having lived under the circumstances for as long as I have and being able to escape those circumstances in Austria, I think I qualify.

Gérard Kohbieter

It was a lifesaver. The Chinese are polite people, and they put up with a lot with us. You were in an environment where *Ausländlerhaß* [hatred of foreigners] existed perhaps, but it was never expressed. Some refugees had it in their head that they were superior to the Chinese, and that's a considerable error in thinking. There were some frictions, but all in all, I must say they were good hosts. I'm grateful to them.

One should perhaps, at a certain age, try to forget what's happening out there. It's such a dangerous thing to do. As a magician I am always interested in how it works. How do they do it? I know what they are doing, but how are they going to put it over, you know? It's like you know somebody is cheating at poker. I want to watch this guy and see how he does it. It's a good comparison, I think. But as a consequence one suffers. If you have a social conscience, if you see injustice, if you see outrageous things are happening. I mean, I wouldn't sit sobbing for hours in a corner, but you push it away, and I think your body reflects it. I'm pretty sure that what I got in my throat is possibly a psychosomatic development from rage and anger about things I've heard and seen, that I've simply repressed, or suppressed, which would be conscious. Perhaps you can't do that.

Renate suggested that I don't read the *Spiegel* anymore, it's really one catastrophe after another. You say, "My God, they've done it all!" They couldn't possibly shock you anymore. Next Monday, there it is, baby. Another hammer! It's like sitting on a sinking ship. And you drive yourself nuts thinking about it. I mean, the feeling of impotence is total. Nothing you can do. You can influence, perhaps, a few people that happen to be around you, by the way you live, by the way you act and think and feel, but I don't think that's terribly effective.

The hippies had a rather exaggerated view of their influence on society, but I think they were naive, they were sweet and wonderful, man. In Haight-Ashbury when that hippie thing started, a young woman, 17 or 18, came up to me and had a bunch of flowers and gave me a flower and wished me a good day, and that was it and then she walked away. She said it smiling, and she meant it. That woman was really concerned whether I had a good day or not. It was touching. It was not a formality. That was her way of spreading love or spreading good. Beautiful. Ain't going to change things in Washington a bit.

It is important that people march. It is important that people protest. Even in Nazi Germany there was an incident where they busted a bunch of Jewish husbands of Christian wives, and the wives got together and went to the police station, and made a fuss and said, "We want our husbands back," and they got them back.[1] Well, now, that gives one room for thought, doesn't it? Didn't happen much, that people protested. Well, I ain't gonna march. And I should stop reading the *Spiegel,* but I don't think I can. I'm too curious, man, I'm like a cat. Besides, you got pretty good book reviews.

I have to consider that I spent eight years, and crucial years, 16 to 24. I mean, you grow up in that period, you learn things, your personality forms, attitudes form. I had a lot of time to observe people and probably got used to doing that. The attitude towards money I attribute to Shanghai. At that time it was, of course, also a mild consolation that everybody was in the same boat. You weren't the only one that was running around with a hole in his shoe and it was raining and didn't have enough to eat sometimes. That was just the way it was. And you learned that being poor isn't the end. I don't have investments, but if I had investments and my stock was worthless suddenly, I don't think I'd jump out the window. I mean, where is it written that you should lead the same life all your life?

In Shanghai I said to myself, when the war was over, this will never happen to me again. I will go to America, and I will make money, baby. I will make money, money, money. And the first time I cried in a movie was in New York, and I discovered that I wasn't really all that tough. It quickly developed that making money wasn't really my thing. A famous economist, I forgot who it was, said that the only way to solve personal economy is to reduce your needs. Or the American saying, "All you need is one dollar more than you need." That too leaves a spectrum, but if you are modest, I'm content.

I did have money once, I come from a family that had money. If you are born into something like that, you accept it. It wasn't that big a carrot to hang before me. Maybe if Hitler hadn't come, I would have inherited the business and found myself somebody to run that properly and gone into moviemaking or something, or maybe an academic career. Psychology had always intrigued me. I like to think Shanghai had something to do with it.

Mark Twain said once, "Broke don't scare me." Well, it doesn't scare me, but I've always taken care that that stage of affairs doesn't happen again. But loosely, without busting my fanny. Looking back, you know, when you are 72, you can sort of look back and see everything and figure, "Well, if you do that right, all in all, yeah." Because I have lots of friends who've been very successful, and I mean money successful, and they seemed to be a little envious of me. I have more time. I laugh more. I do more interesting things.

Alfred Kohn

My father had a brother in Vienna, they found out that a transport went from Yugoslavia to Palestine, and the ship was sunk with all the people aboard. He and his wife and two sons were killed in that thing. My father had a brother in Breslau, he was killed. Another brother went to Cuba. He got sick in Cuba, they took him off the stretcher to America, he died here. His wife committed suicide. Another brother, who was married to a non-Jewish woman in Paris, he got killed by the Nazis. The wife and the children went to a convent, they survived the war.

My mother was six brothers and sisters in Germany, three got killed, my mother survived, my mother's oldest sister survived in Argentina, and my mother's youngest brother lived in Israel with a daughter, who's still alive today. Two of my mother's sisters married two brothers, and the brothers looked like twins. Both of them wore glasses. One brother worked in an underground factory for the Germans as a slave laborer, and one day he broke his glasses, couldn't work anymore, so they shot him. The older brother went to Argentina, and he's walking in the street, [emotional voice] and a man comes over and says to him, "Are you Mr. Mondschein?" He said, "Yes." And he says, "I can't believe this, I saw how they shot you. I saw how they dragged you out from the underground." He said, "That's my brother."

I still speak German, I go back to Germany, I still have German relatives that are not Jewish on my wife's. But I am totally unforgiving for anybody who had anything to do with the extermination of Jews. There was a small minority who didn't participate, but it was very hard not to participate. If you were not a member of the Party, you had no future in Germany. You didn't get a good job, you didn't get a promotion in your company, you were ostracized. So I cannot blame many of the Germans who went along.

In Florida where we have an apartment, I belong to a tennis club and there are a lot of non-Jewish Germans, mostly born after the war or during the war, you know, it's a generation younger. They all know I'm Jewish, and they are sometimes very apologetic. I tell them, "Listen to me. What is done we cannot undo, but it is your responsibility as a German to say and to do that these things don't happen again. Not here in America, but in your little town where you come, where you tell me there are no Jews in your town. For that's where you have to say, 'We made a mistake, we chased people and killed people out of this country who lived here a thousand years, that can never happen again.' You've got to open up your mouth. You're not going to say, 'Gee, I'm sorry, it wasn't me, it was not even my father.'"

Unfortunately my son married a non-Jewish woman, and we do not have a good relationship because of it. She has children from a previous marriage, and I will never accept it, neither will my wife. And we still see our son, he comes, I never go there, I don't want to have anything to do with that, and I told him so. I told him, "You have broken the continuity of Jewish life and I can never forgive you," and I will never forgive him.

It's as we say, *"Schwer zu sein a Jid,"* it's not easy to be a Jew. But I believe it's much easier to be a Jew if you want to be a Jew, than if you don't want to be a Jew.

Ralph Hirsch

My father had vowed that he'd never set foot on German soil again. He had never forgiven the Germans for stripping him of his German citizenship, which I fully understand. He didn't keep that vow by the way, he went back about 25 years later at the urging of my mother, whose family was still over there. And in fact, her mother came over to live with us in the '50s. Her husband had died, my grandfather, had died after the war, and she was alone, so she came over to America. Never really took root there. She didn't speak the language, she felt very isolated. She died perhaps a year later.

I don't think my father was particularly happy that I began to visit Germany and several other European countries, but particularly Germany, in the 50s when I was a student. And it was only after my mother had been back a couple of times, I think that he finally decided he would accompany her back to Germany.

Lisbeth Loewenberg

It was a very interesting experience, I thought, that really showed the difference between people. The ones who had get up and go, and the ones who didn't. Because practically everybody came out with no money. There were very few who had money already outside of Germany. But 90 percent had nothing. Some made it and some didn't. And it had nothing at all to do really with what people used to be. We had friends who were very well-to-do in Vienna. He got here, and he was completely helpless and couldn't do a darn thing. Other people who never had anything before, all of a sudden had it in them to go out and do something about the situation. It sort of separated the men from the boys, or the women from the girls. Because everybody had nothing, and they had to start from scratch in an unknown place, in impossible circumstances. It's amazing what they did.

A theory that I developed in Shanghai and then in San Francisco, that you meet the same type of people wherever you are. Because the others that you are not congenial with, you don't meet. Somehow you will always have the same type of persons around you. Mysteriously or not mysteriously. How did people meet? Well, first of all, it was very close physically, the same kind of fate and destiny. Everybody knew everybody, and there was more gossip going on than you can possibly imagine. Gossip was the main entertainment. But still, naturally, there were groups of friends. We got to know almost everybody, because most people did read. That was the only entertainment, and yet you get to know people, there were many coffee houses, restaurants, and you see people. "Where do you come from?" "From Vienna," "From there," "From there." Or, "Where did you live, and what did you do?" I mean, everybody was in the same boat. So there were no strangers in that sense. But then some people you like and you meet again, and others you don't. There was certainly no difficulty in meeting anybody as far as social life was concerned.

It was a close-knit community, even if, as I say, the main entertainment was gossip, it's because it was so close, everywhere to know who slept with whom. You hardly find as close-knit a community, not in San Francisco, not in Vienna where everybody is very selective, and you only talk to people you have been introduced to. I mean, it has to be somebody's friend or relative or this or that. In Vienna, the first question is, "What's his family, where does he come from?"

All of a sudden, that was the interesting part, all the barriers fell. It didn't make any difference, what does your family do, where did she come from, and so on and so forth, because everybody was there and started from scratch, nil, nothing, in Shanghai. All things being equal, if all people start under the same adverse conditions, this is where your true ability will show or your true survival instincts or your enterprise, whatever you want to call it. They couldn't call on family connections or rich friends or their bank accounts anymore, because it didn't exist. Here they had to show what they could do on their own, without their exalted circumstances. That I realized. Don't ever blame the condition, blame yourself. Because under the most impossible conditions, some people will make it one way or another.

It also taught me one thing: that happiness has nothing to do with possessions. That you can live with minimal possessions or in one room. You can be just as happy in one room as you can be in a house. You don't have to have much.

It was a good experience.

Melitta Colland

There was a difference in the attitude towards this whole Holocaust from one brother to the other. Because Henry, the younger brother, left really before it got so drastically bad. Paul left after Kristallnacht, and I, of course, too. And when we first got together again, I could see that there isn't this utmost hatred in Henry that was in Paul and me. Probably because he has very good friends all over the world, and he is more, how shall I say, willing to forgive and forget. I'm not and neither was my brother Paul.

I was in Vienna once and once only, in 1960, for three days, with Asherah as a teenager and my mother. I couldn't wait to get out. I hated every minute I was there. And my brother Henry, who travels all over Europe continually, and who has friends in Germany and friends in Austria and friends in Switzerland, he called me from Vienna, and I could hear by the tone of his voice that it was even depressing to him. He says, "The city is beautiful. Everything looks lovely." But there was such a sadness in his voice. Well, alone the experience of being back in the town that you lived all your childhood in. You have all your childhood memories, and you had all your friends there. And suddenly you come to the town, and there isn't a soul that you really know.

I used to say, I personally am grateful to Hitler, because he pushed me out of becoming a very middle class, very narrow-minded little nothing. Because that is the feeling I have now, that I would have grown up to be, in that type of life that we lived in Vienna. Vienna, to me, was always, how should I say, a little mediocre in certain respects. Outstanding in others, like music and opera, etcetera. But very mediocre in the world horizon for people. And when you lived there, and you stayed in that kind of life, you became that way, too. I mean, I would not have been the person I feel I am today, with somewhat knowledge for life and world, and other people's feelings and other people's knowledge.

Ruth Sumner

I remember about Shanghai I was young, I was optimistic, we had a good time. I mean, nothing fazed me, nothing bothered me. I did not suffer. I enjoyed my teenage years. They were very uncomplicated when you compare with what the kids are doing these days. So I enjoyed Shanghai. We didn't have much to eat. But everybody was in the same boat, so who cared? I never felt a lack of anything, because I had my friends, I had enough to eat, it wasn't the best, but it was adequate. We made clothing out of blankets and curtains, but I dressed well. So we took in stride with a youthful bouncing back. That's the way the situation was, so we survived.

My life has been enriched because I have been in Shanghai. I don't talk, make a big to-do about it, but I don't hide it. I haven't done this in years, talk that much about the past. We were very fortunate that we weren't killed, that we had enough food.

What have I gotten from Shanghai? I've gotten from Shanghai the realization that you can be down and still be up. You don't have to be afraid. You're the same person, whether you have money or if you don't. It's self-worth that counts. If I would have lived in Europe, I would have been into the best schools. I would have been well chaperoned and had all the advantages, I'm sure, that I did not have. It's nice to have nice things, but if I don't have it, so what? I'm still me. It's what's inside of me that's counting so much, not the possessions that I have accumulated. Unto this day, this is the advantage of ever having been low, you're not afraid of it anymore. I learned to be very frugal. I still sew, I still make my own clothes.

Just like if they were to replant you, you'd take yourself with you. You're still the same person that you are, with your values. This is what I'm saying, this is what's important. It's not what you've got, it's who you are, that's what counts. What your beliefs are, the type of person you are. And if you had children and took your children with you, you'd put into them your values, no matter, the geography has nothing to do with it.

I believe being in Shanghai and having tasted poverty, having tasted being a nobody, makes you a little bit more aware that the veneer is not what's important. You know what the veneer is? Good manners, money, *Kinderstube* [good upbringing]. I had a dickens of a time with that, because I was so raised. My aunt used to teach me, "There's a difference between a woman and a lady, a man and a gentleman. It's breeding." Now that I'm an adult and I'm beginning to judge myself, I am seeing it doesn't really matter. I have gotten over that. Because that is not what's important. So if you don't know what fork to use or if you aren't that educated, but what's inside of you that counts, what kind of person you are. And that bridges all color barriers of people and heritages and backgrounds. It's their inner values. But this is me now speaking. That's how I have changed.

I think Shanghai helped. Because being a stateless refugee is being the bottom of the barrel, so you become a little more tolerant and understanding. I'm proud of my heritage, because it's the soul that I grew out of, matured into the person that I am today. My life, it's part of me, and I'm not ashamed of it. It was a good foundation.

When I went to the Concord, it was a very funny situation. It was all of a sudden you were back, back when, where. I wasn't the only one, I was almost giddy. It was almost a reliving of the past. But yet you were so changed, that you knew that you were like two ships meeting at sea. "Oh good, I'm glad to see you, you've changed." And unless you kept up over the years, it didn't mean that much. It was fun.

I never would have translated that diary had I not gone through that reunion, and begin to realize that my past is different and I wanted to live that. And I wanted my daughter to know about that, and perhaps her children. I've got five granddaughters, but right now they couldn't care less.

You know, they are very proud of their Jewish heritage. My little granddaughter said, "I'm half-Jew." And I said, "No, you're not, you're quarter-Jew, but that's enough." So she's very proud of that, you know. [laughs] But my dead mommy, of course, the older generations are dead.

Conclusion

Within the broad scope of Holocaust history, the refugee experience occupies a subordinate place. Life and death in Auschwitz, Babi Yar, and the Warsaw ghetto continue to demand historians' skills and contemplation. The plight of those who escaped the wartime horrors of Nazi genocide has been overshadowed by the camps, and refugees often refrained from drawing attention to themselves in their efforts to assimilate to new environments. Much of the initial writing about them focused on the difficulties of becoming a refugee, the hurdles placed in the way of Jews who tried to flee. Public exposure of the grimly unsympathetic policies of the Western democracies, motivated by selfishness and antisemitism, has led to much more humane responses to crises of persecution since the creation of the United Nations.[1]

The hundreds of thousands of refugees, scattered across the globe, separated from their extended families and cultural roots, have tended to defy group analysis. The literature on German Jewish refugees has been absorbed into histories of their new host countries, just as the refugees themselves tried to assimilate into American, British, or Israeli society. A recent exception is the attempt by Walter Laqueur to write the history of the younger generation of German Jewish refugees. Some of the niches into which refugees settled have been examined more closely.[2] I am waiting for someone to do research on refugees who returned with the U.S. Army to Europe to fight the Germans, as my father did.

The stories told by our narrators have passed many historical tests: they relate experiences known to the narrators, they are not contradicted by other reliable evidence, and they represent the wider experiences of many Shanghai refugees.

These stories are still only a partial history of refugees in Shanghai. In particular, scarcity of evidence from and about the generation who occupied leadership roles in Shanghai makes it difficult to write the internal history of this community. A fuller picture would include the variety of perspectives brought by all those other groups who jostled with each other in this overcrowded, but exciting city. Someone will tell us one day about the letters that Japanese soldiers in Shanghai wrote home and about the diaries of Shanghai natives. The spectrum of expatriate behavior from official disdain to individual generosity must be filled in. The most we may hope for from the 13 narrators who appear here is a varied, but one-sided narrative. Even that depends on our faith in their memory.

What is the relationship between the experiences of the narrators and the stories they tell? Over the past few decades, analytical discussions of memory as a building block of history have properly complicated our understanding of sources. The unique existence of Holocaust denial, a broad, concerted, and never-ending effort to claim that a major historical event never happened, has made tellers of Holocaust narratives sensitive, even anxious. Every incident of Holocaust fabrication becomes a world-wide cause célèbre, such as the unlikely story of Herman Rosenblat.[3] Oral narratives have been scrutinized with special skepticism, as if any form of written Holocaust document, from Eichmann's report on the Wannsee Conference to the most recently published survival memoir, did not also spring from fallible memory.

Oral histories, once criticized by Raul Hilberg as unreliable, have emerged as a crucial source of evidence to be interrogated in the same ways as documents. Christopher Browning's classic work on Holocaust perpe-trators, *Ordinary Men*, and his more recent *Collected Memories*, examine the congruences and discrepancies among memories of the same events and explain the analytical process he used to arrive at the most plausible recon-struction.[4] Lawrence Langer argues that the "deep memory" of camp sur-vivors preserves more authentic sensations of personal experiences.[5]

The functioning of memory represents one stage of the transformation of experience into narrative. A subsequent stage is telling, the construction of narratives from memories. Henry Greenspan, one of the most thought-ful interviewers of survivors, writes about how the process and setting of recounting, as well as the role of the listener, affects what is told.[6]

In the Introduction, I offered my affirmation of the accuracy of the nar-rators' memories: I believe what they said. That means, I believe that they tried to accurately portray their memories when they talked with me. That is not always the case, especially with Holocaust memories. Browning's *Ordinary Men* depended heavily on judicial interrogations of perpetrators, and thus on his ability to distinguish between testimonies that "had the 'feel' of candor and frankness conspicuously absent from the exculpatory, alibi-laden, and mendacious testimony so often encountered in such court records."[7] All of the interviews excerpted here had the feel of candor.

The discussion of how memory ultimately relates to history, this history and all history, has just begun. Each study offers raw material for that discussion. The story of the death of several newborns in the Ward Road Emigrant Hospital illuminates the complex relationship between memory, telling, and history.

Memories can be truthfully and accurately told, but still be false. When the Greenings debated where to have their baby delivered, they heard about the deaths of several infants at the Ward Road Hospital. Dr. Greening, whom we should assume was a well-informed expert, explained what he remembered: *"The heating in the new baby department was very primitive. They had what they called electric suns, electric heating lamps. And there was a short cut in the electricity and three babies died from exposure to cold."* No matter what form Dr. Greening might use to put his memories into narrative, this is the story he had to tell. But Doris Grey, the head nurse at that hospital, told a better story.

> *Six babies, newborn, died in one night. And, of course, at that time we didn't know any better and they thought because it was not heated. We couldn't heat, we couldn't use any electricity. But we kept them with hot water bottle and blankets and everything. It was a virus, we knew it afterwards. But people were saying they died of frost cold, you know. They didn't.*

Doris Grey's narrative encompasses Herbert Greening's, explains his error, and offers us a different judgment based on better proximity and evidence. Her superior authority brings more details to light. Mrs. Ascher told her years later that two of the babies were her twins. Now we know, too.

There is one more story to tell, which does not appear in any interview transcript. As we wandered on the grounds of the Ward Road Hospital in Shanghai in 1989, a few days after our interview, one of my narrators whispered to me that her baby had also been among those newborns. As in every interview, and every memoir, diary, and letter, crucial historical information had been withheld. Whatever truth we may discover in our sources, each telling displays a negotiation between memory and intention that only the narrator can know about. Based on considerable experience with interviews, both audio and video, and with memoirs, including interviews and memoirs produced by the same person, I believe that the form, and even locale, of telling crucially affects the content. I cannot imagine this former refugee writing of her child's death in any memoir. She did not speak of it in our single interview session. Only a later conversation in a special place allowed the transformation of memory into recounting.[8]

Accepting these caveats, the recounted memories collected here permit us to observe closely one stream of refugees and their interactions with other peoples. Able to create a new German Jewish community in Shanghai, then crammed into a tiny urban space for several years after 1943, the interactions between these Jews and the other national groups they encountered offer unusually clear insight into the social attitudes of a variety of peoples at mid-century. I offer now some generalizations derived from Jewish refugee interactions with Germans, with citizens of Western democracies, with Chinese and Japanese, and with other Jews. Much is revealed about these peoples and about the refugees themselves.

There is little new to say about Germans and Jews in Europe. The Jews who fled to Shanghai were Germans in their own minds. Their family stories often begin with a recitation of generations of life in Germany, with an emphasis on their rootedness in the German landscape. The World War I service of fathers and grandfathers is offered as proof of national allegiance and belonging. German Christians, both Catholic and Protestant, overwhelmingly supported another viewpoint: Jews could never be Germans, no matter how long their families had lived on German soil. While debate about the support of ordinary Germans for genocide goes on, it is clear that the Nürnberg Laws of 1935 excluding Jews from the national community won popular support throughout Germany.[9] Although refugees recount tales of assistance from sympathetic neighbors and friends as persecution intensified, many of these stories are about people who helped them leave.

Interactions with Germans did not end when the refugees escaped from Germany. About 2,500 Germans lived in Shanghai, taking advantage of the colonial privileges of Europeans in Asian outposts. Nazis controlled all administrative posts and published the major German newspapers, so those refugees like Lotte Schwarz, who had to visit the German Consulate, had unpleasant experiences.[10] But most Germans in Shanghai appear to have been much friendlier to Jews than Germans in Germany. If we add Melitta Colland's unexpected story about making dresses for the wife of the German news agency's director, to Gérard Kohbieter's employment by a German bookseller, to the much broader silence across all my interviews about unpleasant interactions with antisemitic Germans in Shanghai, we can tentatively conclude that location made a great difference in the relationship between German Christians and German Jews. Perhaps the Germans who lived in Shanghai in the late 1930s were much more tolerant than those at home. Perhaps Jews were much more tolerable to these Germans once they were no longer in Germany. Generalizations about German antisemitism can be refined by examining the relationships between German Christians and Jews in places outside of Germany.

Germans were a minority among the white Westerners who controlled Shanghai and its economy until the Japanese forcibly took over in 1941. When Jewish refugees arrived in Shanghai, many settled in areas governed by businessmen from England, France, and the United States. Much of the economic life of Shanghai was controlled by these men. Yet our narrators virtually never mention them. There was very little contact of any kind between Shanghai's Western communities and the Jewish refugees outside of exceptional circumstances, such as the boarding of the Reisman brothers with English-speaking families. Most central European refugees seem barely cognizant of the harsh treatment of Westerners by the Japanese, who interned thousands of British and American citizens after Pearl Harbor for the duration of the war.

The Westerners in Shanghai had everything, and the refugees had nothing. Yet the collective reaction of the Western communities to the appearance of the first ships carrying penniless refugees from Nazi Germany in late 1938 was to try to prevent any more from landing. Detective Sergeant Pitts of the Special Branch of the Shanghai Municipal Police reported on the arrival of the first "batches of Germans of the Jewish faith" in November 1933. During 1939, Pitts or one of his colleagues wrote a report about every arrival of a ship with passengers, even just a handful, for the purpose of specifying the number of Jews.[11]

Pitts himself developed considerable sympathy for and understanding of the refugees. He told his superiors that "most of them are with nothing more than their clothes" and reminded them that "Shanghai is at present the only place in the world which refugee Jews may enter without question." Pitts praised the local Jewish committees for their remarkable charitable efforts. The SMC showed no such sympathy. Two weeks later, the Vice Chairman was painfully clear about the official response: "the Council must not take any action which can possibly be interpreted to mean that it is, or ever will be, in many way responsible for the maintenance of the refugees in question."[12] Nowhere in my reading or interviewing have I come across reference to any public effort by the Western elite to help the refugees. Official representatives of the Western democracies acted no more charitably toward the refugees than the German community in Shanghai.

This attitude represents a second form of antisemitism, next to the fanatically murderous ideas of the Nazis. Central European Jews appeared in large numbers in Shanghai because they were not wanted in the West. Western elites in Shanghai displayed the same attitudes toward Jews as the elites in their home countries: they did not like them, they would not help them, but they did nothing to harm them. They were indifferent to Jewish suffering, even when it existed right under their noses.

Their form of antisemitism persisted right through the extraordinary growth and extraordinary crimes of the much more deadly central European antisemitism. The democracies became the heroes of the war by defeating fascism. This victory allowed their form of antisemitism to continue after 1945, politically visible as the continued barriers to Jewish immigration, which only gradually lost force over the next decades.

Although history appears rarely to teach lessons, growing knowledge of the Holocaust has shown Western democracies the tragedy of prejudice. After centuries of deadly Christian antisemitism, the modern world has witnessed a remarkable change of heart. In Europe and America, official antisemitism is finally gone. That transformation may have followed a broader popular acceptance of refugee Jews among ordinary Americans. I will return below to the final stage of the journey of the Shanghai Jews, which casts a different light on their interactions with Westerners, and on themselves.

Facing this wall of indifference, Jewish refugees could rely on the help of other Jews. One charge that antisemites often make about Jews is that they stick together. In the face of such anti-Jewish disdain, that should hardly be surprising. Yet the level of Jewish self-help described here is surprising. Jews across the world went to enormous lengths to help these refugees at every stage of their ordeal. From the Hilfsverein in Germany to the spontaneous generosity of Jewish communities along the ocean voyage to the extraordinary willingness of the Baghdadi and Russian communities in Shanghai to feed and house thousands, Jews helped Jews in need. The unflagging efforts of the American Jewish Joint Distribution Committee throughout the war prevented mass starvation in Hongkou.

As some of the narrators note in the final chapter, being Jewish means feeling a bond with other Jews and acting on that feeling to help Jews in need. In the face of Christian indifference and antisemitism, the Jewish family meant much more than blood relatives. The assistance provided by Jews who had never met these refugees helped them all to survive. This is an extraordinary aspect of the refugee experience that has not received the attention it deserves. These social and economic bonds may partially explain why some refugees preserved the sense of being Jewish over a lifetime devoid of religious practice, as in the case of my own family.

There are, however, limits to this sense of Jews as one extended family. It goes beyond the familiar joke about Jews arguing among themselves: "three Jews, five opinions." The stories in this book separate Jews into clearly demarcated ethnic-national communities. The central European refugees felt themselves to be different from the Baghdadi Jews, the Russian Jews, and the Polish Jews. Much of this separation was religious: the Baghdadi community was Sephardic, and the Poles were Orthodox. Similar experiences of persecution and flight were not sufficient to overcome the historical resentments between the Western Jews, who developed Reform Judaism in German-speaking territories, and the Eastern Jews, who preserved Orthodoxy in Slavic lands. Despite the immense contributions made by the Baghdadi elite and by individual Russian Jews to the survival of central European Jews in Shanghai, relationships among these communities remained distant and superficial. This book contributes little to the history of the other three groups of Shanghai Jews, because the German-speakers knew little about them.

The separation among these Jewish communities continued after the war. Palestine, and then Israel, was the preferred destination for the Baghdadi and Russian Jews, despite material deprivation and continued war with the Arabs. The central European Jews overwhelmingly chose to go to the United States, even if they had to wait longer in Shanghai.[13] Many of the German Jews who did go to Israel stayed only a few years. Just among our narrators' families, Otto Schnepp, Alfred Kohn, and Ruth Sumner's cousin lived in Israel before coming to North America. These divergent group preferences were rooted in the more secular attitudes of the German and Austrian Jews and their lesser interest in Zionism. The most committed Zionists within the German Jewish community had already moved directly to Palestine: nearly 60,000 Jews from Greater Germany, about one-fifth of those who escaped from Europe, went to Palestine.[14]

The trucks that carried newly arrived Jews and their luggage from the piers at the Bund to their first accommodation in barracks set up by the Baghdadi community traveled across the Garden Bridge from the Western architecture of downtown Shanghai to wartorn Hongkou. There they finally encountered a Chinese city. Unlike their silence about the other Shanghai Jews, the refugees could not help but remark on the Chinese among whom they lived. As Lisbeth Loewenberg says, the shock was immediate: *"I saw these masses of people. I thought that there has to be an accident or something going on, there cannot be that many people always, like ants, constantly. I thought that I would never be able to breathe again in my whole life."* Many Chinese in Hongkou were also refugees, seeking safety from the Japanese army. But these parallel circumstances were insufficient to overcome the enormous social and cultural gulf between Jews and Chinese. For central Europeans, most Chinese in Shanghai represented an abject poverty that no longer existed in Berlin or Vienna. This might evoke sympathy from the refugees, as Lotte Schwarz says: *"It was a very bad time in Shanghai for the Chinese people, too. More than for us, I say."*

But shared suffering could not overcome cultural distance. Otto Schnepp summarized relations between the two communities: *"Chinese were all over the place, and Chinese language was all over the place, and the writing was everywhere, you know. And yet the refugees kept completely apart from China."* Exceptions were small children, like Ralph Hirsch, and those adults who met educated middle-class Chinese through work, such as the Greenings. Otto Schnepp had Chinese classmates at St. John's University, and his unusual knowledge of Chinese made all the difference.

Beyond a few individual successes in bridging the cultural gap, Jewish refugees, despite their precarious circumstances, still represented the white European hegemony that had been imposed on Shanghai for a hundred years. The end of colonialism allowed some uglier sentiments to come to the surface, as Schnepp perceptively noted: *"After the war there was great animosity on the part of Chinese towards foreigners, deep-seated animosity. That was there, I think, all the time."*

In spite of the cultural separation, and the occasional thefts, most former refugees feel gratitude for Chinese hospitality. Although the Chinese in Shanghai had little say about the sudden arrival of thousands of Jews in their midst, their utter lack of hostility, at least until 1945, was a welcome contrast to the attitudes of virtually every other nationality the refugees encountered.

After December 1941, the most important external relationships of the refugee community were with the Japanese. Nearly all the refugees I interviewed, except the very youngest ones, told stories about Ghoya to emphasize the brutality of the Japanese as a occupying power. Every slap by Ghoya was felt throughout the community. The pain has lingered for half a century. This form of Japanese violence became part of the narrators' experiences before knowledge of what the Nazis actually were capable of could reach them. The outrage at Ghoya that is apparent in their stories reproduces feelings from their past.

The narrators now know about the Holocaust that they escaped, which is also invariably mentioned at some point during an interview. This newer knowledge does not, however, function to revise the internalized meaning of the Ghoya stories. It is added on, creating one of those contradictions that are part of every confrontation of remembered past experiences with life at the moment of telling.

I see the stories about Ghoya and the nature of Japanese behavior toward Jewish refugees in the comparative context of the Holocaust. For me, the crucial element of Japanese behavior is their refusal to do anything like what the Nazis repeatedly demanded they do. The Japanese military created a situation in Shanghai in which Jewish refugees could survive.

They made life difficult, they forced the Jews into a ghetto around sensitive military installations, and they destroyed the independence of their communal organizations. But they also allowed thousands to enter Shanghai in 1938 and 1939, then a couple of thousand more from Lithuania into Japan itself. Japanese behavior toward Jews came from a mixture of gratitude for past Jewish help to Japan, respect for Jewish culture, exaggerated assumptions about Jewish world power, and desire to maintain an alliance with Nazis. It was equivocal and unpredictable. But it never became deadly.

Official Japanese behavior toward Jews under their control compares favorably not just with Germans and Austrians. Across the European continent, popular hatred of Jews encouraged by antisemitic policies of the political elite created a deadly collaboration with the Nazis. While Ghoya attended Jewish soccer games and slapped some men who requested passes out of the Designated Area, French police rounded up Jews and delivered them to trains headed toward Auschwitz, and Lithuanian mobs publically beat Jews to death. By resisting German pressure to murder Jews and providing a refuge where thousands could survive, the Japanese most clearly resemble the Italians, the Danes, and the Bulgarians. Ghoya was no rescuer of Jews, but he represented a government and a military hierarchy that steadfastly refused to participate in the Holocaust.

Hearing the narrators tell their Ghoya stories in their own way serves two purposes: it demonstrates how they perceived their own experiences, and it helps us understand what the Japanese did not do. I think the contrast is fruitful for our understanding of the lives of these refugees, even if we might not fully share their outrage at Ghoya's petty humiliations. In this way, the narrators' stories have been transmuted into my history of their community.

German-speaking Jews became refugees against their will. Those who went to Shanghai resisted the idea of leaving their homeland for years, hoping that the German people would come to their senses in time to protect them. The events of 1938 forced them to flee for their lives. They did not choose Shanghai as a destination; Shanghai was forced upon them by the lack of alternatives.

But once they landed in China, German and Austrian Jews regained the freedom they had lost at home to shape their own lives. Until 1943, there were almost no restrictions on their behavior, except those caused by a lack of resources. Unlike the bigger streams of refugees to the United States, Britain, Argentina, or Palestine, assimilation into the dominant culture was impossible. The immediate development of a new German Jewish urban culture on the streets of Shanghai tellingly reveals, I believe, the deepest cultural values of the broader diaspora from central Europe.

The most easily noticed manifestation of their own creative impulses was the blossoming of a café culture in Hongkou. Coffee shops, delicatessens, and kosher butchers lined streets rebuilt after the Japanese bombings of 1937. "Little Vienna" was the voluntary re-creation in Asia of central European Jewish life. The new German newspapers, soccer clubs, and intellectual societies did not simply regenerate a familiar culture. They demonstrate what kind of lives the refugees wanted to live: German Jewish lives. There has been little serious investigation of the development of German Jewish culture in Shanghai, with the exception of the theater.[15] It is clear, however, that expulsion from Greater Germany by the self-proclaimed protectors of true Germanic culture did not deter Jewish refugees from trying to recreate the version of that culture to which they felt close allegiance. Just as the so-called German Jewish symbiosis was being violently destroyed in Europe, it was transplanted into the unlikeliest of new homes in Shanghai.

Re-creation was accompanied by assimilation, in this case assimilation into the English-speaking environment of Shanghai. Despite the difficulties with English experienced by many in the older generation, the most impressive refugee institution was the English-language Shanghai Jewish Youth Association school. The school was built by Horace Kadoorie and staffed by refugee teachers, led by Lucie Hartwich, a former principal in Berlin. Hans Cohn's memory that the Kadoorie School was "magnificent" is common among the former students.[16]

Unlike other streams of refugees from the Nazis, the Jews in Shanghai did not have to put all of their energies into assimilation. Their isolation was a spur to creativity, and the refugees' inability to become Chinese turned them inward. The power and the need to be creative were left behind when the refugees left Shanghai after the war. The United States provided an unparalleled freedom, but of a different sort. Able to participate in the long postwar economic boom, these Jews ceased being refugees in order to become Americans, and proud of it. Again, their silences are telling: they do not tell stories about antisemitism, not because it wasn't present in exclusive country clubs, elite universities, and certain businesses, but because there were so many places where it didn't exist. Gérard Kohbieter was not the only one who thought, *"My God, you made it"* in New York, California, or Florida. As Alfred Kohn said, *"America has been good to me."*

Like German immigrants had done since the 19th century, the former refugees founded *Landsmannschaften*, clubs based on their heritage. But this time, the common background was Shanghai. Former refugees and their families continue to meet and even travel together to Shanghai, organized through the organization Rickshaw Reunion. These meetings are about the past, though, not the present. The German Jewish symbiosis no longer exists, in Germany or elsewhere. One of its final manifestations lasted for a few years longer in Shanghai.

The experience of being a refugee is still not well understood, despite the flood of writing about Jews and Nazis. The lingering questions about why so many German and Austrian Jews did not leave the Third Reich, which shade into unspoken criticism of that apparently foolish choice, shows the persistence of misunderstanding. As these stories have demonstrated, leaving was anything but easy. Getting out meant successfully finding a place to go, giving up everything one had, directly facing Gestapo bullies determined to humiliate Jews, and then sailing off into the unknown. Leaving meant splitting families, leaving the elderly, the sick, or the fearful behind.

Each of these stories of escape from Germany is amazing, dramatic, and lucky. These stories are remarkable for us to read in the twenty-first century, but absolutely normal for those who escaped. People without luck, persistence, and then more luck were likely to perish in wartime Europe. Although the refugees themselves often talked about going "into the emigration," these are not stories about emigration, but about survival. The persistent use by historians and the general public of the word emigration as a label for the whole process by which Jews escaped from Nazi Germany before the war demonstrates a profound misunderstanding of what happened to these refugees.

The obstacles to leaving created by both Nazis and other governments around the world were enormous, especially for those ordinary Jews without wealth, fame, or international experience. Unprecedented Nazi violence in 1938 created panic among the hundreds of thousands of Jews still living in the Third Reich. The brave, persistent, and successful efforts by women in these narrators' families deserve our admiration. For that reason, the unsuccessful efforts and the willingness to hope that it might not get worse on the part of tens of thousands of others deserve our understanding. Criticism should be directed at those men in comfortable positions in Washington or London or Shanghai who decided very quickly that they had seen enough Jewish refugees. Those decisions prevented more central European Jews from escaping genocide.

At the same time that powerful people around the world were making it difficult to escape the Third Reich, countless people who have remained largely unknown helped Jewish refugees. The courageous efforts of diplomats in Europe to provide travel documents for Jews between 1938 and 1940, usually in defiance of their governments, saved thousands of lives. Chiune Sugihara of Japan and Jan Zwartendijk of Holland in Kovno, and Feng Shan Ho in the Chinese Consulate in Vienna, were joined by others whose humanitarian work has yet to be fully acknowledged. At a much more personal level, Christian family friends, even just acquaintances, some of them Nazi Party members, offered timely advice or warnings. There were nameless thousands whose sympathy for a human being in danger saved lives. From my conversation with survivors, I would guess that these experiences with helpful Germans made it easier for former refugees to trust non-Jews wherever they finally settled.

We know that those who survived the Holocaust in Europe, in camps or in hiding, were damaged by their traumatic experiences. The refugee experience was also damaging, not so much to the younger generation, but to those who were already adults when they fled Europe. The achievements of former refugees in their new homelands have been remarkable. But my interview partners described long-term health issues, the persistent sense of being homeless, the loss of profession and status, psychological trauma, and the truncation of their families as symptoms of permanent damage. The refugees have been very reluctant to express this openly, for fear of appearing to put themselves on the same plane as camp survivors. Yet it is clear in their stories.

The public silence of former refugees has contributed to ignorance about their experiences. One of my motivations has been to help these survivors better inform the wider world of the full meaning of their experiences. In today's world, knowledge about refugees is more necessary than ever. The refugee experience was not a decade in Shanghai, but a lifetime in which that decade was central. Thus, these Shanghai stories begin and end far from China. That is the way I believe refugees must be understood.

The uniqueness of Shanghai lies behind this whole history. This one city saved more Jews per capita than any other self-governing entity in the world. Who was responsible? The Western elite set the rules that allowed free entry and then wanted to change them when a few hundred Jewish refugees arrived. The Japanese respected and competed with the Westerners for power, until they took it forcibly in 1941. They resisted Nazi pressure to persecute Jews for years, but eventually made life very difficult for the refugees. The Chinese had little legal power and distinguished themselves by a personal and social reserve in which antisemitism did not exist. They were neither friends nor enemies.

Into the spaces between the rival powers in Shanghai slipped 16,000 central European Jewish refugees. They meant only to survive, but they have done much more than that. The stories of their exodus to Shanghai and beyond reveal the evil and good of which the human community is capable, the hatred of neighbors and the kindness to strangers that continue to define our world. They have much more to tell us than I could fit into this book.

Notes

Introduction

1. Translated from my interview with Martin Beutler, Berlin, June 29, 1995, Shanghai Jewish Community Oral History Project, p. 545. This passage is published in my book, *Shanghai-Geschichten: die jüdische Flucht nach China* (Berlin: Hentrich und Hentrich, 2007), p. 241, which uses interviews in German to present the stories of 12 Shanghai refugees who later returned to Germany and Austria.
2. David Kranzler, *Japanese, Nazis and Jews: The Jewish Refugee Community of Shanghai 1938–1945* (New York: Yeshiva University Press, 1976). See also James R. Ross, *Escape to Shanghai: A Jewish Community in China* (New York: Free Press, 1994). Films include *Port of Last Resort* (1999) by Paul Rosdy and Joan Grossman, and *Shanghai Ghetto* (2002) by Dana Janklowicz-Mann and Amir Mann.
3. Among the first were Evelyn Pike Rubin, *Ghetto Shanghai* (New York: Shengold Books, 1993); and I. Betty Grebenschikoff, *Once My Name Was Sara* (Ventnor, NJ: Original Seven Publishing Co., 1993). By combining the details of his own family's stories with considerable research about the whole community, the late Ernest Heppner's *Shanghai Refuge: A Memoir of the World War II Jewish Ghetto* (Lincoln, NE: University of Nebraska Press, 1993) is the best of the memoirs. See the bibliography for this growing literature.
4. The most successful thus far is Michèle Kahn, *Shanghai-la-juive* (Paris: Flammarion, 1997). Vivian Jeanette Kaplan fictionalized her family's experience *in Ten Green Bottles: The True Story of One Family's Journey from Wartorn Austria to the ghettos of Shanghai* (New York: St. Martin's Press, 2004). Most recently, Andrea Alban has written a book for young adults, *Anya's War* (New York: Feiwel & Friends, 2011).
5. Leo Spitzer, *Hotel Bolivia: The Culture of Memory in a Refuge from Nazism* (New York: Hill and Wang, 1998) notes the wide spectrum of estimates for German Jewish refugees to Bolivia, ranging from 7,000 to 60,000. Spitzer's estimate is 20,000 (p. 203, n. 2).
6. These are generally accepted estimates, cited for example in Walter Laqueur, *Generation Exodus: The Fate of Young Jewish Refugees from Nazi Germany* (Hanover, NH: Brandeis University Press, 2001), pp. 20–21; Saul Friedländer, *Nazi Germany and the Jews*, Vol. 1, *Years of Persecution 1933–1939* (NY: HarperCollins, 1997), pp. 62, 245; Marion A. Kaplan, *Between Dignity and Despair: Jewish Life in Nazi Germany* (New York: Oxford University Press, 1998), p. 132; Yehuda Bauer, *A History of the Holocaust* (New York: Franklin

Watts, 1982), p. 109; Ino Arndt and Heinz Boberach, "Deutsches Reich," in *Dimension des Völkermords: Die Zahl der jüdischen Opfer des Nationalsozialismus,* ed. Wolfgang Benz, (Munich: R. Oldenbourg Verlag, 1991), pp. 35; and Jonny Moser, "Österreich," in *Dimension des Völkermords,* ed. Wolfgang Benz, p. 68. But Niewyk and Nicosia, *Columbia Guide to the Holocaust* (New York: Columbia University Press, 2003), p. 419, also cites a much higher set of estimates compiled by the Reichsvereinigung der Juden in Deutschland.

7. Relatively precise estimates exist for the early years of Nazi power, from 1933 through 1937. Beginning with 1938, yearly totals of the masses of Jews who poured out of the Third Reich vary widely, and many sources do not even attempt estimates.

8. Niewyk and Nicosia, *Columbia Guide to the Holocaust,* p. 420, cites a figure of 40 percent from the Reichsvereinigung der Juden in Deutschland, which however seems much too high.

9. This phrase comes from Leo Spitzer, *Hotel Bolivia,* p. 63.

10. Wolfgang Benz, ed., *Das Exil der kleinen Leute: Alltagserfahrungen deutscher Juden in der Emigration* (Frankfurt: Fischer Taschenbuch Verlag, 1994). The poorest Jews were less likely to escape: Stephanie Schüler-Spangorum, "Fear and Misery in the Third Reich: From the Files of the Collective Guardianship Office of the Berlin Jewish Community," *Yad Vashem Studies* 27 (1999), pp. 61–103.

11. Paul Thompson, *The Voice of the Past: Oral History* (New York: Oxford University Press, 2000), 3rd edition, p. 260.

12. Lawrence Langer argues that oral accounts are "rich in spontaneous rather than calculated effects." *Holocaust Testimonies: The Ruins of Memory* (New Haven: Yale University Press, 1991), p. 129.

13. The full transcripts of these and many other of my interviews in the Shanghai Jewish Community Oral History Project are available online through Bates College.

14. A fine general history is Betty Peh-T'i Wei, *Shanghai: Crucible of Modern China* (Hong Kong: Oxford University Press, 1987).

15. Translated from my interview with Heinz Grünberg, Vienna, May 31, 1995, Shanghai Jewish Community Oral History Project, p. 1. This interview, conducted in German, is also quoted extensively in *Shanghai-Geschichten.*

16. For example, the discovery a few years after publication in 1995 that *Fragments: Memories of a Wartime Childhood* (New York: Schocken, 1997) by Binjamin Wilkomirski was an invention.

17. The relationship among event, memory and retelling has recently been the focus of much analysis. A brief summary of the issues by one of the experts on Holocaust interviews is Henry Greenspan, "Survivors' Accounts," in *The Oxford Handbook of Holocaust Studies,* ed. Peter Hayes and John K. Roth (Oxford, UK: Oxford University Press, 2010), pp. 414–27.

18. This is Langer's argument about "deep memory," based on hundreds of Holocaust interviews, in *Holocaust Testimonies.*

19. Translated from my interview with Rita Opitz, Berlin, June 26, 1995, Shanghai Jewish Community Oral History Project, p. 8. Opitz is one of the narrators in *Shanghai-Geschichten.*

20. On this subject, see also Helga Embacher and Margit Reiter, "Geschlechterbeziehungen in Extremsituationen: Österreichische und deutsche Frauen im Shanghai der dreißiger und vierziger Jahre," in *Exil*

Shanghai 1938–1947: Jüdisches Leben in der Emigration, ed. Georg Armbrüster, Michael Kohlstruck, and Sonja Mühlberger (Berlin: Hentrich und Hentrich, 2000), pp. 133–46.

I   In the Third Reich

1. The classic work on restrictive American immigration policies is David Wyman, *Paper Walls: America and the Refugee Crisis 1938–1941* (Amherst, MA: University of Massachusetts Press, 1968). See also Bat-Ami Zucker, "American Refugee Policy in the 1930s," in *Refugees from Nazi Germany and the Liberal European States,* ed. Frank Caestecker and Bob Moore (New York: Berghahn Books, 2010), p. 162.
2. In October, 1934, 32 Jewish doctors from Germany were reported to be practicing in Shanghai: "Refugee Doctors Settle in Orient," Jewish Telegraphic Agency, October 5, 1934, JTA Jewish News Archive. James R. Ross, *Escape to Shanghai: A Jewish Community in China* (New York: Free Press, 1994), pp. 24–25, describes some of the early refugees.
3. The report is reproduced by Moshe Avalon, "'Gegenwaertige Situation': Report on the Living Conditions of the Jews in Germany. A Document and Commentary," *Leo Baeck Institute Year Book* 1998: 271–85.
4. For example, Varian Fry, an American journalist who helped several thousand anti-Nazi and Jewish refugees to escape from Vichy France in 1940, was constantly harassed by American authorities.
5. Ho describes his diplomatic career in *My Forty Years as a Diplomat* (Pittsburgh, PA: Dorrance Publishing Co., 2010), translated and edited by his son, Monto Ho.
6. *Rebetsin* means wife of the rabbi and was a term of highest respect in Jewish communities.
7. On June 14, 1938, the Nazis promulgated an addendum to the Nuremberg Laws, which made it easier to plunder Jewish businesses. On that night, between 1,500 and 2,500 Jewish men who had any kind of criminal record, including traffic offenses, were arrested and sent to concentration camps.
8. In order to get a visa to enter the United States, Jews had to have an affidavit from a U.S. citizen promising to support them in case they could not support themselves.
9. Kurt Schuschnigg (1897–1977) succeeded the assassinated Engelbert Dollfuss in 1934 as Chancellor of Austria. In 1938, he was imprisoned by Nazi Germany following the *Anschluss* and survived Dachau and Sachsenhausen.
10. The *Physikum* is the first major exam during medical study.
11. The first mass rail transports of Jews from Vienna to Poland took place in October 1939.
12. The *Stürmer* was a violently antisemitic Nazi newspaper published by Julius Streicher.
13. This treaty was signed in August 1939.
14. On April 26, 1938, the Nazi government issued the Order Requiring the Declaration of Jewish Property, which forced all Jews to declare their holdings in Germany over 2,000 Mark, including art, jewelry, and businesses.

2 Leaving Home

1. In the city of Worms, nearly every German Jew tried to get out after Kristallnacht, but most only succeeded in securing a place on an interminable waiting list: Henry R. Huttenbach, "The Emigration of Jews from Worms (November 1938–October 1941): Hopes and Plans," in *Rescue Attempts During the Holocaust: Proceedings of the Second Yad Vashem International Historical Conference* (Jerusalem: Yad Vashem, 1977), pp. 267–88.

2. Christiane Hoss, "*Abenteurer:* Wer waren die Shanghai-Flüchtlinge aus Mitteleuropa?" in *Exil Shanghai 1938–1947*, ed. Georg Armbrüster, Michael Kohlstruck, and Sonja Mühlberger, (Berlin: Hentrich und Hentrich, 2000), p. 107. Numbers of arriving refugees come from a compilation of information about ship arrivals and numbers of refugees on board, which were consistently reported by the Shanghai Municipal Police to the Shanghai Municipal Council, the real government of the city run mainly by foreign businessmen and diplomats. The reports are located in the records of the SMP, file D5422(c).

3. For a detailed study of the changing official policies that governed entry into Shanghai, see Steve Hochstadt, "Shanghai: a Last Resort for Desperate Jews," in *Refugees from Nazi Germany and the Liberal European States*, ed. Frank Caestecker and Bob Moore (New York: Berghahn Books, 2010). pp. 109–21.

4. "The Refugee Problem," *North China Herald*, December 28, 1938, p. 529; Cordell Hull's telegram to U.S. Embassy in Berlin, archived in United States National Archives, file number 893.55J/4, microfilm publication LM63, roll 143. I am grateful to the late David S. Wyman for alerting me to this document, which is reprinted in Steve Hochstadt, *Sources of the Holocaust* (Houndmills, UK, and New York: Palgrave Macmillan, 2004), p. 83.

5. Gerhard Krebs, "Antisemitismus und Judenpolitik der Japaner," in *Exil Shanghai 1938–1947*, ed. Armbrüster, Kohlstruck, and Mühlberger, pp. 65–66.

6. Reports of German Consul General Bracklo to Foreign Ministry Berlin, February 24, and March 27, 1939, and to German Embassy Shanghai, March 20, May 24, and June 30, 1939, all in Bundesarchiv Berlin-Lichterfelde, R9208/2329.

7. The literature about Sugihara tends toward the hagiographic: see the book by his widow, Yukiko Sugihara, *Visas for Life* (Sacramento, CA: Edu-Comm Plus, 1995). There is little written about Zwartendijk.

8. The Wiener Schneiderakademie (Tailor Academy) was a major training school for the clothing trade in Vienna.

9. Grey refers to the Centralverein deutscher Staatsbürger jüdischen Glaubens (Central Association of German Citizens of the Jewish Faith), the major national Jewish organization in Germany, and its chapter house in Munich.

10. Lutz Haase also left Germany via the Trans-Siberian Railroad in October 1940, after spending two years in the Oranienburg concentration camp: Debórah Dwork, ed., *Voices and Views: A History of the Holocaust* (New York: The Jewish Foundation for the Righteous, 2002), p. 194.

11. Karl May's many books imagining the lives of cowboys and Indians in the American West were tremendously popular in Germany.

3 Culture Shock and Community Creation in Shanghai

1. Maisie J. Meyer's work is the most thorough description of the Baghdadi Jewish community: *From the Rivers of Babylon to the Whangpoo: A Century of Sephardi Jewish Life in Shanghai* (Lanham, MD: University Press of America, 2003).
2. Rena Krasno's memoirs of the Shanghai Russian community are excellent: *That Last Glorious Summer 1939: Shanghai–Japan* (Hong Kong: Old China Hand Press, 2001); and *Strangers Always: A Jewish Family in Wartime Shanghai* (Berkeley, CA: Pacific View Press, 1992). Marcia Renders Ristaino, *Port of Last Resort: The Diaspora Communities of Shanghai* (Stanford, CA: Stanford University Press, 2001) describes both the Russian Jewish and non-Jewish communities.
3. An excellent synthesis of refugee theater is Michael Philipp, *Nicht einmal einen Thespiskarren: Exiltheater in Shanghai 1939–1947* (Hamburg: Hamburger Arbeitsstelle für deutsche Exilliteratur, 1996).
4. Reisman means the Public and Thomas Hambry School.
5. ORT is a Jewish education and vocational training organization.
6. Because toilets were rare in Hongkou, human waste went into buckets, which were collected by the poorest of Chinese sanitation workers.
7. Richard Tauber was one of the great Austrian tenors. His family had a Jewish background.
8. Ernst Toller was an anarchist playwright who briefly served as president of the Bavarian Soviet Republic in 1919.
9. A small number of doctors' families were allowed to spend the entire war outside of the Designated Area, including Josef and Amalia Hochstadt, my grandparents.
10. The injection was in his right thigh, and soon after, he became lame in that leg below the knee.
11. The *tefillin* or phylacteries are little black boxes containing verses from the Torah to be worn on the forehead and on the upper arm during prayer.
12. See the interview with Herbert Moss in the Shanghai Jewish Community Oral History Project housed at Bates College.
13. Major Gerhard Kahner was head of the Gestapo in Shanghai from 1940 to 1943.
14. The memoir by Sigmund Tobias offers much detail on the distant relationship between the secular German-speaking and the religious Polish refugees: *Strange Haven: a Jewish Childhood in Wartime Shanghai* (Urbana, IL: University of Illinois Press, 1999).
15. Friedrich Hermann Glimpf was an important Nazi, the chief of the German news agency, the Deutsches Nachrichten Büro, until late 1943, when he became chief correspondent for China.
16. The *Hilfsfund*, or the Kitchen Fund, provided free meals for refugees.

4 In the Designated Area

1. David Kranzler, "'The Miracle of Shanghai'. An Overview," in *Exil Shanghai 1938–1947: Jüdisches Leben in der Emigration*, ed. Armbrüster, Kohlstruck, and Mühlberger (Berlin und Teetz: Hentrich und Hentrich, 2000) p. 41.

2. SACRA stands for the Shanghai Ashkenazi Collaborating Relief Association, formed by Russian Jews after the Japanese Proclamation in February 1943 to help with the relocation of Jews into the Designated Area. The SACRA building in which Culman lived was located at Tongshan and Kungping Roads.

3. A number of Polish refugees refused to move into the Designated Area, claiming they were not stateless. Many months after the deadline for moving, they were arrested and put in the Ward Road jail. At least five contracted typhus and died, while others became seriously ill. Kranzler, *Japanese, Nazis and Jews: the Jewish Refugee Community of Shanghai 1938–1945* (New York: Yeshiva University Press, 1976), p. 529.

4. See the interview with Alfred and Eva Zunterstein, Shanghai Jewish Community Oral History Project, Salzburg, May 20, 1995.

5. The refugee Max Buchbaum had been the middleweight amateur champion in Berlin.

6. The Alcock Heim was around the corner from the Ward Road prison.

7. *"Mensch, ärgere dich nicht"* means "man, don't get angry." It is the name of a German board game similar to Parcheesi.

8. The Emigrants Hospital was first opened in the Washing Road Heim in 1939, then moved to the Ward Road Heim. Outpatient clinics also were established at some of the other *Heime*.

9. The actual figure for deaths among the refugees was probably closer to 1,500.

10. Doris Grey here tells from personal experience and with more accuracy the same story about newborns dying that Herbert Greening told a few pages ago from the outside, without direct knowledge. See the conclusion for further discussion of this incident.

11. Dr. Tibor Kunfi from Vienna served on the Medical Committee of the larger Committee for the Assistance of European Jewish Refugees in Shanghai, set up in 1938. This Committee was sometimes known as the Speelman Committee, after its first treasurer, Michel Speelman.

12. *Yecke* is a pejorative word for German Jews used by Austrians. Grey hints here at the continuation in Shanghai of European resentments among national Jewish groups.

13. Sumner here refers to Bruno and Lisbeth Loewenberg.

14. Ruth Sumner's friends were Inge Pikarski and Eva Wolffheim.

15. The same word is used in the Terezin diary of Petr Ginz: Alexandra Zapruder, *Salvaged Paper: Young Writers' Diaries of the Holocaust* (New Haven: Yale University Press, 2002), p. 169.

5 The End of the War

1. Dr. Samuel Didner was a refugee from Graz, in Austria. His story is featured in James R. Ross, *Escape to Shanghai: A Jewish Community in China* (New York: Free Press, 1994).

6 After the War

1. Heinz (Pit) Bergman was Eva's boyfriend.

7 *Auf Wiedersehen*, Shanghai! But Where Do We Go?

1. The information here about how refugees gradually left Shanghai comes from many articles published by the Jewish Telegraphic Agency in this period, newly available online at http://archive.jta.org.
2. For a better understanding of the difficulties, physical and psychological, faced by those who returned to Germany and Austria, see the interviews in Hochstadt, *Shanghai-Geschichten: die judische Flucht nach China* (Berlin: Hentrich und Hentrich, 2007), pp. 175–229.
3. The Jewish Telegraphic Agency published many articles about the delaying tactics of the Consulate in Shanghai and the eventual effort of the State Department in Washington to accelerate approval of immigration to the United States: see dispatches for July 16, September 25, September 30, and December 27, 1946, and January 26, 1947.

8 Another New Life

1. Michael W. Blumenthal became secretary of the Tteasury under President Jimmy Carter. Hans Eberstark was a linguist who founded Mensa Switzerland.

9 My Life as a Refugee

1. This famous incident occurred in February 1943, when nearly 2,000 Jewish husbands of Christian wives were arrested and incarcerated in the Rosenstrasse in Berlin on their way to deportation. The mass protest of hundreds of women resulted in their release.

Conclusion

1. Bat-Ami Zucker extends the discussion of American official behavior beyond Washington, DC, in *In Search of Refuge: Jews and US Consuls in Nazi Germany, 1933–1941* (London: Vallentine Mitchell, 2001).
2. Walter Laqueur, *Generation Exodus: The Fate of Young Jewish Refugees from Nazi Germany* Hanover, NH: Brandeis University Press, 2001); Lewis A. Coser, *Refugee Scholars in America : Their Impact and Their Experiences* (New Haven: Yale University Press, 1984).
3. Penguin canceled the 2009 publication of his "memoir," *Angel at the Fence.*
4. Christopher R. Browning, *Ordinary Men: Reserve Police Battalion 101 and the Final Solution in Poland* (New York: Harper-Collins, 1998); and *Collected Memories: Holocaust History and Postwar Testimony* (Madison, WI: University of Wisconsin Press, 2003).
5. Lawrence Langer, *Holocaust Testimonies: The Ruins of Memory* (New Haven: Yale University Press, 1991), ch. 1.
6. Henry Greenspan, *On Listening to Holocaust Survivors: Recounting and Life History* (Westport, CT: Praeger, 1998).

7. Browning, "Preface," in *Ordinary Men: Reserve Police Battalion 101 and the Final Solution in Poland* (New York: Harper-Collins, 1998), p. xvii.

8. For this reason, I also believe that Greenspan's method of repeated interviews with fewer people, as recounted in *On Listening to Holocaust Survivors*, offers the possibility of revealing a different and broader range of memories than the much more common single interview.

9. One of the best collections of evidence and analysis of popular knowledge and feelings about mass murder of Jews is Eric A. Johnson and Karl-Heinz Reuband, *What We Knew: Terror, Mass Murder and Everyday Life in Nazi Germany: An Oral History* (Cambridge, MA: Basic Books, 2005).

10. For the role of Nazis within the German community in Shanghai, see Astrid Freyeisen, *Shanghai und die Politik des Dritten Reiches* (Würzburg: Konigshausen und Neumann, 2000).

11. Over 60 individual Special Branch reports in D5422(c), Shanghai Municipal Police (SMP) files, running from November 1933 through 1940.

12. D.S. Pitts, "Central European Jews – Arrival in Shanghai," March 15, 1939, D5422(c), SMP files; letter of March 28, 1939, from the secretary of the Municipal Council to the Commissioner of Police, D5422(c), SMP files.

13. The Association of Former Residents of China in Jerusalem (Igud Yotzei Sin) is dominated by Jews with a Russian background. The history of the central European refugees in Shanghai is underrepresented in their *Bulletin*.

14. Aviva Halamish, "Palestine as a Destination for Jewish Immigrants and Refugees from Nazi Germany," in *Refugees from Nazi Germany and the Liberal European States*, ed. Frank Caestecker and Bob Moore, p. 143.

15. The Shanghai Municipal Police files have voluminous records of the meetings of the many clubs that were founded because the police were responsible for ensuring that political issues would not be discussed.

16. Hans Cohn, *Risen from the Ashes: Tales of a Musical Messenger* (Lanham, MD: Hamilton Books, 2006), p. 30.

Bibliography

Interviews (all interviews by Steve Hochstadt, unless otherwise noted)

Colland, Melitta. Portland, ME, September 30, 1989. Transcription by Catherine Bohn, Jennifer Gibson, Steve Hochstadt, Scott Jerome, and Scott Pugh.

Culman, Ernest. Rockville, MD, October 18, 1997. Transcription by Nicci Leamon and Steve Hochstadt.

Greening, Herbert and Ilse Greening. Sarasota, FL, February 19, 1997, transcription by Nicci Leamon and Steve Hochstadt.

Grey, Doris. Laguna Hills, CA, June 26, 1991. Transcription by Jen Sbrogna and Steve Hochstadt.

Hirsch, Ralph. Shanghai, April 22, 1994; interviewers Steve Hochstadt and Christine Lixl. Transcription by Hin-Cheng Wang and Steve Hochstadt.

Kohbieter, Gérard. Berlin, December 9, 1994. Transcription by Leslie Broch and Steve Hochstadt.

Kohn, Alfred. Kiamesha Lake, NY, April 13, 1997. Transcription by Nicci Leamon and Steve Hochstadt.

Loewenberg, Lisbeth. Shanghai, April 21, 1989. Transcription by Natalie Adler and Steve Hochstadt.

Reisman, Eric. Bonita Springs, FL, February 17, 1997. Transcription by Jennifer Gibson, Nancy Masino, Scott Pugh, and Steve Hochstadt.

Schnepp, Otto. Los Angeles, CA, June 7, 1990. Transcription by Nicci Leamon and Steve Hochstadt.

Schwarz, Lotte. Seal Beach, CA, June 11, 1990. Transcription by Meredyth Muth, Jessica Oas, Stefanie Pearson, Philip Pettis, and Steve Hochstadt.

Sumner, Ruth. Tampa, FL, April 17, 1991. Transcription by Matthew Bennett, Jessica Oas, Philip Pettis, Audra Pontes, Robert Yahn III, and Steve Hochstadt.

Other Primary Sources

Avalon, Moshe. "'Gegenwaertige Situation': Report on the Living Conditions of the Jews in Germany. A Document and Commentary." *Leo Baeck Institute Year Book* (1998): 271–85.

Hull, Cordell, telegram to U.S. Embassy in Berlin, United States National Archives, file number 893.55J/4, microfilm publication LM63, roll 143.

Jewish Telegraphic Agency, news articles. JTA Jewish News Archive accessed at http://archive.jta.org/.

List of Foreigners Residing in Dee Lay Jao Police District, August 1944: a Japanese census of 14,794 names, covering most refugees in Hongkou, available as CD-ROM accompanying *Exil Shanghai 1938–1947*, with explanation on pp. 256–59.

"The Refugee Problem." *North China Herald*, December 28, 1938. 529.

Reports of German Consul General Bracklo to Foreign Ministry Berlin, February 24, and March 27, 1939, and to German Embassy Shanghai, March 20, May 24, and June 30, 1939, all in Bundesarchiv Berlin-Lichterfelde, R9208/2329.

Shanghai Jewish Chronicle, March 6, 1940.

Shanghai Jewish Community Oral History Project, Special Collections, Laid Library, Bates College, Lewiston, ME: 99 Taped Interviews by Steve Hochstadt with Jews who lived in Shanghai, available online at abacus.bates.edu/muskie-archives/Collections/OralHistoryFindingAids/ShanghaiOHFA,shtml.

Shanghai Municipal Police, SMP file D5422(c).

Memoirs and Oral Histories

Cohn, Hans. *Risen from the Ashes: Tales of a Musical Messenger*. Lanham, MD: Hamilton Books, 2006.

Grebenschikoff, I. Betty. *Once My Name Was Sara*. Ventnor, NJ: Original Seven Publishing Co., 1993.

Heppner, Ernest G. *Shanghai Refuge: A Memoir of the World War II Jewish Ghetto*. Lincoln, NE: University of Nebraska Press, 1993.

Ho, Feng-Shan. *My Forty Years as a Diplomat*. Trans. Monto Ho. Pittsburgh, PA: Dorrance Publishing Co., 2010.

———. Hochstadt, Steve. "Erinnerungen an Shanghai," edited version of interview with Martin Beutler. *Zwischenwelt: Literatur, Widerstand, Exil* (Vienna) 18 (2001): 28–33.

———. *Shanghai-Geschichten: die jüdische Flucht nach China*. Berlin: Hentrich und Hentrich, 2007.

Iwry, Samuel. *To Wear the Dust of War: From Bialystok to Shanghai to the Promised Land: An Oral History*. Edited by L. J. H. Kelley. New York: Palgrave Macmillan, 2004.

Kneuker, Alfred W. *Zuflucht in Shanghai: Aus den Erlebnissen eines österreichischen Arztes in der Emigration 1938–1945*. Vienna: Hermann Böhlaus Nachfolger, 1984.

Krasno, Rena. *Strangers Always: A Jewish Family in Wartime Shanghai*. Berkeley, CA: Pacific View Press, 1992.

———. *That Last Glorious Summer 1939: Shanghai–Japan*. Hong Kong: Old China Hand Press, 2001.

Lindenstraus, Jerry. *Eine unglaubliche Reise: Von Ostpreussen über Schanghai und Kolumbien nach New York, Jüdische Familiengeschichte 1929–1999*. Konstanz, Germany: Hartung-Gorre Verlag, 1999.

Mühlberger, Sonja. *Geboren in Shanghai als Kind von Emigranten: Leben und Überleben (1939–1947) im Ghetto von Hongkew*, Jüdische Miniaturen, vol. 58. Berlin: Hentrich und Hentrich, 2006.

Rubin, Evelyn Pike. *Ghetto Shanghai*. New York: Shengold Books, 1993.

Stern, Helmut. *Saitensprünge*. Berlin: Transit, 1990.

Strobin, Deborah, and Ilie Wacs. *An Uncommon Journey: From Vienna to Shanghai to America – A Brother and Sister Escape to Freedom During World War II* (Fort Lee, NJ: Barricade Books, 2011).

Tausig, Franziska. *Shanghai Passage: Flucht und Exil einer Wienerin*. Vienna: Verlag für Gesellschaftskritik, 1987.

Tobias, Sigmund. *Strange Haven: a Jewish Childhood in Wartime Shanghai*. Urbana, IL: University of Illinois Press, 1999.

Films

"A place to save your life": the story of the Jewish refugee community of Shanghai, China. Produced and directed by Karen Shopsowitz. Montreith Inn Productions, 1992.

Port of Last Resort. Produced and directed by Paul Rosdy and Joan Grossman. Extrafilm, 1999.

Shanghai Ghetto. Produced and directed by Dana Janklowicz-Mann and Amir Mann. Rebel Child Productions, 2002.

Novels

Alban, Andrea. *Anya's War*. New York: Feiwel & Friends, 2011.

Kahn, Michèle. *Shanghai-la-juive*. Paris: Flammarion, 1997.

Kaplan, Vivian Jeanette. *Ten Green Bottles: The True Story of One Family's Journey from War-torn Austria to the ghettos of Shanghai*. New York: St. Martin's Press, 2004.

Wagenstein, Angel. *Farewell, Shanghai*. Trans. Elizabeth Frank and Deliana Simeonova. New York: Handsel Books, 2007.

Secondary Sources

All About Shanghai: A Standard Guidebook . Shanghai: University Press, 1934. Reprinted by Oxford University Press, 1983.

Armbrüster, Georg, Michael Kohlstruck, and Sonja Mühlberger, eds. *Exil Shanghai 1938–1947: Jüdisches Leben in der Emigration*. Berlin und Teetz: Hentrich und Hentrich, 2000.

Benz, Wolfgang, ed. *Das Exil der kleinen Leute: Alltagserfahrungen deutscher Juden in der Emigration*. Frankfurt: Fischer Taschenbuch Verlag, 1994.

Browning, Christopher R. *Collected Memories: Holocaust History and Postwar Testimony*. Madison, WI: University of Wisconsin Press, 2003.

———. *Ordinary Men: Reserve Police Battalion 101 and the Final Solution in Poland*. New York: Harper-Collins, 1998.

Embacher, Helga, and Margit Reiter. "Geschlechterbeziehungen in Extremsituationen: Österreichische und deutsche Frauen im Shanghai der dreißiger und vierziger Jahre." In *Exil Shanghai 1938–1947: Jüdisches Leben in der Emigration*. Ed. Armbrüster, Kohlstruck, and Mühlberger. 133–46.

Finnane, Antonia. *Far From Where? Jewish Journeys from Shanghai to Australia*. Victoria, Australia: Melbourne University Press, 1999.

Freyeisen, Astrid. *Shanghai und die Politik des Dritten Reiches*. Würzburg: Königshausen und Neumann, 2000.

Geldermann, Barbara. "Shanghai a City of Immigrants: Shanghai und die Gründer der ersten jüdischen Gemeinde, die bagdadischen Juden." In *Exil Shanghai 1938–1947*. Ed. Armbrüster, Kohlstruck, and Mühlberger. 46–57.

Goldstein, Jonathan, ed. *The Jews of China*, 2 vols. New York: M.E. Sharpe, 2000.

Greenspan, Henry. *On Listening to Holocaust Survivors: Recounting and Life History*. Westport, CT: Praeger, 1998.

———. "Survivors' Accounts." In *The Oxford Handbook of Holocaust Studies*. Ed. Peter Hayes and John K. Roth. Oxford, UK: Oxford University Press, 2010. 414–27.

Hochstadt, Steve. "Flucht ins Ungewisse: Die Jüdische Emigration nach Shanghai." In *Exil Shanghai 1938–1947*. Ed. Armbrüster, Kohlstruck, and Mühlberger. 27–33.

———. "Jüdische und nichtjüdische Vertriebene aus Nazi-Deutschland in Shanghai." In Anna-Ruth Löwenbrück, ed., *Auswanderung, Flucht, Vertreibung, Exil im 19. und 20. Jahrhundert*. Berlin: Philo Verlag, 2003. 117–31.

———. "Shanghai: A Last Resort for Desperate Jews." In *Refugees from Nazi Germany and the Liberal European States*. Ed. Frank Caestecker and Bob Moore. New York: Berghahn Books, 2010. 109–21.

———. "The Social History of Jews in the Holocaust: The Necessity of Interviewing Survivors." *Historical Social Research – Historische Sozialforschung* 22 (1997): 254–74.

———. "Vertreibung aus Deutschland und Überleben in Shanghai: jüdische NS-Vertriebene in China." *IMIS-Beiträge*, Institut für Migrationsforschung und Interkulturelle Studien, Universität Osnabrück, 12 (1999): 51–67.

Hoss, Christiane. "*Abenteuerer*: Wer waren die Shanghai-Flüchtlinge aus Mitteleuropa?" In *Exil Shanghai 1938–1947*. Ed. Georg Armbrüster, Michael Kohlstruck, and Sonja Mühlberger. Berlin: Hentrich and Hentrich, 2000. 103–32.

Huttenbach, Henry R. "The Emigration of Jews from Worms (November 1938 – October 1941): Hopes and Plans." In *Rescue Attempts During the Holocaust: Proceedings of the Second Yad Vashem International Historical Conference*. Jerusalem: Yad Vashem, 1977. 267–88.

Johnson, Eric A., and Karl-Heinz Reuband. *What We Knew: Terror, Mass Murder and Everyday Life in Nazi Germany: An Oral History*. Cambridge, MA: Basic Books, 2005.

Kranzler, David. *Japanese, Nazis and Jews: the Jewish Refugee Community of Shanghai 1938–1945*. New York: Yeshiva University Press, 1976.

———. "'The Miracle of Shanghai': An Overview." In *Exil Shanghai 1938–1947*. Ed. Armbrüster, Kohlstruck, and Mühlberger. 35–45.

Krebs, Gerhard. "Antisemitismus und Judenpolitik der Japaner." In *Exil Shanghai 1938–1947*. Ed. Armbrüster, Kohlstruck, and Mühlberger. 58–76.

Langer, Lawrence. *Holocaust Testimonies: The Ruins of Memory*. New Haven: Yale University Press, 1991.

Laqueur, Walter. *Generation Exodus: The Fate of Young Jewish Refugees from Nazi Germany*. Hanover, NH: Brandeis University Press, 2001.

Messmer, Matthias, *Jewish Wayfarers in Modern China: Tragedy and Splendor* (Lanham, MD: Lexington Books, 2011).

Meyer, Maisie J. *From the Rivers of Babylon to the Whangpoo: A Century of Sephardi Jewish Life in Shanghai*. Lanham, MD: University Press of America, 2003.

Philipp, Michael. *Nicht einmal einen Thespiskarren: Exiltheater in Shanghai 1939–1947*. Hamburg: Hamburger Arbeitsstelle für deutsche Exilliteratur, 1996.

Ristaino, Marcia Renders. *Port of Last Resort: The Diaspora Communities of Shanghai*. Stanford, CA: Stanford University Press, 2001.

Ross, James R. *Escape to Shanghai: A Jewish Community in China*. New York: Free Press, 1994.

Schüler-Spangorum, Stephanie. "Fear and Misery in the Third Reich: From the Files of the Collective Guardianship Office of the Berlin Jewish Community." *Yad Vashem Studies* 27 (1999).

Schomann, Stefan. *Der grosse gelbe Fisch: Julie und Robert – eine Liebesgeschichte aus China*. Munich: Wilhelm Heyne Verlag, 2008.

Spitzer, Leo. *Hotel Bolivia: The Culture of Memory in a Refuge from Nazism*. New York: Hill and Wang, 1998.

Sugihara, Yukiko. *Visas for Life*. Sacramento, CA: Edu-Comm Plus, 1995.

Thompson, Paul. *The Voice of the Past: Oral History*, 3rd ed. New York: Oxford University Press, 2000.

Wei, Betty Peh-T'i. *Shanghai: Crucible of Modern China*. Hong Kong: Oxford University Press, 1987.

Wyman, David. *Paper Walls: America and the Refugee Crisis 1938–1941*. Amherst, MA: University of Massachusetts Press, 1968.

Zucker, Bat-Ami. "American Refugee Policy in the 1930s." In *Refugees from Nazi Germany and the Liberal European States*. Ed. Caestecker and Moore. New York: Berghahn Books, 2010. 151–68.

———. *In Search of Refuge: Jews and US Consuls in Nazi Germany, 1933–1941*. London: Vallentine Mitchell, 2001.

The Narrators

Melitta Colland

Melitta Colland (née Sommerfreund) was born in November 24, 1917. One of her brothers left Vienna for Panama, another went to Shanghai in December 1938, and she sailed with her mother, Sarah, on the *Conte Verde* to Shanghai in the summer of 1939. She immediately started her own dress shop. After the war broke out, Colland lost the business and had to move to Hongkou. In 1944 she married Dr. Bruno Meyerowitz, a refugee from Germany. They had a daughter, Asherah, in September 1945.

The family left for Panama in 1947, and soon afterwards for the United States. Melitta divorced Dr. Meyerowitz, and later married Joseph Colland. Melitta Colland died in Connecticut on September 5, 2001.

Ernest Culman

Ernest Culman (formerly Ernst Culmann) was born in Liegnitz on December 2, 1929. His father, Engush, a doctor, was arrested on *Kristallnacht*. Culman, his older brother, Hans, and their parents sailed on a Dutch ship to Shanghai in June 1939. His father had difficulty establishing himself as a doctor, so his family and some friends started a luncheon business. Later his mother, Beth, baked cakes and took in sewing. Culman attended the Shanghai Jewish School, and after 1942 the Kadoorie School. He celebrated his Bar Mitzvah in Shanghai. The Culman family lived in the SACRA building on Tongshan Road, which was bombed by the Americans on July 17, 1945, but none of them were hurt.

After the war, Culman apprenticed in camera repair. The family left Shanghai in January 1947 for San Francisco, and settled in Baltimore. Culman continued in camera repair, was drafted during the Korean War, and later became a manager with Industrial Photo and Pen Camera. He and his wife, Anya Hoffman, live near Washington, D.C.

Herbert and Ilse Greening

Ilse Greening (née Braunsberg) was born in Hannover on July 11, 1919. She began working for a lawyer at age 16. Herbert Grünberger was born in Königshütte on December 13, 1912, and moved with his family to Hindenburg in 1922. He studied medicine in Bonn, Berlin, and Breslau, and graduated in 1936. He became an intern in a hospital in Hannover. Ilse and Herbert were married in December 1938, and took the freighter *Oldenburg* to Shanghai in April 1939, with Ilse's mother, Erna, and younger sister, Eva.

In Shanghai, Ilse's uncle, Bruno Italiener, helped them rent an apartment in the French Concession, but they soon moved to Hongkou, where Herbert set up a medical practice in Kung Ping Road. Ilse worked in the Chartered Bank of India and China. After Pearl Harbor, the bank was taken over by the Japanese authorities. Both Ilse and Herbert attended to the Chinese wounded by the American bombing of Hongkou in July 1945. Their son, Michael, was born in December 1945.

They left Shanghai for Australia in January 1949, changing their name to Greening, and arrived in the United States in August 1950. Herbert joined a medical practice in New York, where their daughter was born. After retirement, they moved to Florida. Herbert Greening died on April 30, 2004, and Ilse Greening on November 18, 2008.

Doris Grey

Doris (originally Dorchen) Grey was born in Hindenburg, Upper Silesia, on June 21, 1912. She studied nursing and worked in Breslau, before moving to Berlin and becoming head nurse at the Krankenhaus der Jüdischen Gemeinde. In Berlin, she married Willy Cohn, born circa 1899. On May 5, 1940, they left Berlin for Genoa, where they sailed to Shanghai on the *Conte Verde*. Doris worked at the Emigrants Hospital in the Ward Road Heim as head nurse, while her husband continued his work as an art dealer. They lived on Point Road.

In January 1947 they left Shanghai on the *Marine Lynx* for the United States. In New York, Doris worked as a nurse and Willy became an art dealer. After becoming widowed around 1955, she married Benny Grey, who survived the war in the Soviet Union. Doris died on January 16, 1999, in California.

Ralph Hirsch

Ralph (originally Rolf) Hirsch was born on December 2, 1930, in Berlin. After attending the Volksschule, he had to transfer to a Jewish school after *Kristallnacht*. The Hirsch family left Berlin in October 1940 by train to Moscow, and then by the Trans-Siberian Railroad to China. They settled in Hongkou. Hirsch attended the Kadoorie School, as did his younger brother, Claus. Their father, Gerhard, worked occasionally for the Joint Distribution Committee and as an accountant for some refugees' small businesses until the war ended. Their mother, Editha, opened a hat shop, and when that did not succeed, a candy store.

In May 1947, the family left for the United States. Hirsch was a city planner in Philadelphia and now lives in Germany. He is married to Angelica Hack, an art historian and museum curator.

Gérard Kohbieter

Gérard (formerly Gerhard) Kohbieter was born in Berlin on May 30, 1922. He sailed alone to Shanghai in March 1939 at age 16. In Shanghai he worked as a magician and lived mainly in the Alcock Heim. He also sold books.

In 1947 he arrived in New York, and later lived in San Francisco, working as a magician under the name Gérard Slaxon. He finally settled in Berlin. Shortly after this interview, he died on January 4, 1995, of complications from an operation. He is survived by his widow, Renate Kohbieter.

Alfred Kohn

Alfred Kohn was born in Berlin in January 1927. His family, including his younger brother, Ingolf, traveled to Shanghai on an Italian ship in late 1939. His father, Chaim, began work as a furrier for a Russian Jewish firm. Kohn played soccer and boxed in the Hongkou ghetto, and became a well-known sports figure, nicknamed Lako, "der lange Kohn," He worked as a radio technician and in a kitchen. After the war, he worked for the US Army.

In September 1947 Kohn arrived in the United States and began work in the fur business in New York. He was the New York Golden Gloves champion in 1948, and was defeated in the championship bout in 1949, after which he gave up boxing. He is retired and lives with his wife, Hedy, in Florida.

Lisbeth Loewenberg

Lisbeth Loewenberg (neé Epstein) was born on January 4, 1922. She and her mother sailed to Shanghai from Trieste in 1940, when she was 18. Her father had already sailed there in 1939 and was teaching music at the Kadoorie School. He died in Shanghai of cancer in 1942. Lisbeth worked in Shanghai as a secretary. There she married Bruno Loewenberg (born 1890) from Berlin, who had spent 13 months in Buchenwald. He ran a lending library on Ward Road.

In 1948 they emigrated to the United States and settled in San Francisco, where Bruno owned the Lion Book Shop and Art Gallery and Lisbeth worked for *Collier's* magazine. Bruno Loewenberg died on October 29, 1986, and Lisbeth Loewenberg on September 7, 1996.

Eric Reisman

Eric Reisman (originally Erich Reismann) was born in Vienna, Austria, on April 26, 1926. His parents, Hermin and Oskar, were born in Theben-Neudorf, Czechoslovakia. At the time of the *Anschluss*, Reisman's mother was forced to scrub the sidewalk outside their apartment. Reisman, his older brother, Paul, and their parents managed to get a Chinese visa from Consul Feng Shan Ho, which helped them get a passage to Shanghai on the *Conte Biancamano* in November 1938. In Shanghai Reisman attended the Public and Thomas Hambry School, then the Kadoorie School. He celebrated his Bar Mitzvah in Hongkou in April 1939. After Pearl Harbor, the house they had bought was confiscated by the Japanese. Reisman worked in a pharmacy and learned to box. The family lived on Tongshan Road. After the war ended, he worked for Northwest Airlines at Kiangwan airport.

His parents came to the United States in 1947. His brother, Paul, married Trude Zalusky in Shanghai, and they went to Bolivia, and eventually to the United States. Reisman came to the United States in 1949. He got married and worked many years for Sikorsky Aircraft. Eric Reisman died on June 30, 1999.

Otto Schnepp

Otto Schnepp was born in 1925 in Austria. In January 1939, at age 13, he left Vienna, and met his parents, Bruno and Elisabeth, in Shanghai, where they had arrived a month earlier. Schnepp attended the Shanghai Jewish

School, then the Public and Thomas Hanbury School, and finally graduated from St. John's University in 1947. He earned money by teaching English to Chinese.

He received a doctorate from Berkeley in 1951 and taught at the Technion in Haifa for 13 years. In 1965 Schnepp took a position in the Chemistry Department at the University of Southern California, where he eventually became chair. Schnepp returned to China as science advisor to the United States Embassy in Beijing in 1980. He retired from the USC Chemistry Department in 1992, and became director of the USC East Asian Study Center in 1994.

Lotte Schwarz

Lotte Schwarz (neé Cohn) was born in Halle on September 7, 1910, and grew up in Nordhausen. She worked for the Hilfsverein in Hannover. In February 1938 she married and moved to Berlin. On June 14, 1938, her husband was arrested and sent to Buchenwald. In August they sailed to Shanghai from Trieste on the *Conte Verde*. The Schwarzes opened a small coffee shop, the Quick Restaurant, in Hongkou. Their daughter was born in 1940.

They sailed to San Francisco on the *General Meigs* in 1948, and then settled in southern California. Lotte Schwarz worked for many years for the Judy Crib Sheet Company. She died on October 3, 2005.

Ruth Sumner

Ruth Sumner (neé Wendriner) was born in Silesia on August 24, 1927, and grew up in Bobrek and then Beuthen. When she was six, her mother was killed by an intruder to their home. Her father, Kurt, owned a bar, but sold the business and retired to Beuthen. On *Kristallnacht*, her father's brother was arrested and killed at Buchenwald. Her father and she then sailed to Shanghai on the *Hakone Maru* in January 1939; shortly afterward, her sister left for the United States. In Shanghai, her father opened the Roof Garden Mascot restaurant on Wayside Road. They lived together with her aunt, Erna Schaie, on Tongshan Road.

After the war ended, Ruth got married in Shanghai to an American soldier, Forrest Sumner, and had a child within a month of arriving in the United States in 1947. They live in Florida.

Index